D1858624

ENGLISH network

Refresher

Lynda Hübner
Carolyn Kilday Wittmann
mit Donald Porsché

Langenscheidt-Longman
ENGLISH LANGUAGE TEACHING

English Network Refresher

Autoren:
Lynda Hübner (Units, Extras)
Carolyn Kilday Wittmann (Units, Language & Culture)
Dr. Donald Porsché (Homestudy)

sowie
Dr. Dieter Kranz (Grammatikanhang)
Michael Rutman (Grammatikübungen)

Beratende Mitwirkung:
Dr. Dieter Kranz, Dr. Donald Porsché, John Potts, Gaynor Ramsey, Michael Rutman

Projektteam:
Lynda Hübner, Kursleiterin, München
Carolyn Kilday Wittmann, Kursleiterin und Lehrbeauftragte, München
Dr. Dieter Kranz, Kursleiter und Akademischer Direktor, Münster
Dr. Donald Porsché, Programmbereichsleiter, Frankfurt
John Potts, Kursleiter und Lehrerfortbildner, Zürich
Gaynor Ramsey, Autorin, Kursleiterin und Lehrerfortbildnerin, Hove
Michael Rutman, Lehrerfortbildner und Landesbeauftragter, Zürich

Verlagsredaktion:
Doris Michels

Redaktionelle Mitarbeit:
Christiane Gsänger, Agnes Gschwind, Wolfgang Kaul

Graphik und Layout:
Beate Andler
Kathrin Hälbich

Desktop-Publishing:
Kathrin Hälbich

Umschlag:
Kathrin Hälbich

Lehrwerkskomponenten:	
Kursbuch	50 406
Textcassette	57 501
Text-CD	57 515
Lehrerhandreichungen	50 407
Homestudy-Cassette	57 502
Homestudy-CD	57 516
Lehrwerksbegleitend:	
Network Grammar	50 412
Grammar Workbook 1	50 413

Der Innenteil dieses Buches wurde auf chlorfrei gebleichtem Papier gedruckt.

1. Auflage 1997

Druck: Landesverlag Druckservice, Linz
Printed in Austria

ISBN 3-526-50406-7

1 2 3 4 5 / 2001 00 99 98 97

Wegweiser

Sie haben das Gefühl, Englisch einigermaßen verstehen zu können? Sie erfassen Zusammenhänge und auch Einzelheiten, aber dann treten einige Vokabeln auf, an die Sie sich nur schwer erinnern können? Vermeintlich komplizierte Dinge verstehen Sie dagegen recht gut? Und plötzlich gibt es Probleme mit einfacher Gegenwart und Verlaufsform? Wie war das eigentlich noch? Überhaupt – wenn es darum geht, selber zu sprechen und zu schreiben ... Da würden Sie sich schon eine Wiederholung „von Grund auf" wünschen. Am besten mit anderen in einem richtigen Kurs, allerdings kompakter, zielgerichteter als früher!

English Network Refresher bietet Ihnen genau das.

Vor dem Unterricht haben Sie die Möglichkeit, sich selber zu überprüfen. Ein einseitiger Checkpoint enthält Aufgaben mit wichtiger Grammatik und Ausdrucksweisen. Über einen Lösungsschlüssel überprüfen Sie Ihre Antworten. Wenn Sie meinen, noch ein wenig üben zu müssen, können Sie im Anhang noch einige zusätzliche Aufgaben machen oder in der zusammenfassenden Grammatik schmökern.

Durch diese „Selbstdiagnose" auf den Unterricht vorbereitet, können Sie dann die Stunde mit den anderen Kursteilnehmern und -teilnehmerinnen zum Auffrischen Ihrer kommunikativen Skills optimal nutzen!
Wichtig ist, dass Sie Ihre Kenntnisse schnell auffrischen möchten und bereit sind, zu Hause etwas dafür zu tun. Die Vor- und Nachbereitungsarbeit gehört nämlich unbedingt dazu.

Der Unterricht selber vermittelt Ihnen, wie Sie Inhalte von Texten schnell und sicher erfassen können – ob es sich nun um Lese- oder um Hörtexte handelt.
Mit *English Network Refresher* lernen Sie also sowohl allein als auch in einer Gruppe mit anderen. Im Unterricht hören Sie die Textcassetten oder -CDs (=), üben das Sprechen, lesen Texte und schreiben Sätze oder kurze Texte über sich auf. Sie arbeiten mal zusammen, mal alleine, mal mit einem anderen Kursmitglied, mal mit einer kleinen Gruppe von Kursmitgliedern zusammen. Das gibt Ihnen viel Übung und mehr Sicherheit in der englischen Sprache. Durch abwechslungsreiche Übungen wird Ihr englischer Wortschatz systematisch erweitert, und grammatische Strukturen erscheinen Ihnen dann auch nicht mehr kompliziert. Im Gegenteil: Vieles wird Ihnen wieder vertraut und in Ihren aktiven Sprachgebrauch überführt.

Wie ist das Buch aufgebaut ?

Das Buch besteht aus 20 kurzen Units d. h. Lerneinheiten, die verschiedene Themenschwerpunkte haben. Jeder Unit vorangestellt ist die daraufvorbereitende *Checkpoint*-Seite. Nach jeder Unit folgt eine *Homestudy*-Seite, die zusammen mit der Homestudy-Cassette oder -CD (=)für die Nachbereitung der Stunde und die Festigung des zentralen Lernstoffes zu Hause gedacht sind, bevor erneut über den nächsten Checkpoint die nächste Unterrichtsstunde vorbereitet wird. Zwischen der Nachbereitung der vergangenen und Vorbereitung der neuen Stunde sollte etwas Zeit vergehen, damit Sie Abstand gewinnen.

Diese 4-Seiten-Kombinationen sind die Bausteine Ihres Kurses. Sie bieten aktuelle und interessante Themen als Rahmen für Aufgaben und Übungsmaterial in den Bereichen Grammatik, Wortschatz, Lese- und Hörverstehen, Sprech- und Schreibfertigkeit.

Nach jeder 4. Unit folgt eine etwas andere Sequenz. Im Mittelpunkt hier steht *Panorama*, Texte, die interessante landeskundliche Aspekte englischsprachiger Länder beschreiben. Weitere Bestandteile diese Sequenz sind *Lerntipps* und *Test yourself*. Hier können Sie in regelmäßigen Abständen Ihre Fortschritte und Ihren Lernerfolg selbst überprüfen. Vier optionale, zusätzliche *Extra*-Units, die verschiedene Aspekte der vier Jahreszeiten zum Thema haben, und vier Geschichten für die unterhaltsame Lektüre schließen das Angebot an Lernmaterial ab.
Unter der anschließenden Rubrik *Language & Culture* erhalten Sie nützliche Tipps und Hintergrundinformationen über das Leben in englischspachigen Ländern. Danach finden Sie im Anhang eine Nachschlagegrammatik mit Übungsmaterial, die in Kombination mit den Checkpoints und dem Refresher-Verweissystem in den Units und Homestudy-Teilen die notwendige Sicherheit bietet. Eine Zusammenfassung wichtiger Redemittel (*How to say it*) erleichtert Ihnen beim Sprechen das Nachschlagen der passenden Redewendung. Am Ende des Buches steht das *Dictionary*. Hier sind alle Wörter des Kurses aufgeführt, die über die 1000 Wörter des Grundbausteins hinausgehen, jeweils mit phonetischer Umschrift und deutscher Entsprechung in alphabetischer Reihenfolge.

Wenn Sie sich in der englischen Grammatik noch mehr vertiefen wollen, so steht Ihnen die *English Network Grammar* zur Verfügung, die die Grammatik speziell für deutsche Lerner aufbereitet hat: Dem, was deutschsprachigen Lernern erfahrungsgemäß Lernprobleme bereitet, wird besondere Aufmerksamkeit geschenkt. Sie erhöhen Ihren Lernerfolg zusätzlich mit dem *English Network Grammar Workbook 1*, dessen Einsatz Sie selber steuern können, zumal ein Lösungsschlüssel zur Selbstkontrolle enthalten ist.

Viel Spaß und viel Erfolg beim Lernen
wünschen Ihnen
Autorenteam und Verlag

Inhalt

Work and skills

Where you live

Spending time and money

Influences on your life

Stages of your life

Anhang Unitteil

Anhang Homestudy

Anhang Grammatik und Wortschatz

Texte und Übungen mit diesem Symbol finden Sie auf der Textcassette bzw. -CD

Texte und Übungen mit diesem Symbol finden Sie auf der Homestudy-Cassette bzw. -CD

CHECKPOINT 1

What you learn
Diese Unit behandelt die kleinen Probleme im Alltagsleben. Sie wiederholen hier u.a.:
- die einfache Gegenwart (*present simple*)
- die Stellung der Adverbien (*frequency adverbs*)
- Vorschläge machen und darauf reagieren (*making suggestions and reacting*)

Grammar 1: The present simple (*do / does*)

1 Grammar check
Write down the 3rd person singular of these verbs, like this: *start - starts*.
carry / catch / dance / do / fly / go / have / wash

2 A different kind of 'waiter'
Choose the correct word.

(1) **Does/Do** it make you angry when you (2) **has/ have** to wait in a queue for something? An agency in New York (3) **helps/help** people with this problem. Now busy New Yorkers (4) **doesn't/don't** have to wait in queues any more. When they (5) **needs/need** a new passport or they (6) **wants/want** theatre-tickets, they just (7) **rents/rent** someone from this agency to queue for them. If a customer (8) **have/has** to sign a document, the 'waiter' (9) **takes/take** it to the customer and then (10) **go/goes** back with the signed document. The customer doesn't (11) **has/have** to queue or wait. For business people, time (12) **is/are** money.

3 Negatives and questions
Make a negative sentence and a question from these sentences.

He goes to the theatre once a month.

1 negative: ....

....

2 question: *How often* ....

....?

They book tickets by phone.

3 negative: ....

....

4 question: *How* ....

....?

Grammar 2: Frequency adverbs

Number these frequency adverbs 1-6 in the order of frequency, beginning with *always*.

☐ always ☐ often ☐ sometimes
☐ never ☐ seldom ☐ usually

Put a cross (✗) in these sentences to show where a frequency adverb could go.

a) My neighbour goes to the theatre.

b) He is late for work on Mondays because of the heavy traffic.

c) Do you take a taxi when it rains?

How to say it: Making suggestions

Two people want to go to the theatre, but they have got a problem: their car has broken down!
Look at their conversation. A suggests how to get to the theatre. B's answers are in the wrong order.
Number the answers 1-4 in the correct order.

1 A: O.K. We can't use the car. That's not a problem. **Let's** take a taxi.
2 A: Yes, you're right. But **we could** go by bus.
3 A: Well, **why don't you** phone your brother and ask him for a lift?
4 A: **Shall we** ask Mother if we can borrow hers?

☐ B: No, because, he's always so busy. **Perhaps we could** borrow someone's car.

☐ B: **We can't do that**. It's too expensive.

☐ B: **Yes, let's**. That's a good idea.

☐ B: No, **I don't really want to** use public transport.

page 112

Language & Culture: page 109
If you have any problems with these exercises, ask your teacher in the next lesson.

Life's little problems

Unit 1

1 Starter: Problem solving

When do you have to queue? Does queueing make you angry? Tell the class about other situations which make you angry. Think about travelling, shopping, your family, school, and work.

Suggest ways of solving other students' problems. Do it like this:

A: *I usually work until six o'clock and the banks are always closed when I finish work.*
B: *What about going to the bank during your lunch-hour?*
A: *Yes, that's a good idea. / No, I can't do that because ...*

Use expressions like: *You could ... / Why don't you ...? / What about ...?*

2 LETS 1

LETS is an interesting new organisation which helps people solve some of their every day problems.
Look at the LETS poster on the left. What do you think the LETS organisation does?

To find out more about LETS, try to match questions 1-6 with answers a) -f).

Questions:
1 What is LETS?
2 What kind of services do people give?
3 How much do I ask for my services or goods?
4 How do I pay for a service?
5 Can young people offer any services to LETS?
6 Do I have to pay tax?
7 Who can become a LETS member?
8 How do I join?
9 How do I know what goods and services I can get?

Answers:

- ☐ a) You 'pay' for services with a LETS cheque.
- ☐ b) You can decide the price.
- ☐ c) People do jobs for you which you can't do or don't enjoy doing.
- ☐ d) Yes, they can babysit or look after animals.
- ☐ e) Private people don't have to pay tax but firms sometimes do.
- ☐ f) LETS is an organisation for local people who give and receive services without paying money.

Now listen to Sarah and Peter who are talking about LETS. Check if your answers are correct.

Listen to the conversation again and fill in the answers to questions 7-9.

7 g) ....

....

8 h) ....

....

....

9 i) ....

....

....

3 Vocabulary

➤ Money

In the conversation about LETS we heard a lot of words connected with money, like *cheque, pay, account*.

In groups, make a list of words that you think of when you hear the word 'money'.

➤ Word focus: *borrow* or *lend*?

Fill in the missing words.

Don't .... Graham any money. He always .... money and never pays it back.

You've left your bag at home and you need things like: a dictionary, a pen, a course book, a newspaper, some money.

Ask other students for what you need. Make questions with *borrow* or *lend*. Begin like this: *Could I ...?* or *Could you ...?*

4 How often do you do these things? 2 3

Choose three things from the list below and write down how often you do them. Use phrases like: *every day / once a week / twice a month / three times a year.*

Do it like this: I go to the bank once a week.

cook a meal	travel by taxi
clean the windows	go to the dentist's
go shopping	do homework
wash the car	go to the hairdresser's

Now write sentences about any of these things that you seldom or never do.

Work in pairs and find out how often your partner does some of these things. Ask questions beginning with: *Do you ever ...? / How often do you ...?*

Tell the class about some differences between your routines and your partner's, like this: *I usually travel by bus but Anna doesn't often travel by bus. She usually goes by car.*

5 Talking points

When we listened to Sarah and Peter talking about LETS, we heard that Gillian earns extra pocket-money.

- To earn extra pocket-money, many English teenagers have Saturday jobs. Do you think this is a good idea? Why? / Why not?
- How can young people earn extra money in your country?
- What do you think they spend their money on?
- Why do you think they want extra money?

Today's grammar

The present simple → *p. 128 + 137*

1 is used for explanations and general statements: *We don't pay our bills immediately, we pay them at the end of the month.*

2 is used to talk about habits and routines: *Sarah doesn't work in the garden; Jack does the gardening for her twice a month.*

3 is often used with frequency adverbs: *Gillian doesn't often go out on Saturday evenings so she usually babysits for her neighbours.*

Life's little problems

Homestudy

1 Write the sentences.

Write a sentence for each of the pictures. Use the words below the pictures. Sentences 7 and 8 are questions.

1
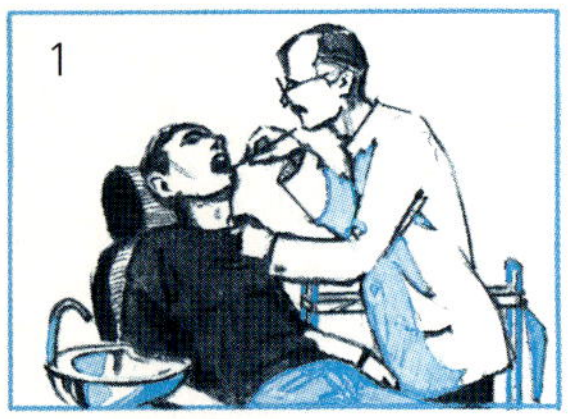
not often / go

2

never / go

3

sometimes / on Saturdays / go shopping

4

not usually / travel

5

always / travel

6

not / on Sundays / wash

7
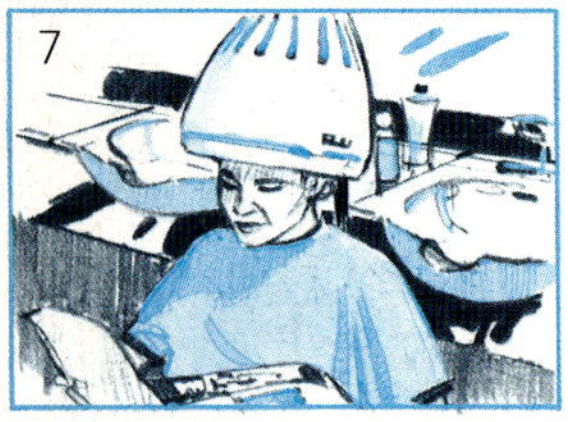
every week / go / ?

8

How often / clean / ?

1 *He doesn't often go to the dentist.*

2 ....

3 ....

....

4 ....

5 ....

6 ....

7 ....

....?

8 ....

....?

2 Suggestions

Use expressions from Unit 1 to make suggestions. Write one letter on each line.

Your friend seems unhappy. You suggest:

1 *L* _ _ ' _ go to the cinema.

2 *S* _ _ _ _ *w* _ go out for a nice meal?

3 *W* _ *c* _ _ _ _ get tickets for the new musical.

4 *W* _ _ _ *a* _ _ _ _ going for a walk in the park?

5 You look tired. *W* _ _ *d* _ _ ' _ *y* _ _ go to bed early?

3 Remember the words.

Find fifteen more verbs from Unit 1.

W	O	R	K	E	D	E	C	I	D	E	T
R	P	U	T	N	G	F	Z	T	R	W	H
I	F	L	Y	J	O	I	N	A	I	A	I
T	B	C	O	O	K	N	Q	L	V	L	N
E	H	T	R	Y	M	D	O	K	E	K	K

Four of these verbs have an irregular 3rd person singular (with *he, she* or *it*) in the simple present – not only with an *-s* at the end. Write the four irregular verb forms here:

He/She/It ...., ..., ..., ...

4 Pronunciation

Sarah and Peter used these words in their conversation about LETS. Do the underlined letters sound the same (✓) or different (✗)?

1 ☒ bobbins – money
2 ☐ member – cheque
3 ☐ account – could
4 ☐ woman – nobody
5 ☐ name – tax
6 ☐ simply – skills
7 ☐ sometimes – comes
8 ☐ earns – easy
9 ☐ good – cooking
10 ☐ come – on
11 ☐ girl – list
12 ☐ you – young

Now listen to the words.

5 Listening

Yvonne, a French student, and Hans, a German businessman, are in an English course together. They are talking about organisations like LETS in their countries. Listen and decide if each sentence is true (T) or false (F). Circle T or F.

1 There are only two SEL groups in France. T / F
2 "Grains of salt" are like bobbins. T / F
3 Germany has got about 300 trading circles. T / F
4 In Kassel a *Talent* is for 5 minutes' work. T / F
5 They say *bobbins* only in Manchester. T / F
6 Some German groups use the word *Kreuzer*. T / F
7 Peanuts are not only something to eat. T / F

CHECKPOINT 2

What you learn
Sie erfahren hier mehr über die Selbsthilfegruppe LETS. Sie wiederholen u.a.:
- die vollendete Gegenwart (*present perfect*)
- seit *(for* and *since)*
- (sich und andere) vorstellen (*introducing yourself and others*)

Grammar 1: The present perfect (*have / has gone*)

1 Grammar check
Do you remember the past participle of these verbs?
Example: *go - gone*.
be / buy / catch / fall / feel / forget / get / know / show / think / wear

2 Helping the community
Fill in the correct form of the verb.

.... you (1 *hear*) .... about the school problem in some British villages? Many schools (2 *close*) .... because a lot of people (3 *leave*) .... the villages to work in towns. In one village in England a mother, who (4 *live*) .... there for ten years and (5 *have*) .... three children herself, (6 *ask*) .... other mothers to have more children to save the local school. The school must close if there are not at least 13 children for each school year. So far they (7 *not find*) .... enough children. But there is hope for the future! Six women (8 *say*) .... they are expecting babies. It is not known how many mothers and fathers (9 *agree*) .... to help the community!

3 Which sentence is correct?
Cross out the wrong one.

He's an old friend of mine ...
1 I know him for 20 years.
2 I have known him for 20 years.

Grammar 2: *for* and *since*

Choose the correct word (*for* or *since*) in each sentence.
1 I have been a member of LETS *for/since* 3 months.
2 I have been a member of LETS *for/since* January.

Put in the correct word, *for* or *since*.

We use .... to talk about a period of time.

We use .... to talk about a point of time.
Which word(s) do you use for *for* and *since* in your language? ....

How to say it: Introducing people

Match the phrases.

1 Mr Leason, I would like to introduce you to my boss, Mathew Herriot.
2 Peter, I'd like you to meet my wife, Susan.
3 Jim, this is Julia.

☐ a) Hi, there! I've heard a lot about you.
☐ b) How do you do, sir?
☐ c) Hello, nice to meet you.

Which situation is the most formal and which is the least formal?

Most formal: ....

Least formal: ....

What is the correct answer to 'How do you do?'
a) How do you do?
b) Very well, thanks.

page 112

Language & Culture: page 109
If you have any problems with these exercises, ask your teacher in the next lesson.

Helping each other

Unit 2

1 Starter: What have you done? 1

Interview another student about some things that he/she has done or has never done. Ask questions with: *Have you ever ...?*

Here are some verbs to help you: *drink / eat / fly / go to / learn / live / meet / see / speak to.*

Do it like this: A: *Have you ever ridden a horse?*

B: *Yes, I have. / No, I haven't.*

Then introduce your partner to the class and tell them the most interesting piece of information you have found out.

Use expressions like: *I'd like to introduce ... to you. / I'd like you to meet ... / This is ...*

MEETING PEOPLE

This week 'MEETING PEOPLE' is talking to three members of the self-help organisation LETS – an organisation whose members do jobs for each other and don't charge money.

Hello, my name's Len Cartwright and I'm a milkman. I know this town really well because I've been a milkman here since 1985. My job has changed a lot over the last few years. When I first started this job, we only delivered milk but now we sell everything you need for breakfast, from eggs to orange-juice. Many people like the service but they haven't got a lot of money. That's why my dairy has joined LETS. Have you ever heard of this organisation? Members don't have to use money – they can pay their bills with a LETS cheque. And the dairy is very happy because we have 'sold' a lot more milk recently. Even the garage has become a member of LETS and they have serviced all our milk-vans and so they'll get free milk for one year! And the local cleaners get free milk, too because they wash all our coats.

Hi! I'm Lin Wang and I'm 22. I was born in China but I've lived in England since I was six. When I left school, I worked for a big department store and then it closed down. I've had two or three other jobs since then but I'm unemployed at the moment. I've been out of work for almost a year. I *am* looking for a job but I haven't found anything yet. Because I'm always short of cash, my mother suggested that I should join LETS and do odd jobs for people. You don't get money but other members do jobs for you. Up to now, I've repaired two bicycles, a broken lawn-mower and I've mended an old lady's garden-gate. I've earned a lot of 'bobbins' and tomorrow I'm going to 'spend' some of them on a really cool haircut!

Let me introduce myself: I'm Mary Duckworth and I'm 82 years old. I can't walk very well and so it's difficult to do the housework or go shopping. I joined LETS two years ago and it has changed my life completely! Two young women, Sue and Ann, come to my home three times a week to help me with the housework. They are both young mothers who haven't got a lot of money for extras so they joined LETS about six months ago – it was just before Christmas – and they've done a lot of little jobs for me since then. And, look, I've just knitted a pullover for Sue's daughter. I've knitted a few pullovers for LETS. It doesn't cost me anything to advertise them in the local newspaper and LETS people come and 'buy' them. I've lived in this town all my life but I have never known people to be so friendly and helpful!

2 Helping each other

Make three groups. Each group will read about one member of LETS in the magazine article on page 6. In your group, discuss how the LETS members that you have read about have helped each other or have helped local businesses.

Then work with two people from the other groups and tell them about the person in your passage and about his/her role in LETS.

3 How to pay

Read the last three sentences of each passage. Why are the words '*sold*', '*spend*' and '*buy*' in inverted commas? What ways do you know of paying for things?

4 How long ...? 3

Read about Mary Duckworth and then answer these questions with *for* and then with *since*:
How long has Mary Duckworth lived in that town?
How long have Sue and Ann been members of LETS?

Look at the list below. Find someone in your class who can answer *yes* to your questions. Write down the student's name on the line. Then ask another question with *How long ...?*
Do it like this: *Do you live near the school?*
How long have you lived there?

Find someone who ...

- lives near the school ....
- is a member of a sports club ....
- has got a car ....
- works in an office ....
- has got a dog or a cat ....
- is married ....
- has got a computer ....

Now tell the class what you have found out, like this:
Sue has got a car. She has had a car for three years.

5 Have already done / Haven't done yet

Read the passage about Lin Wang and write down one thing Lin Wang has *already* done and one thing he hasn't done *yet*. Then compare your sentences with a partner.

Now tell the class one thing you have already done this week and one thing you are planning to do but haven't done yet. Think about your work, your home, your school, your family and friends.

6 What has just happened?

In small groups complete these sentences in at least two different ways. Say what has just happened, like this:
Len is happy because ... he has just won £50 / his daughter has just had a baby.

1 Len is going to turn off the TV because ...
2 Len has got oil on his hands because ...
3 Len feels cold because ...
4 Len is making a cup of coffee because ...
5 Len isn't hungry because ...

7 Vocabulary

➤ Plurals

Many different groups of people use LETS services. They may be teenagers, housewives, young mothers, unemployed people, businessmen and business women, employees, senior citizens, or children.
Underline the irregular plurals in this list and then write down the singular of these words. Check your answers with a partner.

Now with your partner, write down the plural of these words: *boss / box / boy / bus / church / factory / family / foot / hobby / holiday / knife / lady / life / potato / secretary / tax / tomato / tooth.*

➤ Word focus: *been* or *gone*?

Lin Wang has been to China; his mother has gone to China. Where is he now? Where is she now?

Tell the class two places you have been to this week.

8 Talking points

- What skills have you got which you could offer to an organisation like LETS?
- How do you think could LETS help you?
- What organisations do you know in your country/ town/area which help people? What do they do? For example, is there an organisation like *Meals on Wheels* in England? They take meals to old people at home.

Today's grammar

The present perfect → p. 129 + 130

1 is used to talk about experiences we have had at some time in our lives (but we're not interested in *when* these things happened): *I've had two or three different jobs.*

2 is used to talk about the result of an action which is finished: *Look! I've just knitted a pullover.*

3 is used to talk about situations which started in the past and continue up to the present: *I've been a milkman since 1985 / since I moved here. I've been a milkman for over 10 years.*

Helping each other

Homestudy

Jobs to do this week:

1 repair Ann's bicycle ✔
2 mend Mary's garden-gate
3 do Mary's shopping ✔
4 wash Len's milk-van ✔
5 clean Sue's windows

1 What has he done?

Write what Lin Wang has already done (✔) and what he hasn't done yet.

1 *He has already repaired Ann's bicycle.* ....

2 ....

3 ....

4 ....

5 ....

2 Write the sentences

Sue and Ann are talking about Mary Duckworth. Write the words in the correct order. In each list there are two words you don't need. Cross them out.

1 all / has / her / here / life / lived / lives / Mary / since

....

2 1986 / alone / been / died / for / has / her / husband / in / is / she / since

....

3 a / been / for / has / is / LETS / member / of / she / since / two / years

....

4 for / have / know / known / Mary / months / now / six / since / we

....

5 December / for / have / her / joined / know / known / last / LETS / since / we / we

....

3 Introductions

Listen to the four dialogues and write the number of the dialogue in the box next to each picture.

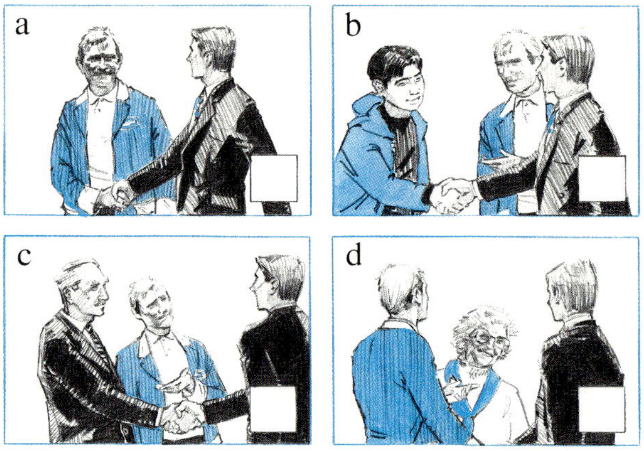

Listen to the dialogues again and write the number of the dialogue in the box next to each expression.

☐ Hello, my name's Cartwright, Len Cartwright.
☐ How do you do?
☐ I would like to introduce you to ...
☐ I'd like you to meet a new neighbour.
☐ I'm happy to meet you.
☐ Nice to meet you.
☐ Pleased to meet you.
☐ This is ...

4 Plurals

These words were all in Units 1 and 2. Write the plural form after the correct spelling rule.

baby	church	dictionary	taxi
boy	class	lunch	wife
business	community	milkman	woman
child	country	Saturday	yourself

Add *-s* (regular): ....

Add *-es*: ....

Change *y* to *i* and add *-es*: ....

Change *f* to *v* and add *-s* or *-es*: ....

Irregular plurals: ....

CHECKPOINT 3

What you learn

Diese Unit behandelt unsere Arbeitswelt, heute und damals. Sie wiederholen hier u. a.:

- die einfache Gegenwart (*present simple*) und die einfache Vergangenheit (*past simple*)
- früher (*used to*)
- Zustimmen und Widersprechen (*agreeing and disagreeing*)

Grammar 1: The past simple (*went*)

1 Grammar check

Do you remember the past tense of these verbs?
begin / catch / check / do / drink / eat / fall / feel / find / hire / lose / meet / pay / put / recommend / see / spend / tell / think / wear.

2 The skating doctor

Fill in the missing verb.

Some years ago, when Doctor Graham Hutchison (1) *s* _ _ _ _ _ _ _ work in a big hospital in the north of England, he (2) *u* _ _ _ to wear roller-skates to go from one part of the hospital to another. It (3) *w* _ _ quicker than walking. An interviewer (4) *a* _ _ _ _ Dr. Hutchison, "Did all the doctors (5) *w* _ _ _ skates?" Dr. Hutchison (6) *a* _ _ _ _ _ _ _ _, "No, of course we didn't all (7) *w* _ _ _ skates – the children's doctor (8) *w* _ _ _ rollerblades!"

Grammar 2: used to

Write these sentences again with *used to*.

1 One doctor had rollerblades.

……………………………………………………………

2 He didn't wear skates.

……………………………………………………………

3 Did he ride a bike at work?

……………………………………………………………

Now put *use to* in one of these sentences:

a) He didn't ………… ride a bike.

b) He didn't ………… break his leg.

Why can't we have *use to* in the other sentence?

How to say it: Agreeing and disagreeing

Put the words into the right order to make sentences.

1 sorry / I'm / wrong / but / that's

…………………………………………………………… ☐

2 sure / right / I'm / you're

…………………………………………………………… ☐

3 true / that's / very / yes

…………………………………………………………… ☐

4 must / I / you / afraid / disagree / I'm / with

…………………………………………………………… ☐

5 that / you / look / say / can't

…………………………………………………………… ☐

6 right / you're / quite

…………………………………………………………… ☐

Now write A next to the sentences we can use to agree with someone and D next to the sentences for disagreeing.

page 112

Language & Culture: page 109
If you have any problems with these exercises, ask your teacher in the next lesson.

Benson's clothes factory

is looking for a well-dressed man, between 21 and 30 years old, for the position of

Assistant Manager.

He must have experience in office-work and in shorthand and typing.
Working hours: Mon. - Fri. 8 a.m. - 6 p.m. Saturdays 9 a.m. - 3 p.m.
Salary: £500 a year and 2 weeks paid summer holidays.

Please write to: The Manager, Benson's Clothes Factory, Stockwell Rd., Ealing.

Work – then and now

Unit 3

1 Starter: Years ago

Look at the list of jobs and think what the people used to do / didn't use to do 100 years ago.
nurse / teacher / farmer / factory-worker / policeman / secretary / shop-assistant
Then ask each other questions, like this:
A: *What did / didn't nurses use to do?*
B: *Nurses used to wear long dresses.* or *Nurses didn't use to have much training.*
C, what did / didn't teachers use to do?

2 Then and now

Look at these two job advertisements. What kind of person did the company want 50 years ago? What kind of person does the company want today? What did the company offer then? What does it offer now?

3 In the canteen

You are going to hear a conversation between two colleagues in Benson's canteen. Mr Read has worked for the company for over 40 years and Nigel has only been with the firm for a short time. Mr Read and Nigel are talking about their work. Listen and underline the things in the adverts that they talk about. What are the differences between Benson's 40 years ago and now? Talk about office technology, working hours, canteen and clothes.

Now read the sentences below.
Tick (✓) the sentences which are true.

- ☐ 1 Nigel doesn't like machines.
- ☐ 2 Nigel thinks modern technology is wonderful.
- ☐ 3 Mr Read started work there 50 years ago.
- ☐ 4 Office work used to be quicker in those days.
- ☐ 5 Mr Read started work at seven o'clock, from Mondays to Saturdays.
- ☐ 6 Nigel went to the dentist's before work yesterday.
- ☐ 7 Nigel arrived at work at ten o'clock.
- ☐ 8 The workers brought coffee to work.
- ☐ 9 Mr and Mrs Read were rich in those days.

Listen to the conversation again and check your answers. Then correct the sentences which are not true. Do it like this: *Mr Read didn't have a computer, he had a typewriter.*

4 Going to work

Last Thursday evening Nigel went to a party and came home very late. Look at the pictures and say what happened the next morning. You can use these verbs: *arrive at / be / drink / drive / eat / get dressed / get up / go / have a shower / have breakfast / look at / not wait / pay / phone / read / ring / run / see / wake up.*

5 Agreeing and disagreeing

Write down phrases that you can use when you want to agree or disagree with someone, like the phrases on the Checkpoint page.

In groups of three, say how you feel about the things below and give your reasons, like this:
I'm sorry, I can't agree with you. I think ... .
I think you're quite right because ... .

Mobile phones are fantastic! • Doctors are underpaid. • They should ban smoking in all public places. • Computers make life easier. • It must be great to be a stewardess. • All people should stop work at 60.

6 What did you do? 1

Write down on a piece of paper the year (and, if you can remember, the date) when something important happened to you. Then exchange your paper with a partner. He/She will ask you ten questions and try to find out what happened to you in that year.
Ask and answer questions beginning with *Were you ...?* or *Did you ...?* like this: *Were you at school at that time? Did you start school in that year?*

Now tell the class what happened to your partner in that year (or, if you didn't find out, your partner can tell the class).

7 Vocabulary

➤ Word focus: *chief, boss* or *chef*?

Match the words to the pictures:

☐ chef ☐ boss ☐ chief

➤ Men and women

A boss / teacher / doctor can be a man or a woman.
Look at these jobs: waiter / landlord / policeman / teacher / office-boy.
What do we call women who do these jobs?

8 Talking points

- When you think of a pilot, do you think first of a man or a woman? Why?
- Are there any jobs you think are 'men's jobs' or 'women's jobs'?
- Which jobs can men/women do today which they didn't normally do a hundred years ago?
- Can you think of any jobs that women never, or seldom, do today?
- Why were there very few women in the business world 60 or 70 years ago?

Today's grammar

1 The past simple → p. 130

- is used to talk about what happened at a certain time in the past (last week / a month ago / yesterday / in 1991): *Nigel arrived at work at ten o'clock yesterday.*
- is used to talk about things which often happened in the past: *We always brought sandwiches to work.*

2 Used to → p. 130

- is also used to talk about things which often happened in the past but do not happen any more now: *We used to bring sandwiches to work but now we eat in the canteen.*

Work – then and now

Homestudy

1 The old days

Write in the correct forms of these verbs. Use *used to* with three of the verbs and *not (n't)* with three others.

be	decide	earn	learn	rain	spend	tell
buy	drink	fly	like	save	take	wear
can	drive	have	pay	say	take	work

When Mr Read (1) .... a young office worker in the 1950s he (2) .... tea to work in a flask every day. Now he usually (3) .... coffee in the canteen. He sometimes (4) .... his colleagues how he (5) .... many years ago. They (6) .... any computers in those days, only typewriters. Mr Read (7) .... type very well, and one year he even (8) .... a course at night school and (9) .... to write shorthand.

With his first salary Mr Read (10) .... a new suit. He (11) .... £35 for it, and he (12) .... it for about fifteen years until his wife (13) .... that she (14) .... it any more. Even though he (15) .... very much money at first, he (16) .... some money every week. In 1959 he (17) .... to buy a car. He and his wife (18) .... to Brighton that summer and (19) .... their holiday by the sea. But it (20) .... the whole time, so the next year they (21) .... to Majorca for their summer holidays.

2 What was the question?

Nigel is asking Mr Read about his life as a young man in the 1950s. Write Nigel's questions, using *use to* in all four.

1 *Did* ....

....?

By underground? No, I used to travel to work by bus.

2 *How* ....

....?

I used to earn £500 a year. That doesn't sound like much, but a pound was worth more in those days.

3 .... *work?*

We used to start work at eight o'clock every morning, nine on Saturdays.

4 *What* .... *to work?*

We used to wear suits and ties to work every day.

3 Agreeing and disagreeing

Which of these expressions can you use
1 to agree with someone?
2 to disagree politely?
3 to disagree strongly?
Write the correct number in each box.

- ☐ Actually, I'm not so sure about that.
- ☐ I think that's totally wrong!
- ☐ I can see your point, but ...
- ☐ I think so, too.
- ☐ I'm sorry, I can't quite agree with you there.
- ☐ That's interesting, but don't you think ...
- ☐ That's not true at all.
- ☐ Well, I wouldn't really say that.
- ☐ You're absolutely right.

What do you think this man might be saying?
Tick (✓) two expressions from the list above.

4 Pronunciation

These words are all from Unit 3. Some of them look the same in German, but the stress (= *Betonung*) is in a different place. Underline the stressed part of each word.

ad<u>ver</u>tisement	coffee	experience	recommend
appointment	colleagues	important	secretary
assistant	conversation	modern	technology

Now listen and check your answers.

CHECKPOINT 4

What you learn
Diese Unit beschäftigt sich mit der Bewerbung um einen neuen Arbeitsplatz. Sie wiederholen hier u.a.:
- die vollendete Gegenwart (*present perfect*) und die einfache Vergangenheit (*past simple*)
- den bestimmten und den unbestimmten Artikel (*the definite and indefinite article*)
- Telefonsprache (*telephoning*)

Grammar 1: The present perfect (*have / has gone*) and the past simple (*went*)

1 What's the difference?
Tick (✔) the sentence that tells you where Minh lives now.
1 ☐ Minh lived in Vietnam for over 20 years.
2 ☐ Minh has lived in Britain for over 10 years.

2 Translate these sentences.
1 Er ist in Vietnam geboren.

....

2 Er hat Vietnam 1980 verlassen.

....

3 Bis jetzt hat er viele Berufe gehabt.

....

3 Success story
Read this true story of Minh Cuong, a Vietnamese boat-person. Put the verbs into the present perfect or the past simple.

Minh Cuong (1 *be*) .... many things in his life: a soldier, a boat-person and a student. Minh (2 *be*) .... born in Vietnam in 1953. When he (3 *be*) .... a boy he (4 *fight*) .... as a soldier in the Vietnam war. In 1982 he (5 *come*) .... to Britain and he (6 *live*) .... here ever since. During his first two years in Manchester he (7 *go*) .... to courses to learn English and he (8 *use to*) .... do all sorts of part-time jobs to earn money. In 1984, Minh (9 *start*) .... a small business which (10 *give*) .... work to 20 people. In the first year he (11 *make*) .... £150,000. And, a few years ago, Minh (12 *become*) .... the first Vietnamese millionaire in Europe.

Grammar 2: The indefinite and definite article (a, an, the)

There are two mistakes in each sentence. Correct them.

1 When Minh was soldier, he wore an uniform.

2 He has travelled a lot in the Switzerland and in U.S.A.

3 The Minh learnt to play guitar when he was young.

4 He had a lunch a hour ago.

How to say it: Telephoning

Look at these pairs of sentences. Write F in the box to show which sentence is more formal.

1 a) ☐ Hello, this is John Leason.
b) ☐ Good morning, John Leason speaking.

2 a) ☐ Could you put me through to Eve Daniels, please?
b) ☐ Can I speak to Eve, please?

3 a) ☐ Wait a minute, I'll tell her you're on the phone.
b) ☐ Could you hold on a moment, please, I'll see if she's there.

4 a) ☐ I'm sorry, she's just gone out.
b) ☐ I'm afraid she's not in at the moment.

5 a) ☐ Would you like to leave a message?
b) ☐ Can I take a message?

6 a) ☐ Would you like to call back later?
b) ☐ You can ring again later if you like.

page 112

Language & Culture: page 109
If you have any problems with these exercises, ask your teacher in the next lesson.

Getting a job

Unit 4

1 Starter: Have you ever ...?/What was it like? 1

Ask other students about things that they have done in their lives. Begin your questions with *Have you ever ...?* When the answer is *Yes, I have,* find out some details about the experience by asking: *When did you ...?*

Do it like this:

A: *Have you ever been to America?*
B: *Yes, I have.*
A: *When did you go there?*
B: *I went there in 1995.*
A: *What did you ...?* *Why did you ...?*
Where did you ...? *Were you ...?*

Here are some ideas to help you:

an interview	in another country
a computer course	a lot of money
another foreign language	a very boring/ interesting job
a holiday job	

2 Telephoning about a job

Leason Industries needs a new receptionist. A woman is telephoning the factory about the job. Listen to the conversation and make notes about her name / her age / job experience / language skills / her family situation / her reasons for changing jobs / other points.
Then compare your notes with a partner.

3 The best one for the job

John Leason, the manager, has interviewed three people. Read the notes that he made during the interviews.

In small groups, look at the notes that you made about Jane and the notes about the other three people. Discuss who is the best person for the job and say why. Which person would you not choose? Why?

After five minutes, compare your answers with other groups. Can you agree on the person that you would offer the job to?

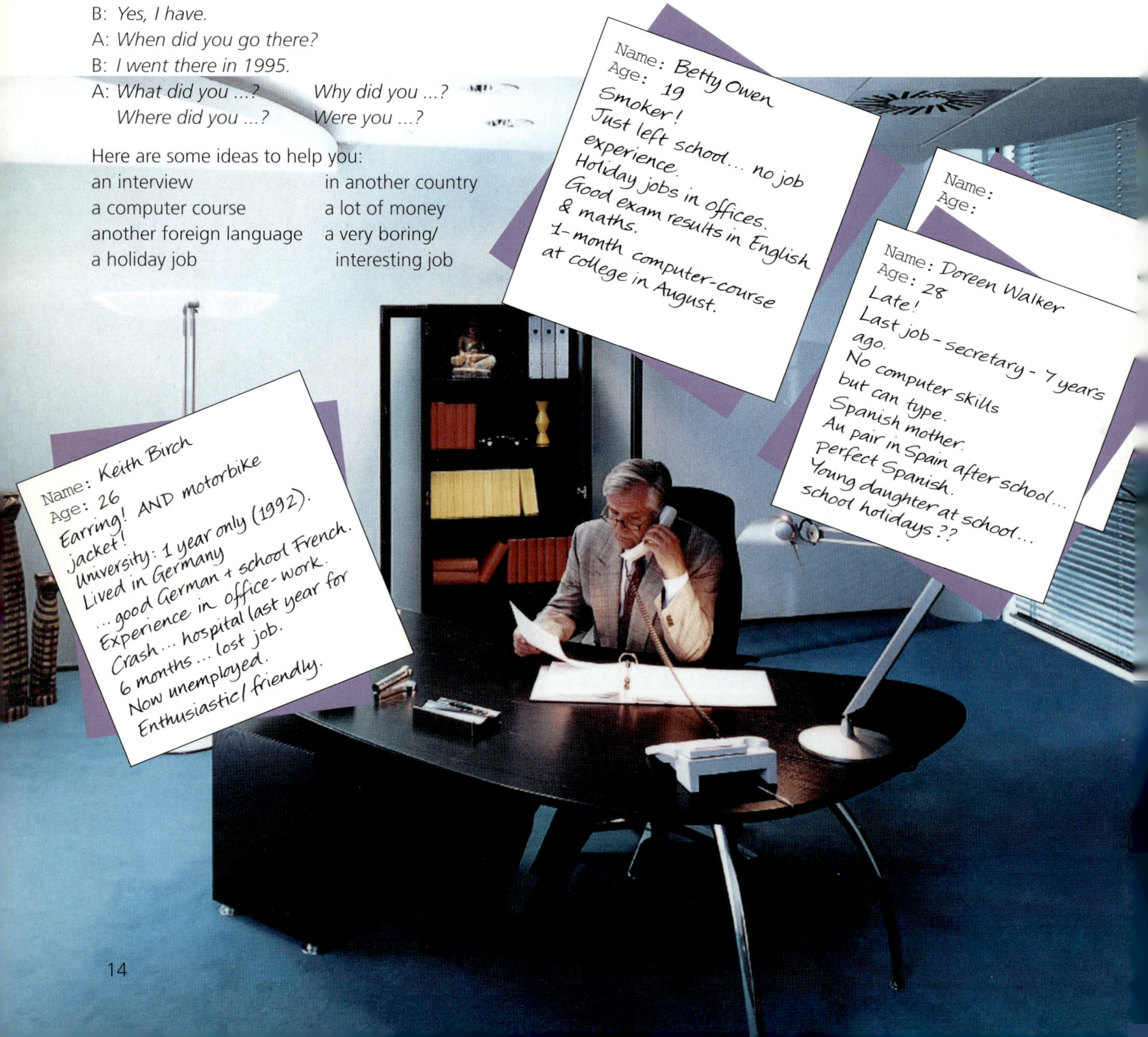

4 What would you say?

You try to phone Mr Leason about the job but he isn't there. You speak to the receptionist (your partner) who will write down your message. The telephone phrases on the Checkpoint page will help you.

5 Vocabulary: Idiom bank

She's up to her eyes in work.

What do you think this expression means?
Is there an expression like this in German?

Can you think of a situation where you could use one of the following expressions?

He's a workaholic.
Job-sharing is ideal for her.
She's work-shy.

6 The article

6a What's his job? 2a

Say what his job is, like this: *He flies planes ... he's a pilot.*

1 He types letters and answers the phone.
2 He takes food to the customers in restaurants.
3 He takes out bad teeth.
4 He cuts your hair.
5 He sells things in a shop.
6 He paints pictures.

6b Where have you been? 2b

Underline the places in this list that you have been to:

U.S.A. / St. Peter's Square, Rome / U.K. / Oxford Street / Switzerland / 5th Avenue / Greece / Sunset Boulevard / Netherlands / Broadway / Austria / Italy.

Now tell the class which places you have been to. Then say when you were last there. Do it like this:
I've been to Hollywood. I was there a few years ago.

6c Where did they go? 2b

In pairs, say where these people went.

1 The burglar
2 The mother
3 The schoolboy
4 The workmen
5 The couple
6 The firemen

went to

☐ a) the school to repair the broken windows.
☐ b) church to get married.
☐ c) the church to put out the fire.
☐ d) prison for a very long time.
☐ e) the prison to see her son.
☐ f) school when he was five.

Why do we use the word *the* in some sentences and not in others?

7 Talking points

- Which professions do you think earn the highest salaries? Which groups of people do you think are overpaid/underpaid?
- Is there any job you would love/hate to have? Why?
- Tell the class about a job that you have had. What interested you most about the job when you chose it?
- What is your job situation at the moment? Has it changed at all in the last two, five or ten years? How?

Today's grammar

1 The present perfect and the past simple → p. 131

- The present perfect is used to find out if people have had a certain experience at any time in their lives: *Have you ever worked in a hotel before?*
- The past simple is used to find out more details about the situation: *Why did you leave your last job?*
- The present perfect is used to talk about things we have done in our lives (but *when* it happened is not important): *I've been a waitress and I've worked in a factory.*
- The past simple is used to talk about when we did things: *I was a waitress in 1994 and I worked in a factory three years ago.*

Remember: With a past time, use the past tense.

2 The article

a) The indefinite article → p. 135

A / An is used before professions: *She's a receptionist.*

b) The definite article → p. 135

- *The* is not normally used before the names of people, roads, streets or squares: *Jane lives in Green Square.*
- *The* is not used before most countries but is used before groups of states: *He went to Canada and to the United States.*
- *The* is not used before *prison / school / church / university / work / hospital* when the function of the place is being used: *The student went to university (to study French)* but: *The professor went to the university (to interview a student).*

Getting a job

Homestudy

1 Past simple or present perfect?

Choose a verb for each sentence and write in the correct form. Use each verb only once.

~~decide~~	~~hear~~	~~leave~~	~~not send~~	~~take~~
~~have~~	~~learn~~	~~not get~~	~~ring~~	~~work~~

1 Jane ....left.... school in 1984.

2 She ....worked.... in the office at Benson's Clothes Factory from 1984 to 1990.

3 She ....has had.... a job at a hotel since 1990.

4 Now she ....has decided.... to look for a new job.

5 Last week she ..rang.. up Leason Industries.

6 She ....hasn't sent.... them her CV yet.

7 She ....didn't get.... home until midnight yesterday.

8 ....Has.... Mr Leason ever ....heard.... of Benson's?

9 ....Did.... Jane ....learn.... French when she was at school?

10 ....Has.... she ever ....taken.... any French courses at night school?

2 Telephoning

Jane has been hired as a receptionist at Leason Industries. Listen to this telephone call and take down the message for Mr Leason.

MESSAGE FOR ....

FROM ....

TEL. NUMBER ....

....

....

....

....

....

....

....

3 Pronunciation

These verbs are all from Units 3 and 4. How should you pronounce the *-ed* ending? Write each word in the correct place.

changed	enjoyed	interviewed	travelled
checked	finished	lived	wanted
decided	happened	started	washed
dressed	interested	talked	worked

/d/ as in *called*: ....

/t/ as in *asked*: ....

/id/ as in *needed*: ....

Now listen to the words.

4 Articles

Put in *a, an* or *the* in the spaces. If you don't need any of these words, put a ✗ in the space.

That evening (1) .... Jane and her husband went out to (2) .... dinner at (3) ..a/the.. Tandoori restaurant in (4) .... Broad Street. They had (5) ..an.. excellent meal, and then (6) .... Jane told her husband about her first day at her new job. "I got to (7) .... work at 9 o'clock," she said. "My colleague, (8) .... Tina, showed me what to do. She's actually (9) ..a.. student, and she's going back to (10) .... university next term, so that's why I got her job. It was (11) ..a.. busy day and (12) ..the.. time went very quickly. There were phone calls from (13) ..the.. Netherlands, (14) .... Switzerland, (15) .... Canada and (16) ..the.. United States. And (17) ..~~the~~ a.. professor rang up. He wants Mr Leason to give (18) ..a.. talk at (19) ..the.. university."

Lerntipp

*Liebe Englisch-Expertin,
jetzt mache ich zum wievielten Mal einen Anlauf, mein Englisch zu verbessern. Ich habe mich für einen Kurs angemeldet und auch das Buch gekauft. Wie kann ich die Sache nun richtig angehen, damit sie diesmal besser klappt?*

*Yours sincerely
(so viel kann ich noch!),
Romy, Wolfsburg*

Liebe Romy,
dass Sie sich für einen Kurs angemeldet haben, finde ich prima, denn es lernt sich leichter und effektiver in der Gruppe als immer nur alleine. Jetzt sollten Sie aber ganz fest beschließen, keine Ausreden mehr gelten zu lassen und wirklich regelmäßig in Ihren Kurs zu gehen. Wenn Sie einen guten Kontakt zu den anderen Kursteilnehmern entwickeln, wird Ihnen der regelmäßige Kursbesuch bestimmt nicht schwerfallen. Nutzen Sie die Kursstunden, indem Sie aktiv mitmachen, auch und vor allem in der Partner- und Kleingruppenarbeit. Machen Sie die Übungen mit verschiedenen Partnern, dadurch lernen Sie alle Leute kennen und hören zu Ihren Fragen nicht immer die gleichen Antworten. Reden Sie in der Partnerarbeit konsequent nur Englisch. Sie werden es bald merken, der Übungseffekt ist enorm.

Yours sincerely,
Your English Expert

P.S. Was Sie zu Hause machen, ist natürlich bei dieser Art von Kurs auch **sehr** wichtig. Arbeiten Sie **vor** jeder Stunde die Checkpoint-Seite durch und **nach** jeder Stunde die Homestudy-Seite. Dazwischen können Sie in den Grammatik- und Wortschatz-Anhängen nachschlagen. Und wenn Sie Fragen haben, schreiben Sie sie auf und fragen Sie gleich in der nächsten Kursstunde Ihre/n Kursleiter/in.

Wordfield

Jobs

Write the jobs in this puzzle.

1 He finds burglars.
2 He / She flies a plane.
3 He delivers milk to people's houses.
4 He (or she) is in the army.
5 He / She types, phones, sends faxes.
6 She serves people on a plane.
7 He / She decides how to build roads and bridges.
8 He / She helps doctors and patients.
9 He / She works in a garden.
10 He / She works in a shop or helps other people to do a job.

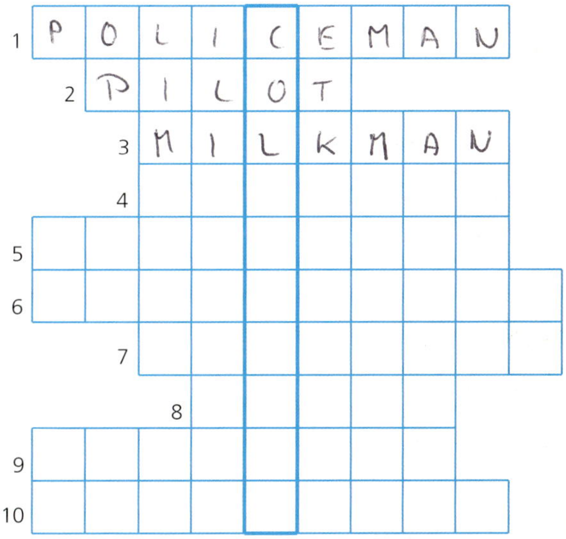

Key word: ....

PANORAMA 1

Living and working in New Zealand

1 Maoris

When the Polynesians – later called the Maoris – came to New Zealand from the north more than a thousand years ago, they found a country empty of people. The Europeans did not make their home there until the 19th century. For a number of years there were wars because the Europeans took away land from the Maoris. But slowly the Europeans began to respect the Maoris for their love of art and nature. Today the Maoris (about 9.5 per cent of New Zealanders) still have a very strong culture and most of them speak their own language and English, too. The New Zealanders are proud of their ethnic mix. 'We're all Kiwis,' they say.

2 Quiz

1 What is the capital of New Zealand?
- Wellington
- Christchurch
- Auckland

2 Which ocean is New Zealand in?
- The Pacific Ocean
- The Atlantic Ocean
- The Indian Ocean

3 What is the currency of New Zealand?
- pounds
- shillings
- dollars

4 Who first landed in New Zealand?
- Cook
- Magellan
- Columbus

3 Did you know?

- New Zealand was the first country to give the vote to women. (1893)
- 74% of New Zealanders live on the North Island.
- In New Zealand, they drive on the left.
- New Zealand is about the same size as Britain but only three and a half million people live there. (About fifty-seven and a half million people live in Britain).

Which piece of information surprised you most? Why?

4 Kiri te Kanawa

Put in the missing words: *at, into, from, on, since, of, of, of, to, to, to, in, in, in, in, in, in, in.*

The opera-singer Kiri te Kanawa is one .... New Zealand's most famous exports. Kiri was born .... Gisbourne .... March 6th, 1944. Her mother was European and her father was Maori. Kiri's music-loving mother pushed her talented daughter .... a musical career and even moved the family .... Auckland so that Kiri could have singing lessons .... one of the best teachers .... New Zealand. She soon became a star .... her own country, but her international career started .... 1966 when she began to study music .... London. She became well-known .... many non-opera-goers when she sang .... Prince Charles's wedding .... July, 1981 in front .... a TV audience of six million people! Kiri has recorded traditional Maori music and also classical music and pop songs .... many different languages. She has been married .... an Australian, Desmond Parks, ... 1967 and they have two adopted children.

New Zealand needs you!

Thinking of emigrating to New Zealand and becoming a Kiwi?

- Enjoy our relaxed lifestyle
- Clean water and clean air
- Beautiful countryside
- Own home and garden
- Pleasant climate
- Friendly people
- Start a business
- Use your skills

Find out what New Zealand needs from you. Please feel free to call us.

NEW ZEALAND EMBASSY
TEL. 0171 / 555 2846

Immigration Form

This form must be completed in English.

Sex: male ☐ female ☐

Full name: ....

Date of birth: *23* day *January* month *1960* year

Country of birth: ....

Nationality: ....

Marital Status: never married ☐ now married ☐ widowed ☐ separated ☐ divorced ☐

Address: ....

....

Telephone number: ....

What is your usual occupation?

....

What kind of work do you want to do in New Zealand?

....

Details of family members who want to travel with you:

Name: ....

Relationship: ....

Have you ever been to New Zealand? yes ☐ no ☐

If yes, please say: where ....

when .... how long for ....

Do you have family or friends in New Zealand?

yes ☐ no ☐

If 'yes', please give details:

Name: *Barbara Gordon*

Address: *35 Summer Drive, Wellington*

Relationship: ....

5 Ringing the embassy

Jean saw the above poster about New Zealand and decided to ring the embassy to get some more information. Listen to the conversation and tick the things on the poster she talks about.

Now read the immigration form on the right. Then listen to the telephone conversation again and fill in the information you get about Jean.
In groups of three, compare your information.

6 Talking points

- Would you like to live in another country? Why? / Why not?
- If you left this country, which country would you choose to live in? Why?

Think about things like the language, the climate, jobs, your family, the food, the lifestyle, the people.

Test yourself

1 Write the questions.

This is Doreen Walker. Use these words to write questions about her. The first word of each question is missing.

1 a / as / secretary / she / to / use / work

....

....?

2 a / computer / course / ever / she / taken

....

....?

3 a / find / job / new / now / she / to / want

....

....?

4 for / her / interview / late / she / yesterday

....

....?

5 her / her / often / parents / to / write

....

....?

6 her / phoned / they / today

....

....?

2 Test your spelling.

Listen to the text and write in the missing words. Can you spell them correctly?

Doreen can (7) .... very well – but she doesn't (8) .... anything about computers. Now that her young (9) .... has started school, she thinks that she'll soon have (10) .... time to go back to work again. Yesterday she phoned Leason's Industries about a job. She's got an (11) .... for an interview tomorrow. She has to be there at ten (12) ....

3 Test your tenses.

Len Cartwright, Lin Wang and Mary Duckworth all live in Manchester. They are all members of LETS. What is the correct tense in each sentence. For each sentence, mark your answer like this: (a)

13 Mary is 82. She ...in Manchester all her life.
a lives **b** has lived **c** lived

14 Her husband ... several years ago.
a dies **b** has died **c** died

15 He ... in Manchester all his life, too.
a lives **b** has lived **c** lived

16 Mary's husband ... in a factory for many years.
a has worked **b** works **c** worked

17 Len Cartwright ... a milkman since 1985.
a is **b** has been **c** was

18 He ... milk and other things every morning.
a delivers **b** has delivered **c** delivered

19 When he was younger, he ... a bus.
a drives **b** has driven **c** used to drive

20 Lin Wang ... Ann's bicycle yesterday.
a has repaired **b** repaired **c** used to repair

21 He ... Mary's garden-gate yesterday.
a didn't mend **b** hasn't mended **c** mended not

22 He ... at the department store any more.
a doesn't work **b** hasn't worked **c** works not

23 He ... unemployed for almost a year now.
a is **b** has been **c** was

24 He ... a new job yet.
a doesn't find **b** hasn't found **c** used to find

4 What's the right word?

After each number, cross out the word *in italics* that is wrong.

Mr Read has worked at Benson's (25) *for / since* many years. When he came for his interview he had to (26) *borrow / lend* a tie, because he didn't have one. His first (27) *boss / chef* was old Mr Benson, who retired in 1958. Mr Read used to travel to work (28) *by / with* bus, but now he (29) *always / ever* takes the underground. He used to use (30) *a / an* typewriter for his work, but he has had a computer on his desk (31) *for / since* 1994. He had problems with the new technology at first, but now he is (32) *a / an* expert.

MY SCORE OUT OF 32: ....

Checkpoint 5

What you learn

Sie erfahren etwas über Nachbarschaftshilfe und Bürgerinitiativen. Sie wiederholen hier u.a.:

- die vollendete Vergangenheit *(past perfect)*
- Hilfsverben *(modal verbs of obligation)*: must, needn't, have to, don't have to, mustn't
- Warnungen und Verbote aussprechen *(telling people not to do things)*

Grammar 1: The past perfect (*had gone*)

1 Leaving the house

Which event happened first (F) and which second (S)?

1 After he had shut the door ( ), he locked it ( ).
2 He remembered ( ) he had left a window open ( ).
3 He left the house again ( ) when he had closed the window ( ).

2 What's the difference in meaning?

In which situation, 1 or 2, did the burglar see the police? Tick (✔) this sentence.

1 ☐ When the police arrived, the burglar ran away.
2 ☐ When the police arrived, the burglar had run away.

3 The stranger

Put the verbs in these sentences into the past simple or past perfect.

My neighbour (1 *phone*) .... the police on Wednesday because he (2 *see*) .... a stranger in our garden. The police (3 *not catch*) .... the man because he (4 *already, drive*) .... away when they (5 *arrive*) .... When I (6 *come*) .... home, I (7 *find*) .... a note which a friend (8 *write*) ....:

Hello Lynda,
I called to see you but then I (9 remember) .... you (10 go) .... away for a few days. Oh yes ... do you know that your neighbour watches your house from his upstairs window??? Be careful!!
See you next week!
Love, Roy.

Grammar 2: must / have to / needn't / don't have to / mustn't

1 Neighbours help neighbours.

Cross out the wrong word or phrase *in italics*.

When you go to work or on holiday or just go out for the evening, and you *have to / needn't* leave your house empty, you *have to / needn't* worry because your neighbours keep an eye on your home.

2 Necessary or not necessary?

Put these words under the correct heading:

necessary: ....
not necessary: ....

1 don't have to, 2 have got to, 3 haven't got to, 4 have to, 5 must, 6 needn't

3 Mustn't and needn't

Translate these sentences into German.

1 You mustn't do that. ....
2 You needn't do that. ....

How to say it: Telling people not to do things

Write the opposite of these sentences. Then underline the sentence which sounds the strongest.

1 You can leave the door open.
....
2 You should leave the door open.
....
3 Please leave the door open.
....
4 You must leave the door open.
....

page 113

Language & Culture: page 109
If you have any problems with these exercises, ask your teacher in the next lesson.

Improving your town

Unit 5

1 Starter: Keeping your home safe

What should / shouldn't you do if a stranger comes to your door to check the gas / sell you a carpet / check your phone?
Which other strangers come to your door? How do you react? Why?

2 Be careful!

Look at the picture on the right. What do you think he / she is saying?
Now read the extract from the Neighbourhood Watch book.

3 Comprehension

Why did Mary Duckworth use to feel worried?
What did she find out about Neighbourhood Watch?

Mary has now got a door-viewer and a chain. What about you? Have you got these things? If so, do you use them? Why? / Why not?

4 Safety tips

The Neighbourhood Watch book also gives useful tips about safety in different situations. Write down two warnings (*Don't ... / You shouldn't ...*) or suggestions (*Remember to ... / You should ...*) that you would give in one of these situations:

- travelling alone on a bus or a train at night
- going for a walk in the evening
- going on holiday and leaving the house empty
- getting money from the bank
- parking the car

Compare your ideas with a partner.

BE CAREFUL!

People often worry when strangers come to their doors. But there are a lot of different ways to make your home secure. Here are some useful tips:

- Look through the door-viewer before you open the door.
- Remember to put the chain on the door.
- Don't forget to check identity cards.

Here is part of a letter from one of our new members, Mrs Mary Duckworth from Heaton Moor:

... And, like many people who live alone, I was very worried because there had been so many break-ins in our neighbourhood. Then I found out that a lot of the people in our street had become members of Neighbourhood Watch so I asked my neighbours about it and I decided to become a member, too. The idea that we should keep an eye on each other's homes is really neighbourly. I feel much safer now that I am a member ... and I also found the tips in the Neighbourhood Watch book very helpful. ...

5 Signs 2

We need both a safe neighbourhood and a pleasant one. Look at these signs. They remind us to take care of our neighbourhood, our neighbours and ourselves.

Where would you see these signs? Use some of these phrases to explain what the signs mean:

You must ...	*You can't*	*Don't forget to ...*
You mustn't ...	*You should ...*	*Don't ...*
You have to ...	*You shouldn't ...*	

6 Improving the neighbourhood 1

You're going to hear part of a radio phone-in programme. You'll hear five people talking about the ways they have tried to improve their neighbourhood. First, look at the list of different things people did. Then listen and put the numbers 1-5 in the boxes, in the order that you hear them.

Caller ☐ helped to clean up a park.
Caller ☐ decorated the trees.
Caller ☐ made the streets safer.
Caller ☐ painted pictures on the walls.
Caller ☐ cleaned the steps.

Now read these questions. Listen to the five people again and write down the answers. Use the past perfect. Then check your answers with a partner.

Conversation 1: How long had the woman lived in her house before she decided to clean the steps?
Conversation 2: Why did the police arrest his friend?
Conversation 3: Why did the park look so terrible?
Conversation 4: Why was the woman dissatisfied with the council?
Conversation 5: The young mother organised a meeting. What had happened to make her do this?

Discuss with your partner which improvement you liked most, and why.

7 Vocabulary

➤ Public buildings and shops

Where do you go when you want to ...

- send a parcel?
- cash a cheque?
- watch a film?
- catch a bus?
- buy some aspirins?
- do the weekend shopping?

Now work with a partner and make a list of the different kinds of shops, facilities and public buildings in your area, like an open-air swimming pool, an airport or a kindergarten.

What other facilities would you like to have in your area?

8 Talking points

- What could you do to make your neighbourhood more pleasant and, perhaps, safer?
- Do you live in the city centre / the suburbs / a small town / the country ? What do you enjoy / not enjoy about living there?
- Are there any public places or buildings you would not like to live near, such as a beer-garden or a prison? Why?
- Have you ever been back to a place which you knew as a child? How had it changed?

Today's grammar

1 The past perfect → p. 131

Remember: The past simple is used to talk about events which happened in the past: *He arrived home at 6 o' clock.*

The past perfect is used to talk about events which had happened before that: *When he arrived home, he saw that someone had broken into his house.*

2 Modals of obligation → p. 127

These phrases tell us what it is necessary or not necessary to do.

necessary ↓

You **must / have to / have got to** leave before 6 o'clock but you **needn't / don't have to / haven't got to** leave yet.

↑ not necessary

Improving your town

Homestudy

1 Past perfect or simple past?

Complete each sentence with the correct forms of *clean, not paint* or ~~*plant*~~. buy Use each verb twice.

1 When Mrs Gordon got home, the steps were still dirty, so she .... them.

2 When I got home, the steps weren't dirty any more. Mrs Gordon .... them.

3 When Michelle moved in, she noticed that her new neighbours .... their houses for a long time.

4 Michelle .... her front door white, she painted it pink.

5 .... Mary already .... a door viewer before she became a member of Neighbour hood Watch?

6 .... she .... a chain for her door after she had read the Neighbour hood Watch book?

2 Modal verbs of obligation

Put in one of these expressions in each sentence: *don't have to, have to, mustn't, needn't.*

1 The steps are already clean. You .... clean them.

2 You .... feed those terrible birds. We don't want them here. They make the steps dirty.

3 Our street is very dangerous. We .... do something about it.

4 The joggers .... pick up the rubbish, but sometimes they do, just to be helpful.

3 Remember the words

Match these words from Unit 5 with their meanings. Write the right letter in each box.

1 ☐ cash	a) a person you don't know
2 ☐ facilities	b) a person who has joined a group
3 ☐ identity	c) for everybody
4 ☐ improve	d) help a person remember
5 ☐ member	e) not dangerous
6 ☐ public	f) things and places for us to use
7 ☐ remind	g) to get money for a cheque
8 ☐ safe	h) to make something better
9 ☐ stranger	i) what we say when there is danger
10 ☐ warning	j) who a person is

4 Past perfect

Write one sentence instead of two. Use the past perfect once in each sentence.

1 There were several break-ins in her neighbourhood. Mary was worried after that.

Mary .... because ....

....

2 Mary joined Neighbourhood Watch. Then she felt safer.

Mary .... after ....

....

3 Two children died in accidents. Eileen organized a meeting.

Eileen ....

after ....

....

5 Listening

Listen to Eileen and her neighbours at their meeting. Decide if each sentence is true or false. Circle T or F.

1 They met at six o'clock.	T / F
2 The room was too small for so many people.	T / F
3 They had never had a meeting like this before.	T / F
4 Eileen had already written a letter.	T / F
5 She had already sent the letter to the council.	T / F
6 The neighbours had already painted some signs.	T / F
7 Eileen had already talked to a council member.	T / F
8 A man offered to ring up the local newspaper.	T / F

6 Pronunciation

In each of these words from Unit 5 there is a silent letter (you don't pronounce it). Draw a circle around each silent letter.

1 could	3 people	5 sign	7 window
2 mustn't	4 should	6 walk	8 would

Now listen to the words.

CHECKPOINT 6

What you learn

Diese Unit behandelt das Thema Nachbarn. Sie wiederholen hier u.a.:

- die einfachen Zeitformen (*simple tenses overview: present, present perfect, past, past perfect*)
- die Steigerung des Adjektivs (*the comparison of adjectives*)
- Angebote aussprechen und Bitten äußern (*offers and requests*)

Grammar 1: Tense overview

1 My neighbour

Put these verbs into the sentences: *had lived / has lived / lived / lives.*

My neighbour and I go jogging in Hyde Park every morning. He (1) .... next door to me. He's American but he (2) .... in London for about five years. When he was a student he (3) .... in New York and, before that, he (4) .... in Chicago for eighteen years.

2 The soap opera, "Neighbours"

Put these phrases into the story: *before that / five times a week / for years / in 1985 / since then / some years ago / two years later.*

„Neighbours, everybody needs good neighbours,
just a friendly wave each morning
helps to make a better day."

This is part of a song which 20 million Australian and British people hear (1) .... when they turn on their televisions to watch the soap opera, "Neighbours". (Even the Queen has been a fan (2) .... !) The programme started in Australia (3) .... and then came to Britain (4) ....

(5) .... it has become the most popular soap opera on TV. There had been many soap operas (6) .... but most people like "Neighbours" best because it is about normal people with everyday problems.

(7) .... the programme offered a "Best neighbour prize". Members of the public could telephone the TV studio and say how their neighbour had been helpful to them. The winner got a prize – a TV, of course!

Grammar 2: Comparison of adjectives

1 Comparatives and superlatives

Do you remember the comparative and the superlative of these words? *a little / bad / big / boring / good / interesting / many / noisy / small*

Example: *quick - quicker - quickest / expensive - more expensive - most expensive.*
(Be careful. There are also some irregular forms.)

2 *As* or *than* ?

Cross out the wrong word.

1 His garden is more attractive *as / than* mine.
2 Their house isn't as nice *as / than* mine.
3 Her car was as expensive *as / than* mine.

How to say it: Offers and requests

First complete the words. Then write F next to the most formal offer and request. Write I next to the most informal offer and request.

Offers:

1 ☐ S __ __ __ __ I carry that for you?
2 ☐ L __ __ me do that for you.
3 ☐ C__ __ I help you?

Requests:

1 ☐ C __ __ you do that for me, please?
2 ☐ Do you think you c __ __ __ __ possibly help me,please?
3 ☐ W __ __ __ __ you carry that for me, please?

page 113

Language & Culture: page 109
If you have any problems with these exercises, ask your teacher in the next lesson.

People around you

Unit 6

1 Starter: People around you

You and a partner have got five minutes to find out the answers to as many of these questions as you can and to write the person's name on the line.

In your class, who ...

... has got the most children? ....

... is the tallest? ....

... has got the heaviest bag? ....

... has got the longest way to school? ....

... can speak the most languages? ....

... is wearing the most modern watch?........................

Check your answers with the others in the class and see if you all agree.

2 For and against

Read the text on the right about the programme "For and against" which is on the radio at 7.30 this evening. Two people, Mrs Monk and Mrs Wood, are going to talk for one minute about a problem they have.

Before you listen, work in pairs and match these sentences.

1 We bought this house ☐ a) it was big enough.
2 Mr Monk has been out of work ☐ b) a year ago.
3 We had seen cheaper houses ☐ c) my husband takes care of the children.
4 The council has never asked us ☐ d) he'd earned good money as a steel-worker.
5 When we moved into our old house five years ago, ☐ e) but we decided to pay more so we could live in a nicer area.
6 Before he lost his job, ☐ f) two days a week.
7 I work part-time at the local school ☐ g) for seven years.
8 While I'm at work, ☐ h) what we think about it.

You are now going to hear part of the radio programme "For and against". Listen and check your answers.

Whose side are you on? Vote now for Mrs Monk or Mrs Wood.
After your teacher has counted the votes, write down the three most important reasons why you voted for Mrs Wood and her husband or Mrs Monk and her large family.
Then compare your list with a partner and talk about your decisions.

3 Vocabulary

➤ Opposites

We have used some these words to talk about neighbours and neighbourhoods: *attractive / clean / happy / expensive / good / interesting / rich / safe / difficult / strong / heavy / young.*
What are the opposites of these words?
(Remember: you can sometimes make opposites with *un*).

Now write down the comparative and superlative forms of the above words.

➤ Word focus: *difficult or heavy*?

Which word, *difficult* or *heavy*, goes with these nouns?

.... neighbour .... traffic

.... problems .... lives

.... smokers .... bag

4 Help!

Work with a partner. You are having a housewarming party and your guests are going to arrive in half an hour but you aren't ready! Ask your partner to help you with the preparations. Use phrases like: *Could you ...? / Would you ...? / Can you ...?*
Your partner will offer to help you, using phrases like: *Shall I ...? / Can I ...? / Let me ... .*

Now look at these ways to accept help (*yes, please*) and to refuse help (*no, thank you*). Underline the phrases that you can use when you accept help.
That's very nice of you. / Oh, it's O.K., thanks. / You're very kind. / Thanks very much. / It's no problem, I can do it. / Thanks for offering but it's all right. / Thank you, that would be a big help.

Now work with a different partner. One of you offers help in the following situations and the other answers, using the phrases above.

- You have got a cat and a lot of plants and you are going on holiday.
- You have just moved into a new flat. The fridge is empty and you still haven't got a phone.
- You have broken your leg and you are alone for the weekend with your two young children.
- You are not going to be here for next week's English lesson

Stereo. **6.00am** Sarah Kennedy **7.30** Wake Up to Woga...

7.30 p.m.

This evening Angus Mcphee, in his series "For and Against", looks at the problem of council housing. About 25% of people in England live in the 5,000,000 council-owned homes. Recently Chipham Council moved a family of ten into a large council house on a private housing estate. This has caused some trouble with the neighbours! Tonight you can hear two people give their side of the story and Angus wants to know: "Whose side are you on?"

London Symphony Chorus, Berlin Philharmonic Orchestra, under Claudio Abbado. Mahler (Symphony No 2, Resurrection)

5 Talking points

- People say that neighbours who live in the country are friendlier and more helpful than people who live in towns. What do you think? Are *your* neighbours friendly?
- Talk about the best/worst neighbour you have ever had. Why is/was this person such a good/bad neighbour?
- If you live with other people, are there things which make you angry? Talk about some of these things. Think about cleaning, noise, the bathroom, smoking, visitors, the fridge, telephoning.
- Have you ever seen a TV programme like "Neighbours"? What programmes are there in your country about families and neighbours? Do you watch these programmes? Why? / Why not?

Today's grammar

1 Simple tenses overview → p. 128–131

- The present simple is used to talk about routines and habits: *She meets her neighbour twice a week and they always have coffee together.*
- The past simple is used to talk about what happened in the past: *We moved into this area last year.*
- The present perfect is used to talk about situations which started in the past and continue up to the present: *We have been neighbours for two years.* It is also used when we can see the result of a finished action: *They have just painted their house.*
- The past perfect is used to talk about what had happened before a situation in the past tense: *She had already left when we arrived.*

2 Comparison of adjectives → p. 136

Comparatives and superlatives of adjectives are made by

- adding *-er* and *-est*: *Diane is older and prettier than Gillian but Sarah is the oldest and the prettiest.*
- using *more* and *most*: *The Browns' house is more expensive than the Greens' house, but the Whites' house is the most expensive.*

Some irregular adjectives are: *good (better - best), bad (worse - the worst), a little (less - least), much/many (more - most).*

People around you

Homestudy

1 Pronunciation

These words are all from the radio programme "For and against". In each group of three there is one word in which the underlined letters make a different sound. Which word is the different one?

1 bought	council	house
2 background	enough	found
3 football	good	school
4 children	listen	quiet
5 baby	name	want
6 future	husband	luck
7 forgotten	job	work
8 do	oldest	so

Now listen to the words.

2 Offers and requests

Write these words in the correct order to make offers (1-3) and requests (4-6).

1 for - I - open - shall - the - window - you

....?

2 for - let - me - on - radio - the - turn - you

....?

3 can - drink - get - I - something - to - you

....?

4 bicycle - borrow - can - I - please - your

....?

5 could - do - I - phone - think - use - you - your

....?

6 fax - for - me - please - send - this - would - you

....?

3 Comparison of adjectives

These four families all live in the same street. Their names are Black, Brown, Green and White.

Complete the sentences below, using the correct forms of these words: *beautiful, expensive, heavy, many, old, short, tall, thin, young*. Use each word once.

1 Mr and Mrs Black are the .... couple*.

2 Mrs Brown is .... than her husband.

3 The Blacks haven't got .... children as the Whites.

4 The Greens have got the .... clothes.

5 Mrs White is .... than her husband.

6 Mrs Green is .... than her husband.

7 Mr Brown is .... as his wife.

8 Mr and Mrs Green are the .... couple*.

9 Mrs Black is .... than Mrs Brown.

**couple = (Ehe)Paar*

4 Correct the mistakes.

The text below has ten lines. Four of them are correct, but in the others the tenses are wrong. Tick (✔) the lines that are correct. If the line has a mistake, cross out the wrong verb form and write the correct form in the space at the right.

1 Mr and Mrs Wood have bought their house a year ago.
2 They had seen cheaper houses, but they
3 decide to pay more for a nice area. Now they
4 are angry because the council wants the Monk
5 family to live next door. Mr Monk is out of
6 work for seven years now. His wife works part-
7 time while he had stayed at home. Mrs Wood and
8 Mrs Monk have talked on the radio yesterday.
9 They have been very angry yesterday, and they
10 are still just as angry today.

1 *bought*..............................

2 ....

3 ....

4 ....

5 ....

6 ....

7 ....

8 ....

9 ....

10 ....

CHECKPOINT 7

What you learn
Diese Unit beschäftigt sich damit, wie man sich in einer Stadt zurechtfindet. Sie wiederholen hier u.a.:
- Verhältniswörter (*prepositions*)
- *some* und *any* und Zusammensetzungen mit diesen Wörtern (some *and* any *and compound words*)
- Befehlsformen (*imperatives*)
- nach dem Weg fragen und Wegbeschreibungen geben (*asking the way and giving directions*)

Grammar 1: Prepositions

1 Problem prepositions
- *in* or *into*?

1 He drove .... his garage.

2 His car is .... the car park.

- *before* or *in front of*?

3 He parked in front of the shop just before 6 pm.
When is *before*, and when is *in front of* used?

- *by, by the time, to* or *until*?

Translate these sentences.
4 Wir fahren bis Rom und nicht weiter.

....

5 Es muß bis Freitag fertig sein.

....

6 Sie blieben bis 6 Uhr.

....

7 Bis wir ankamen, hatten wir alles gesehen.

....

2 Prepositions of time
Which prepositions are used with the phrases below?
1 = at, 2 = in, 3 = on

☐ *1967*	☐ *the weekend*	☐ *Monday*
☐ *summer*	☐ *6.30 a.m.*	☐ *Christmas*
☐ *the morning*	☐ *January*	☐ *January 3rd*
☐ *night*	☐ *autumn*	☐ *Easter*
☐ *two years*	☐ *midnight*	☐ *the afternoon.*

Grammar 2: *some* and *any*

Put these words in the text: *any (2x) / anybody / anything / anywhere / some (1x) / somebody / something / somewhere.*

Are there (1) .... cities in the world without parking problems? Tokyo used to be one of the worst cities to park in and people thought there wasn't (2) .... you could do about it. You just couldn't find (3) .... car parks or (4) .... to leave your car because there were "No parking" signs everywhere. Then (5) .... thought of (6) .... original – car-parking machines! These machines look like mini skyscrapers. Each machine holds hundreds of cars, each in a little box. When the driver wants his car, he puts (7) .... coins into the machine and his 'box' comes down in a lift, automatically. The machines don't need (8) .... to look after them and drivers can easily find (9) .... to park their cars.

In the story about Tokyo there are positive sentences, negative sentences and questions. Where do you use *some* and where do you use *any*?

Grammar 3: Imperatives

Make this sentence negative:

Park here. ....

How to say it: Asking the way

Put these sentences in the right order:
1 Excuse / me / tell / you / me / the / the / can / to / station / way / please?

....

....

2 Excuse / me / you / could / me / to / station / tell / get / to / how / the / please?

....

....

page 113

Language & Culture: page 109
If you have any problems with these exercises, ask your teacher in the next lesson.

Getting around town

Unit 7

1 Starter: What is it? 1a

Think of a place or a building in your town. Tell the class *where* it is and they will try to guess *what* it is. Do it like this:

Remember: It's opposite ~~of~~ ~~to~~ ~~from~~ the station

2 A London bus tour 1b

You have won a tour of London on your birthday. Tell a partner when your birthday is and he/she will look at the bus timetable below and give you information about the tours that you could go on. Then do the same for your partner.

3 Sightseeing 3

Look at the map of London. There are a lot of tourist attractions in Central London. Talk about places in London which you have seen or would like to see.

Choose a place on the map which you would like to see. Draw the route from Speakers' Corner to this place. Describe the route to a partner. He/She will try to follow your directions and find out the place that you would like to go to. Here are some phrases to help you:

Take the first / second / third road on the left / right ...
Go along ...
Turn right / left at ...
It's near / past / opposite / next to ...

Now you try to follow your partner's directions.

London's open-top bus tours

Spring tours:	March 1st - May 31st Mon-Sat (no Sunday service) Depart: 9 a.m. & 2 p.m.
Summer tours:	June 1st - Sept. 30th Mon-Sun Depart: 10 a.m. & 3 p.m.
Night special:	9.30 p.m. (Fri/Sat/Sun only)
Winter tours:	Oct 1st - Feb 28th/29th 10.15 a.m. (no open-top service)
	All buses leave from Speakers' Corner.

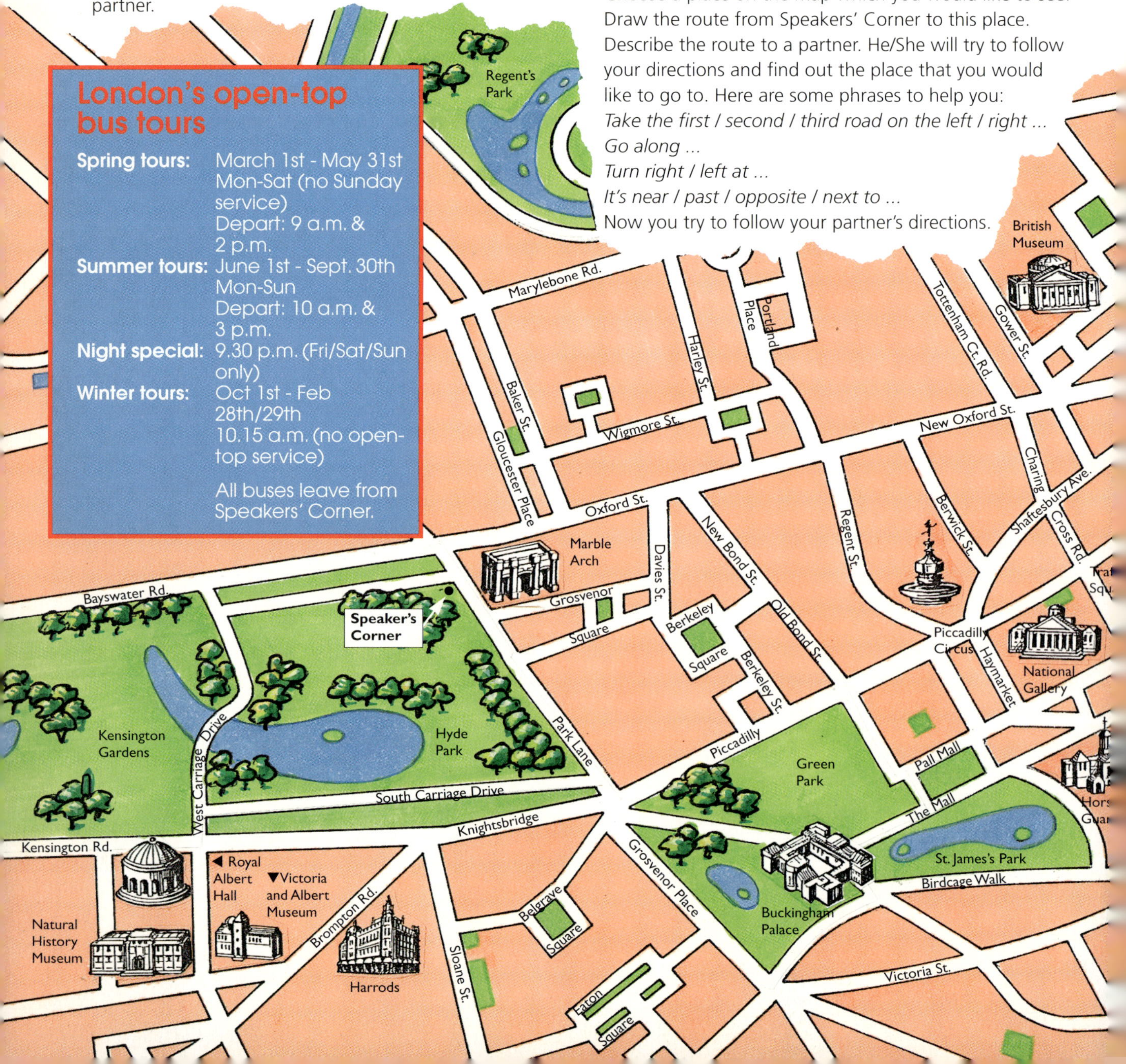

4 Your town 2

What is there in your town to interest visitors? Make sentences with:

There is / isn't a ... *There aren't any ...*
There are a few ... *There are a lot of ...*
There are some ...

Talk about things like parks, museums, cathedrals, churches, beer-gardens, restaurants, palaces, camping sites, art galleries, zoos, swimming pools, airports.

You have a visitor to your town for one day. With a partner, decide where to take him and how to get there. Then compare your 'day out' with another pair.

5 Vocabulary: Travelling

➤ Word focus: *get on + get off / get in + get out of*

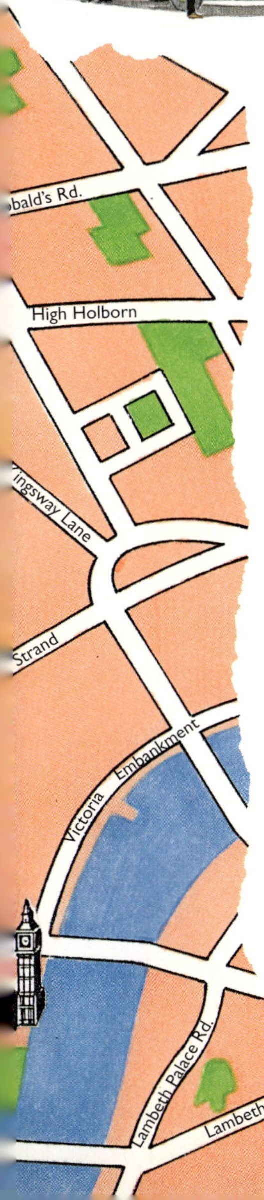

What are the people in the picture doing?

Remember: You get on + off a horse / a bicycle / a train / a plane / a ship / a tram. **But:** You get in + out of a car/ a taxi / a lorry.

Tell the class exactly how you come to school, like this: *I come to school by bus. I get on the bus at Victoria Square and get off at Peter's Street. I go the rest of the way on foot.*

➤ Travelling phrases

Here are some words and phrases connected with three different ways of travelling: *boarding card / Customs / non-smoking compartment / driving licence / filling-station / passport / petrol / platform / porter / season ticket / street map / window seat.*

With a partner, put these words into three groups and make a heading for each group. Check your answers with other students and try to explain any difficult words to each other (in English!).

6 Problem prepositions

Work with a partner. Cross out the wrong preposition.

1 I've been in / to England twice.
2 He saw her at / in the afternoon.
3 I came here by / on foot.
4 Put your chair before / in front of mine.
5 It must be ready by / until 6 o'clock.
6 She bought it at / by the supermarket.

7 Talking points

- How do you come to school? Why do you choose to travel this way?
- Do you have any parking problems in your town? If so, where?
- When was the last time you travelled by taxi? Why did you take a taxi?
- What things would you change in your town to make travelling around easier? Think about: cycle paths / cheap tickets / frequency of buses and trains.

Today's grammar

1 Prepositions → p. 141

a) Prepositions of place and direction

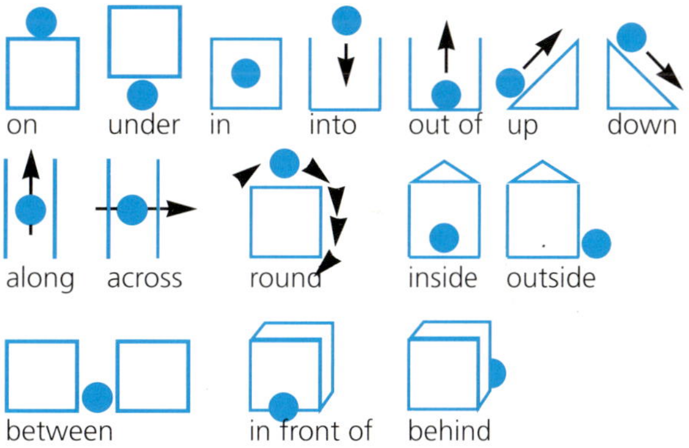

b) Prepositions of time

- ***At*** is used with times: *I catch the bus at 8.30.*
- ***On*** is used with days: *There is no tour on Sunday.* and with dates: *My birthday is on January 23rd.*
- ***In*** is used with months: *His birthday is in February.* with seasons: *I often go by bike in summer.* and with years: *I visited London in 1995.*

2 *Some* and *any* → p. 139

- ***Some*** is used in positive sentences: *There are some tourists in our town.*
- ***Any*** is used in negative sentences: *There aren't any trams in our town.*
- ***Any*** is normally used in questions: *Are there any shops near here?*

3 Imperatives → p. 127

- are used to give instructions: *Turn left. / Don't stop.*

Getting around town

Homestudy

1 Some or any?

At each number, cross out the word that is wrong.

Marc didn't have (1) *some / any* luck yesterday. He wanted to see (2) *some / any* pictures at an art gallery, but he couldn't find (3) *somebody / anybody* who knew where it was. A woman at the station gave him (4) *some / any* directions, and she seemed very sure of herself, but her directions were wrong. Marc couldn't find the art gallery (5) *somewhere / anywhere.* Finally he saw (6) *some / any* people waiting at a bus stop. "Excuse me", he said, "I'd like to ask you (7) *something/ anything.* Do (8) *some / any* of you happen to know where the Bank Art Gallery is?" (9) *Some / Any* of the people knew where it was, but when he finally found the art gallery there wasn't (10) *somebody / anybody* there, because they had all gone out to lunch.

2 Asking the way

Look at the map and complete these directions from the station to the art gallery.

Go (1) .... on and turn

(2) .... at the (3) ....

corner. The art gallery is (4) .... the

(5) ....

Now listen to the woman who gave Marc the wrong directions, and fill in the missing words:

The woman said he should turn (6) ....

at the (7) .... corner. She said the art

gallery was (8) .... the

(9) .... No wonder Marc couldn't find it!

Look at the map. Where did Marc find himself after following the woman's directions?

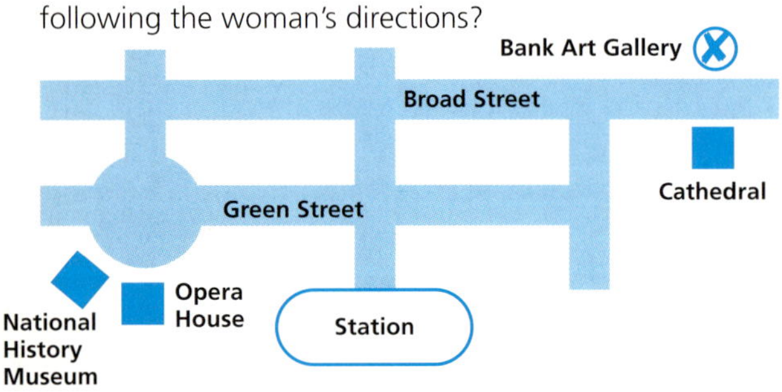

Now listen again and write down the words Marc used to ask for directions.

10 *"Excuse* ....

....

....

3 Prepositions

Write in one of these prepositions in each gap: *at, at, by, by, for, into, off, to, until.*

Marc got (1) .... the train (2) ....

eleven o'clock. He wanted to get (3) .... the

Bank Art Gallery (4) .... eleven thirty, but he

didn't know where it was. A woman (5) .... the station told him the way, but she was wrong. He walked exactly the way she had told him,

(6) .... eleven thirty. Then he went

(7) .... a shop and asked the way again.

(8) .... the time he finally found the art gallery

it had closed (9) .... lunch.

4 Nouns

Here are some nouns from Unit 7. Write the plural form next to each noun, or put an ✗ if there is no plural form.

1 birthday ....

2 box ....

3 bus ....

4 city ....

5 information ....

6 lorry ....

7 luggage ....

8 timetable ....

Now write *a, an* or *some* in the gaps in this sentence:

Your travel agent can give you (9) ....

timetable and (10) .... information

about (11) .... interesting London bus tour.

5 Pronunciation

These words are all from Unit 7. Underline the part of each word where the main stress comes.

at<u>trac</u>tion	direction	imperative	instruction
cathedral	gallery	information	restaurant

Now listen and check your answers.

CHECKPOINT 8

What you learn

Sie erfahren etwas über Haustausch, eine Möglichkeit, preisgünstige Ferien zu verbringen. Sie wiederholen hier u.a.:

- die Fragebildung *(making questions)*
- die Quantität anzeigende Wörter *(quantifiers): all of them, some of them, none of them, etc.*
- Sachen beschreiben *(describing things)*

Grammar 1: Making questions

1 A new home

Read this story and make questions with the underlined information. You are given the first word of the question and you should end it with a preposition.

One day, when Mrs Bailey was on a bus-ride through the village of Bucknall, she saw a lovely old farmhouse. She told her son Ian about it because (1) **<u>he was interested in</u>** old houses. He went to see it and (2) **<u>fell in love with</u>** it. The owner didn't want the house because he had already started to build a bungalow in the grounds of the old house. So he sold the house to Ian for £1! During the next 10 years, Ian numbered all the stones and (3) **<u>he moved them to</u>** the next village. His Chinese-born wife, (4) **<u>Su Ning, has helped him with</u>** the work. They have re-built the house and they have just moved in. (5) **<u>They are now proud of</u>** their wonderful 400-year-old farmhouse.

1 What ....*was he interested in*.........?

2 What ....?

3 Where ....?

4 What ....?

5 What ....?

2 Question words

Put in the correct question word.

1 Q: .... did she tell Ian about it?
A: Because he likes old houses.

2 Q: .... was Su born?
A: In China.

3 Q: .... idea was it to re-build the house?
A: Ian's.

4 Q: .... happened?
A: They bought the house.

5 Q: .... old is the farmhouse?
A: 400 years old.

3 Who ...?

Su helped Ian. We can make two questions, beginning with *Who,* about this sentence.

a) *Who helped Ian?* b) *Who did Su help?*

Translate questions a and b into German.
Now make two questions, beginning with *who,* about this sentence.

1 Mrs Bailey told Ian about the house.

....

....

Grammar 2: Quantifiers

Put these phrases in order, starting with the biggest (=1)

☐ *a few of them* ☐ *both of them* ☐ *one of them*
☐ *a lot of them* ☐ *most of them* ☐ *some of them*
☐ *all of them* ☐ *none of them*

How to say it: Describing things

1 What's it made of?

odow .... tocnot ....
clipsat .... lowo ....
rapep .... letam........................

It's made of *salgs* = glass

2 How big is it?

The opposite of small is large. What's the opposite of:

high .... *thick* ....
long .... *wide* ....

3 What's it for?

Cross out the incorrect words.
A pen is for *write / to write / writing.*

page 113

Language & Culture: page 110
If you have any problems with these exercises, ask your teacher in the next lesson.

Home from home

Unit 8

Homeswapping

1

Get out of the suburbs and into town! Student can offer a bedsit (with separate bathroom and toilet) in central London for any time in August or September. The flat is small, clean, noisy and very basic ... (no dishwasher or video-recorder!) but it is only 3 minutes from Earl's Court station. London is waiting for you ... I'd like some SUN! Write to Gillian. Box number: L11

A

B

2

Modern, 2-bedroomed house in the centre of Oxford – can sleep 4 – no garden but a balcony and a garage – bus and train service to London (about one hour). Sorry, no animals. Married couple & baby want peace and quiet – not too far from home. Any offers? Box number: O34

C

1 Starter: Guessing game 1

One student should think of something in his / her home. Members of the class can ask 20 questions to try and find out what the thing is. The student can only give short answers. Here are some ideas:

Is this thing made of metal?
Yes, it is.

Do you use it every day?
No, I don't.

Do you use it for cooking
No, not really.

Is it bigger than a book?
No, it isn't.

Was it expensive to buy?
No, it wasn't.

Have I got one?
Yes, I think you have.

2 Home-swapping

When you go away on holiday, do you feel worried about leaving your home empty? Some people ask their neighbours to keep an eye on their homes but others have found a different answer to the problem. Over 50,000 people a year, from all over the world, just swap homes for a few weeks. They advertise their homes in newspapers and magazines and say what kind of holiday home they would like to have.

Read the adverts above from the magazine "Home-swapper" and match three of the adverts to the pictures.

In small groups, look at the adverts again and decide which two could easily swap their homes and why.

The owners of these two homes telephone each other and ask for more information. With a partner, act out the conversation. Ask and answer as many questions as you can.

3 Symbols 2

You saw these symbols in the adverts. Decide what the symbols could mean.

3 Who wants to visit beautiful Bavaria? Large country cottage in the village of Blindheim, South Germany. 10 minutes walk to the lake. Ideal for 2 families: 2 double bedrooms + a living-room + a bathroom upstairs; 1 bedroom, living-room, bathroom, dining-room, kitchen and a cat downstairs! We (4 professional people) want to practise our English and visit different towns. Interested? Box number: B46

Homeswapping

4 Luxury flat on the 39th floor of an apartment block in the centre of New York. (Safe area.) Enjoy the high-life of New York. There's enough room for 4 ... no kids, please. I want something different for a few weeks in September ... possibly in Europe. Can we swap?? Contact Don. Box number: NY14

5 2 teachers would love to have a cultural holiday in any interesting city for 2 or 3 weeks in early August. Our comfortable 2-bedroomed cottage is in the pretty Welsh town of Llanfairfechan and is only 5 minutes walk from the beach so it is ideal for families with young children or elderly people. Box number: W 22

• Now look at the symbols in the adverts. Work with a partner and complete these sentences about the homes. Use some of these phrases: *a few / a lot / all / both / most / none / one / some.*

1 Only .... of them has got facilities for old people.

2 .... of them have got a telephone and .... of them have got a dishwasher.

3 Look at the advert from Wales and the one from Bavaria. .... of them say that children are welcome.

4 .... of them have got a swimming pool.

Now ask your partner questions about the adverts. Begin with: *How many of them ...?* Use the phrases from the list to answer your partner's questions.

4 Where can we go?

Jeff and Doreen Brown are looking at these adverts in the magazine. Write down the box numbers of the adverts in the order they talk about them.
Then listen again and write short answers to these questions (not more than three words).

1 Who doesn't like the idea of homeswapping at first?
2 Who wants to go to the USA?
3 Who learnt German at school?
4 Who was ill in Spain?
5 Who would rather travel by car than by plane?
6 Who wants a city holiday?

Jeff and Doreen telephone the teachers in Wales for more information. Write down three questions that you think they would ask.
Compare your questions with the rest of the class.

5 Vocabulary

➤ Different kinds of homes

Describe one of these homes to the class: *bedsit / bungalow / cottage / igloo / houseboat / lighthouse / tent.*
The others will try to guess which one you are describing.

6 Talking points

- Which room do you like best at home? Why?
- If you could have only three of these things in your home, which would you choose, and why?

washing-machine	television	fridge	radio
dishwasher	computer	stereo	fax
microwave	freezer	video	

- Talk about the nicest home you have ever been in.
- What do you think the advantages and disadvantages of living in a flat or a house are?

Today's grammar

1 Questions

a) ... with prepositions → *p. 125*

Put the preposition at the end of the question: *Which advert is she looking at? / Who is she talking to?*

b) ... with *Who* ...? → *p. 125*

She saw **John**. (We want to know the *object*).
Who did she see?
John saw her. (We want to know the *subject*).
Who saw her?

2 Quantifiers → *p. 139*

Who wants to swap homes this summer?

All of us. 100%
Most of us.
A lot of us.
Some of us.
A few of us.
Both of us.
One of us.
None of us. 0%

Home from home
Homestudy

1 Listening

Two of the home owners who have advertised in the Homeswappers magazine are talking on the telephone.

Listen and write down the questions they ask about the things in brackets:

1 *(dates)* ....

....?

2 *(sailing)* ....

....?

3 *(car)* ....

....?

4 *(quiet)* ....

....?

5 *(children)* ....

....?

2 Questions with *Who* ...?

Read B's answers and then write A's questions. All of her questions begin with the word *Who*.

A: You look very upset. What's wrong?
B: It's nothing. Somebody rang up, that's all.

A: (1) ....?
B: Gillian did. She's angry with somebody.

A: (2) ....?
B: With somebody who came to look at her flat.

A: (3) ....?
B: A friend of mine. And she took somebody with her.

A: (4) ....?
B: She took her brother with her, and he said Gillian's flat was noisy and dirty.

3 Quantifiers

A reporter in England asked 30 home owners some questions. Here are the answers they gave:

	Yes	No
"Have you owned your home for over a year?"	30	0
"Do you like your home?"	27	3
"Do you spend your holidays at home?"	21	9
"Have you got a swimming pool at home?"	0	30
"Have you got a sauna at home?"	4	26
"Have you ever swapped homes with anybody?"	2	28
"If so, were you satisfied with the swap?"	2	0

Complete the sentences, using seven of these words: *a few, a lot, all, both, half, most, none, one, some, two.*

(1) .... of the home owners I interviewed have owned their homes for over a year. (2) .... of them like their homes. Surprisingly, (3) .... of them spend their holidays at home. (4) .... of them have got a swimming pool, but (5) .... have got a sauna. Only (6) .... of them have ever swapped homes, and (7) .... of them said they were satisfied.

4 Questions with prepositions

Use these words to ask three questions about a woman who wants to buy a house. Cross out each word when you have used it.

at	has	in	looked	she	to
did	houses	interested	she	talk	yesterday

1 *What is she* ....? (5 words)

2 *How many* ....

....? (7 words)

3 *Who* ....

....? (6 words)

5 Describing things

Choose something out of each of the three boxes to make a sentence.

1 A bungalow	☐ are for	☐ a car.
2 A lorry	☐ are made of	☐ heating food.
3 A magazine	1 is a kind of	1 house.
4 Cities are	☐ is bigger than	☐ paper.
5 Coffee	☐ is made of	☐ to drink.
6 Igloos	☐ is something	☐ snow and ice.
7 Microwaves	☐ noisier than	☐ villages.

Lerntipp

Liebe Englisch-Expertin,

wenn ich neue Wörter lerne, will ich ganz genau wissen, was sie bedeuten, deshalb verlange ich immer eine Übersetzung. Meine Kursleiterin sagt, sie gibt uns gerne mal eine deutsche Übersetzung als erste Annäherung, aber wenn wir das Wort richtig lernen wollen, müssen wir es auf Englisch lernen. Kann das sein?
With friendly greetings,

Katja, Rüsselsheim

Liebe Katja,

Ihre Kursleiterin hat recht. Übersetzungen sind nützlich, aber oft ungenau oder nur von begrenzter Gültigkeit. Mein Vorschlag: Versuchen Sie schon jetzt, Ihren Wortschatz nicht <u>nur</u> durch Übersetzung zu lernen.
Wenn Sie Ihre englischen Vokabeln auf Karteikarten schreiben, muss auf der Rückseite der Karte nicht unbedingt eine deutsche Übersetzung stehen. Oft ist es nützlicher, einen kurzen <u>Beispielsatz</u> mit einer Lücke zu schreiben. Wenn z.B. auf der Vorderseite das Wort neighbour steht, könnten Sie auf der Rückseite schreiben: "My nearest … lives next door." Üben Sie, indem sie den Satz anschauen und versuchen, sich an das fehlende Wort zu erinnern.
Im einem Heft können Sie verwandte Wörter zusammen aufschreiben, z.B. neighbour, neighbourhood, neighbouring, neighbourly … Oder auch <u>Gegensätze</u>: hot/cold, winner/loser, upstairs/downstairs …
Notieren Sie auch kurz den <u>Zusammenhang</u>, in dem Ihnen ein neues Wort begegnet ist, z.B. swap → Homeswapper Magazine.
Es hilft auch, wenn Sie Ihre Vokabeln zu <u>Wortfeldern</u> zusammenstellen. Sammeln Sie z.B. Wörter, die mit Häusern zu tun haben, und teilen Sie sie in weitere Kategorien auf (siehe unten).
Manche Lerner finden es nützlich, neue Wörter laut aufzusagen oder mehrmals zu schreiben.
Und schließlich: Entscheiden Sie selbst, welche Wörter für Sie persönlich am wichtigsten sind, und konzentrieren Sie sich darauf, diese einzuprägen und auch zu benutzen.

All the best,
Your English Expert

P.S. Sie schließen Ihren Brief "With friendly greetings", was zwar ganz nett und freundlich, aber auf Englisch doch ein Bisschen ungewohnt klingt. Das haben Sie wörtlich aus dem Deutschen übersetzt, nicht wahr? "Best wishes" oder "All the best" sind gebräuchlicher.

Wordfield

Houses

Write the numbers next to the words or expressions.

1 Rooms of a house (six words or expressions)
2 Kinds of houses (four words or expressions)
3 People (three words)
4 Things people can <u>do</u> to houses (four words)
5 Things to make a door safe (three words)
6 Other things that are often in houses (six words)
7 The closest house on the same side of the street is … .

...... balcony
...1... bathroom
...... bedroom
...... bungalow
...... carpet
...... chain
...9... chimney
...... cottage
...... decorate
...... dining room
...... dishwasher
...... door
...... door-viewer
...... downstairs
...... farmhouse
...... fence
...... freezer
...... fridge
...... garage
...... gate
...... igloo
...... key
...... kitchen
...... landlord
...... lawn
...... lawn-mower
...... living room
...... microwave
...... neighbour
...... next door
...... owner
...... paint
...... re-build
...... repair
...8... roof
...... telephone
...1... toilet
...... upstairs
...... window

PANORAMA 2

Europe's street people

1 European cities

In your class, try to name big European cities. Do it in alphabetical order, like this: Amsterdam, Bordeaux, C ...

(There is a town called Queensferry in Scotland and Xanten in Germany is a useful town to know!!!)

2 Capital cities

The pictures show two capital cities in Europe. Which cities are they? How did you recognise them?

Which European capitals have you visited? What tourist attractions did you see there?

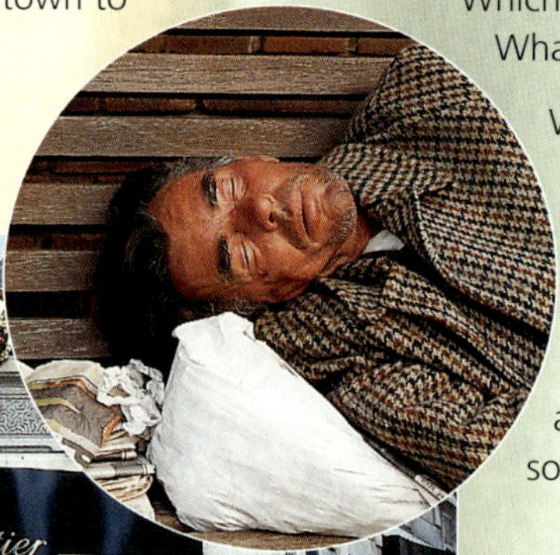

When we visit cities as tourists, we usually stay in hotels, eat in restaurants and visit tourist attractions. But we seldom see the backstreets of these cities where thousands of homeless men, women and children live. How do you think some of them have become homeless?

3 The tip of the iceberg

Read these numbers out loud and then write them down in words:

$\frac{1}{2}$ – $\frac{1}{2}$ million – $\frac{3}{4}$ – 40 – 10,000 – 500,000 – 29% – 31% – 1990.

With a partner, try to put the above numbers into the text. (Some of the numbers have already been done for you.) Then compare your answers with other students.

In .... there were ...., that is *500,000*, people living on the streets of Britain! Less than .... of these were men. *29%* of them were women and a shockingly high percentage, ..., were children. And *$\frac{3}{4}$* of these people were under .... years old. This is not only a problem in Britain – in Germany and the Netherlands there are about .... *children* who live on the streets. And, every year, the number of homeless people rises.

- What do you think the heading of this text means?

4 Street magazines

Look at theses international magazines – *The Big Issue* from London, *Biss* from Munich, *La Rue* from Paris ... Have you ever seen or heard of any of these magazines?

Here's the story of one of them.

The Big Issue

In 1991 when Gordon Roddick (husband of Body Shop millionairess, Anita Roddick) was on holiday in New York, he bought the magazine *Street News* from a man on a street corner. The articles in the magazine were interesting, but the *most* interesting thing was that this was a magazine *by* and *about* homeless people.

Gordon brought the idea back to England and asked a friend of his, John Bird (who had once been homeless himself), to start a similar magazine in England. The first copy of *The Big Issue* was sold in London in September, 1991.

This magazine now sells 250,000 copies *a week,* and there are 7,000 trained salespeople who sell the magazine on the streets of most big towns in Britain. 60% of the price goes to the homeless salesperson and 40% goes back to the magazine or to pay for job-training projects for the unemployed.

The idea was so successful in Britain that many other European cities have started their own street magazines. There are now over 30 of these magazines in Germany alone.

Would you buy a magazine like *The Big Issue*? Why? / Why not?

Here are some headings of articles in *The Big Issue*. What do you think they are about?

MISSING
HEALTH CARE
LETTER OF THE WEEK
PERSONALITY PROFILE
EATING ON £1 A DAY
WHAT'S ON IN TOWN

What other kinds of articles do you think there are in *The Big Issue?*

5 The Big Step

The Big Issue organization has a self-help programme called *The Big Step* which gives practical support and information to their salespeople who want to re-train or who have ideas for their own businesses. You are going to hear Mike's story of how he became homeless, how selling *The Big Issue* helped him to find a job and how *The Big Step* helped him to start his own business.

After you've listened to Mike's story, answer these questions.

1 Where is Mike from?
2 Why did he move to London?
3 Where did he stay at first?
4 How did he become homeless?
5 How did selling *The Big Issue* help him to find a job?
6 What practical help did *The Big Step* give him?
7 What do you think Mike's future could be?

6 Idiom bank

"He ate me out of house and home."
"Make yourself at home."
"There's no place like home."

Can you think of a situation where you would use any of these idioms?
Do you know any more idioms in English or German with the words *home (Heim)* or *house (Haus)* ?

7 Talking points

- Are there any facilities in your town for the homeless?
- Where do many street people sleep?
- What are other problems homeless people have?
- Do you give money to people on the street who ask for it? Why? / Why not?

1 Test your tenses

Put the verbs in these sentences into the simple present, present perfect, simple past or past perfect.

Eileen is a young mother who (1 *live*) .... on our street. She (2 *live*) .... here for three years. Last month she (3 *organise*) .... a meeting. She was angry because there (4 *be*) .... two very serious accidents near her home. They (5 *never have*) .... a meeting like that before. Eileen (6 *give*) .... everybody copies of a letter that she (7 *write*) .... to the council. She (8 *not post*) .... the letter because she (9 *want*) .... everybody to sign it.

2 Write the questions

Use these words to write questions about Eileen. The first word of each question is missing.

10 does / live / she...
....?

11 has / here / lived / long / she ....
....?

12 angry / she / so / was...
....?

13 a / did / letter / she / to / write ....
....?

14 decide / did / do / else / she / to ....
....?

3 What's the right word?

After each number, cross out the word or expression that is wrong.

My car is (15) *in / into* the garage for repairs, I'm afraid, so I can't pick you up, but you (16) *mustn't / needn't* take a taxi, because it isn't (17) *difficult / heavy* to get to our house by public (18) *traffic / transport*. There's a bus stop (19) *before / in front of* the post office. Take the number 62 bus, because it's faster (20) *as / than* the other buses. Get (21) *off / from* the bus at Green Street. There are (22) *some / any* shops near the bus stop, and our house is (23) *against / opposite* the hairdresser's.

4 Test your spelling

Listen to the text and write in the missing words. Can you spell them correctly?

Last summer we decided to (24) .... houses with an Australian (25) .... After a long flight we arrived there on (26) .... morning. When we got to the house we (27) .... that it was absolutely (28) .... – and we had a lovely surprise on the first night: the (29) .... had organised a 'Welcome to Australia' party for us.

5 Which one is correct?

For each sentence, mark your answer like this: (a)

30 The report must be finished … two o'clock.
a by **b** by the time **c** until

31 She's got two brothers. … are singers.
a All of them **b** Both of them **c** The both

32 … I arrived, the others had already left.
a By **b** By the time **c** Until

33 You … park here, there's a 'No Parking' sign.
a don't have to **b** mustn't **c** needn't

34 A car is for …
a drive **b** driving **c** to drive

35 The steps are already clean. You ... clean them.
a have to **b** mustn't **c** needn't

36 That's the ... film I've ever seen.
a bad **b** worse **c** worst

37 They stayed at the park, ... midnight.
a as far as **b** by **c** until

MY SCORE OUT OF 37: ....

What you learn
Diese Unit behandelt das Thema Freizeit und Hobbys. Sie wiederholen hier u.a.:
- die einfache Form und die Verlaufsform der Gegenwart (*present simple and present progressive*)
- rückbezügliche Fürwörter (*reflexive pronouns*)
- sich begrüßen und sich verabschieden (*saying hello and goodbye*)

CHECKPOINT 9

Grammar 1: The present simple (*go / goes*) and the present progressive (*is / are going*)

1 Grammar check
Five of the following verbs are not normally used in the progressive tenses. Cross these verbs out. Then write the progressive form of the other verbs.
Example: *wait - is / are waiting.*
dance / die / give / go / know / lie / like / love / run / want / win / understand

2 Translate these sentences.
1 Was machst du gerade? Arbeitest du?

....

2 Nein, momentan arbeite ich nicht – ich sehe fern.

....

3 Machst du jede Woche deine Hausaufgaben?

....

4 Nein, ich mache nie meine Hausaufgaben.

....

3 An unusual hobby
Put the verbs into the present simple or the present progressive.

"I (1 *collect*) .... miniature bottles of whisky. Although there (2 *be*) .... over 300 bottles in my collection, I haven't got as many as a man in Upham, England who (3 *have*) .... got more than 7,000! At the moment my brother (4 *travel*) .... round the USA and he (5 *look*) .... for miniature bourbon bottles for me. But he (6 *like*) .... whisky so I (7 *hope*) .... he won't drink them on the way home!

Grammar 2: Reflexive pronouns

1 Who did they see?
Cross out the wrong word(s).

1 They looked at *themselves / each other.*
2 They looked at *themselves / each other.*
3 We can look after *us / ourselves.*

2 Have a good time!
Put in a word ending in *self* or *selves.*

1 "Goodbye, Peter. Enjoy .... !"
2 She enjoyed .... at the sports club.
3 I'm enjoying .... at the moment.
4 He always enjoys .... at our parties.
5 I'm sure they'll enjoy .... tomorrow.

How to say it: Saying goodbye

Look at these situations and decide which of the phrases below you would use to say goodbye.
1 To your colleagues after a day's work.
2 To a good friend after a party.
3 To a friend who is going on holiday.
4 To someone after a telephone conversation.
5 To your boss after dinner at his / her house.

☐ a) Take care. Have a good trip.
☐ b) Bye. See you tomorrow.
☐ c) Bye-bye. Thanks for your call.
☐ d) Bye. Thanks a lot. I had a great time.
☐ e) Goodbye. I really enjoyed the evening and the food was lovely.

page 114

Language & Culture: page 110
If you have any problems with these exercises, ask your teacher in the next lesson.

Leisure time

Unit 9

1 Starter: Saying hello

You meet someone who used to be in your English course. He greets you. What would you answer?

Think about things like your work, your hobbies, your home, your English course.

2 Things are changing

Look at the pictures below and say what the people in the pictures are doing. Now tell a partner how often you do some of the things in the pictures. Use words like: *often / sometimes / seldom / never*.

3 Leisure time in Britain

The ways in which people spend their leisure time in Britain are changing. In the graph below, the blue blocks show how much of their free time people spent on different leisure activities twenty years ago. The green blocks tell you about how much time people spend on these leisure activities today.

Look at the graph and answer these questions.

1 What's the most popular way of spending free time nowadays?
2 What do you think some of the 'other hobbies' are?
3 What do you think 'entertaining at home' means? How do *you* 'entertain' friends at home?
4 Which activities are becoming more and more popular in Britain?

Now use the present progressive to talk about how and why leisure activities are changing in your country in areas like holidays / computers / sports / evening classes / hobbies. Begin your sentences like this:

More and more businessmen ... these days because ... .
Nowadays more retired people ... because ... .
These days more and more young people ... because ... .
Not as many people ... nowadays because ... .

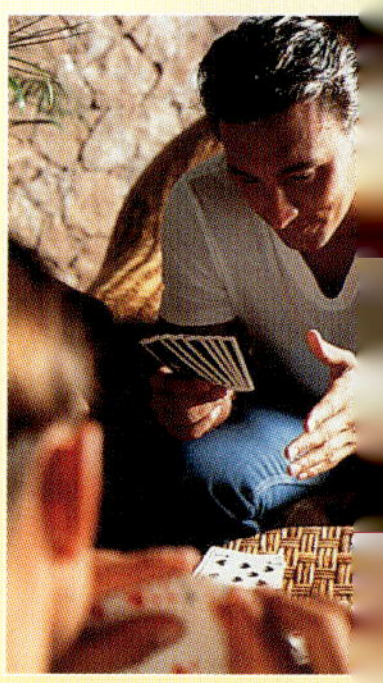

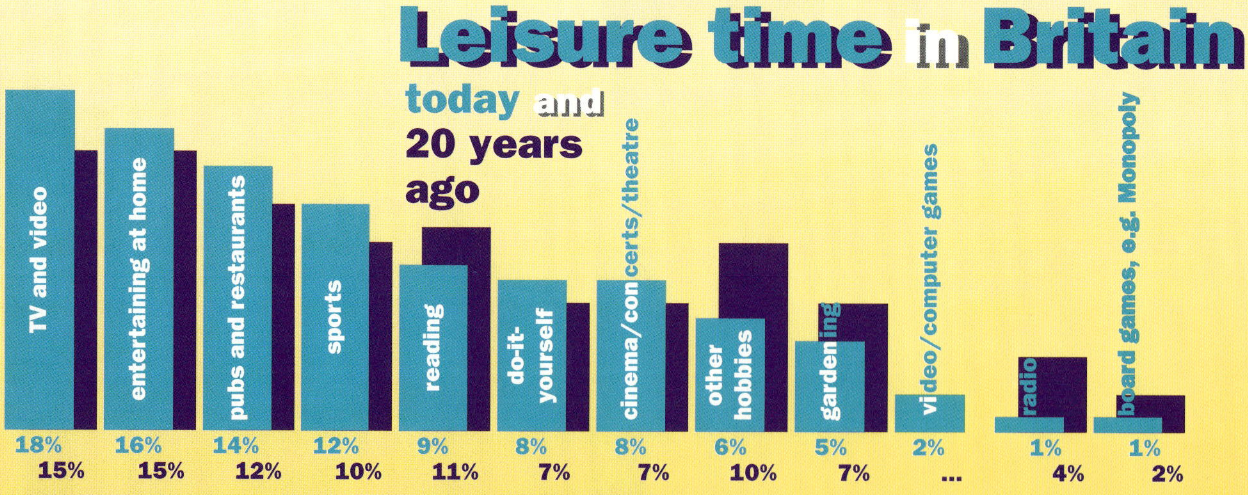

4 Leisure centres 1

These days people are spending more and more time and money on leisure activities. People are living longer, working fewer hours and earning higher salaries. The leisure industry has become big business and new sports clubs and leisure centres are opening all over the country.
Listen to Robin, who wants to join his local leisure centre. He is speaking to Pamela, who runs the centre, and she is giving him some information.
Write down what she says, using these figures, and then check your sentences with a partner.

- £10 a year
- in their twenties or thirties
- at 7.30 a.m.
- twice a week

Listen to the conversation again. Pamela tells Robin about three members of the centre, Len, Anna and Sarah. Make notes so that you can tell the class one thing that each member does and one thing that each member is doing, like this: *Pamela runs the Leisure Centre. At the moment she is showing Robin round the centre.*

5 Help yourselves or help each other? 2

Think of a way to re-phrase these sentences.
1 Jeff often writes to Sue and she writes back. *They ...*
2 I saw him and he saw me. *We ...*
3 She spoke to him and he spoke to her. *They ...*

Now answer these questions. Use a word which ends in *self* or *selves*.
4 Sarah is alone in the café but she is speaking! Who is she talking to? Do you ever do this?
5 Do the 60-plus group have a good time at the leisure centre? What about you and the other students in your English lessons?
6 Did anyone help you with your homework?

Explain these phrases: *do-it-yourself, self-employed, a self-service café, a self-help organisation.*

6 Vocabulary

➤ Word focus: *do* or *make*?
With a partner, put in the verb *do* or *make*. Use the present simple or the present progressive.

1 I never .... my homework so I often .... mistakes in the lesson!
2 He .... a lot of sports and .... a lot of friends when he goes on those adventure holidays.
3 We're all busy. Mother .... the beds, my brother .... the shopping and I .... lunch.

Now tell the class something you often *do* and something you often *make*, like this: *I do the shopping every Saturday and I sometimes make my own bread.*

7 How to say it: Saying hello and goodbye

Match these phrases to the times.

1 Good afternoon.	☐ a) It's 7 p.m.
2 Good evening.	☐ b) It's 9 a.m.
3 Goodnight.	☐ c) It's 3 p.m.
4 Good morning.	☐ d) It's bedtime.

After the lesson, say goodbye to your teacher and another student. Use one of these phrases: *Bye, see you next week. / Goodbye, have a nice week. / Bye. Have a good weekend.*

8 Talking points

- Are you a member of a club or a group? If so, tell the class things like what kind of group it is / how often you go there / how many people are in the group / why you joined. If not, what kind of club would you like to join?
- What other hobbies have you got? Is there anyone in your class who shares your hobby? Who has got an unusual or a dangerous hobby?
- How can teenagers in your area spend their free time? What facilities are there for young people? And what is there for retired people

Today's grammar

1 The present simple and the present progressive

a) The present simple → p. 128

- is used to talk about routines: *He goes to the sports club once a week.*
- is used to talk about timetables and schedules: *The centre opens at 6 a.m.*
- is used with 'non-activity' verbs like: *forget / hate / know / like / understand / want: He likes sports.*

b) The present progressive → p. 132

- is used to describe a scene: *Look! He's drinking whisky.*
- is used to describe things which are happening now: *You are learning English.*
- is used for trends: *Leisure centres are becoming popular.*

2 Reflexive pronouns → p. 140

- are used when the subject and object are the same: *He hurt himself during the match.*
- are not used with the verbs: *concentrate / feel / relax / meet: We met at the sports club.*

Leisure time
Homestudy

1 Present simple or present progressive?

Pamela (P) and Robin (R) are talking about Anna, who has gone to her photography class.

Write in the correct forms of these verbs.

come	do	play	speak	try
come	do	play	stay	try
come	know	play	think	

P: That's Anna. She (1) .... from Brazil, but now she (2) .... with friends in England.

R: Yes, I (3) .... her. We met at a party. How often (4) .... here?

P: Quite often. She (5) .... a photography course right now, and sometimes she (6) .... some sports here, too.

R: (7) .... tennis?

P: No, she (8) .... tennis, but she (9) .... vollyball sometimes. And she always (10) .... to talk to everybody, because she (11) .... to improve her English this year.

R: How many languages (12) ....?

P: Five, I (13) .... But look, she (14) .... out the door now, so you can ask her yourself.

2 Hello and goodbye

Which expressions do they use? Listen and tick (✔) the boxes.

1 ☐ Good morning, Claire.
2 ☐ Hello, Anna, how are you?
3 ☐ Hi, Len, where've you been?
4 ☐ Oh, hi, Len, I'm fine, thanks.
5 ☐ Hello, Robin.
6 ☐ Bye, Robin, see you later.
7 ☐ Bye-bye, see you at the party.
8 ☐ Goodbye, have a nice day.
9 ☐ Take care. Have a good trip.

3 Reflexives

Write in a word ending in *-self* or *-selves*, or put in an ✘ if such a word cannot be used.

Len always enjoys (1) .... at the leisure centre. He likes to relax (2) .... there, and he can concentrate (3) .... on his music better than at home. Sarah feels (4) .... good in her 60-plus group, although once she fell and hurt (5) .... Anna and Robin first met (6) .... at a party. Now they sometimes meet (7) .... at the leisure centre to enjoy (8) .... with their friends.

4 Find the differences

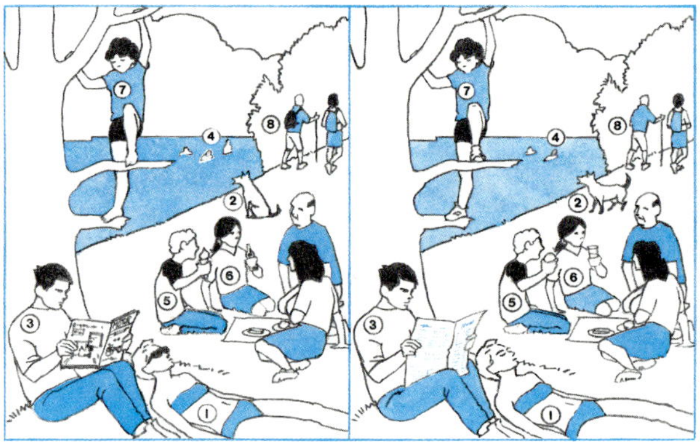

In the second picture, eight things are different. What are they?

1 *The woman isn't wearing sunglasses*
2 ....,
not ....
3 ....,
not ....
4 Only ....,
not ....
5 ....,
not ....
6 ....,
not ....
7 ....
8 .... rucksack.

What you learn

Diese Unit stellt Ihnen ungewöhnliche Urlaube vor.
Sie wiederholen hier u.a.:

- Eigenschafts- und Umstandswörter (*adjectives and adverbs of manner*)
- die Steigerung der Adverbien (*comparison of adverbs*)
- Begründungen abgeben (*giving reasons*)

CHECKPOINT 10

Grammar 1: Adjectives and adverbs of manner

1 Grammar check

Adjectives tell us about a thing or a person: *His car is **slow***. Adverbs tell us *how* someone does something: *He drives **slowly***. What are the adverbs from these adjectives. (Be careful. Some are irregular.)
Example: *slow - slowly*.

bad / careful / clear / fast / good / happy / hard / terrible

2 A letter

Complete the adjectives or adverbs in this letter.

Dear Sarah,

We're having a (1) w................f....... time at this (2) unu.................. igloo-hotel in Sweden. Everything is made of ice – even the beds (which are really (3) c....m...........t.............). Of course, it's not very (4) w............. but we dress (5) wa................. so we don't feel the cold. The people here are very (6) fr.......d........ – but their language is so (7) st..........g....... that we can't understand a word! Luckily, most of them speak English very (8) w.......... . Say hello to everyone in the office – I hope you're all working (9) h............! See you on Monday. (These two weeks have passed so (10) qu............ !)

All the best, Pamela.

3 Look here

Cross out the wrong word.

1 He looked at the holiday brochure *careful / carefully*.
2 The holiday brochure looked *interesting / interestingly*.

Write the correct sentence number on the line.

Sentence ..... gives information about a verb.

Sentence ..... gives information about a noun.

Sentence ..... needs an adverb.

Sentence ..... needs an adjective.

3 ☐ She looked *good*.
4 ☐ She looked *well*.

Tick (✔) the sentence which tells you about her health.

Grammar 2: Comparison of adverbs

Do you remember the comparative and superlative forms of these adverbs? Example: *slowly - more slowly - the most slowly*. (Be careful! Some are irregular.)

badly / carefully / clearly / fast / hard / well

How to say it: Giving reasons

I wanted to enjoy the good weather – that's why I went on holiday in August.
Now match these phrases to answer the question:

Why did you go on holiday in August?

1 So ☐ a) to enjoy the good weather.
2 In order ☐ b) I wanted to enjoy the good weather.
3 Because ☐ c) that I could enjoy the good weather.

page 114

Language & Culture: page 110
If you have any problems with these exercises, ask your teacher in the next lesson.

Murder & Mystery Weekend

The Swan Hotel, Fleetport

Join us for an exciting weekend of MURDER and MYSTERY at the luxurious SWAN HOTEL, Fleetport, from Friday, October 4th - Sunday, October 6th.

When you arrive at the hotel, everything seems normal ... you meet the other guests and have a wonderful dinner. But, some time during the evening, one of the guests dies dramatically ... MURDER!
You must question the other guests carefully to try and find out who the murderer is. But, be careful, they might look like guests but, in fact, be actors! After dinner there is time to discuss your theories in our comfortable bar ... but, when you go to bed, don't turn the lights off or sleep too deeply – you don't know what could happen next! People have disappeared mysteriously from The Swan Hotel ... .

A different kind of holiday

Unit 10

1 Starter: Packing your suitcase

Tell the class what you put into your suitcase when you go on a summer holiday. Do it like this:

A: *I always pack my sunglasses.*
B: *I always pack my sunglasses and a camera.*
C: *I always pack my sunglasses, a camera and ...*

See how long you can make the list before someone forgets to 'pack' something.

2 Murder mystery weekend

Most people work hard during the week and they want to relax at the weekend so many hotels in Britain offer Weekend Breaks. These are short holidays, from Friday to Sunday, and they often have a theme to suit their guests' interests. As England is the home of Sherlock Holmes and Miss Marple, one very popular Weekend Break theme is ... MURDER!

Read the holiday brochure on the left. What kind of people do you think would enjoy a Murder and Mystery Weekend? Would you like it? Give your reasons. Use some phrases from the checkpoint page.

3 Adjectives and adverbs 1

Underline the adverbs in the text which end in 'ly'. Put a ring around the verb it is giving you information about. Write down another adverb you could use with each verb. Do it like this: *You must (question) the guests carefully / politely.*

In a different colour, underline the adjectives in the text. Put a ring around the noun or pronoun it is giving you information about. Write down another adjective you could use with each noun. Do it like this: *The (hotel) is luxurious / expensive.*

4 Weekend Breaks

Here is a list of Weekend Breaks which the Swan Hotel is offering this winter:

Chocoholic Weekend: Nov. 1st - 3rd. Start the day with chocolate eggs and end it with a visit to the local chocolate factory ... with drinking chocolate and chocolate cake between!

Antique Weekend: Nov. 22nd - 24th. Bring your grandmother's treasures (and your grandmother!) and our expert will give you information about them (no ... not about your grandmother). Antique market on Saturday ... in the grounds if the weather is fine.

Unhealthy Weekend: Nov. 29th - Dec. 1st. Sounds crazy? Relax and live decadently for a few days. Look good and feel good: beauty therapy and breakfast in bed – nothing energetic is allowed!

Conservation Weekend: Dec. 13th- Dec. 15th. Your Christmas present to the environment. Work hard and improve the countryside. Help us to build stone walls, clean rivers and repair old buildings.

You can book easily. Just phone.

Romantic Weekend: Jan. 3rd. - 5th.

Olympic Weekend: Jan. 17th. - 19th.

French Weekend: Jan. 24th. - Jan. 26th.

Make three groups. Each group should write down what the hotel could say about one of the above weekends. Then read it to the class.

5 Booking a hotel room

You are going to hear someone booking a room at the Swan Hotel. Write the information on the booking form or put a tick (✔) in the correct box.

The Swan Hotel			
Name(s):			
Dates of stay:			
Theme weekend:			
Room:	☐ *single*	☐ *double*	
	☐ *shower*	☐ *bath*	
Payment:	☐ *cash*	☐ *cheque*	☐ *credit card*

Work with a partner. One of you chooses a Weekend Break and telephones the hotel to book a room. The other is the hotel receptionist and writes down details for the booking form. Begin like this: *Receptionist: Good morning. The Swan Hotel. Can I help you?*

6 More quickly and faster 2

You and two other students have decided to go on the Olympic weekend. In groups of three, compare your sporting talents! Then tell the class what you have found out. Make sentences like this: *Sue can't play tennis as well as I can, but she can run faster than me.*

Use phrases like: *not as well / fast / far / quickly as* – and – *better / faster / further / more quickly than.*

7 Vocabulary

➤ What's the weather like?

Complete these words.

1 It's r _ _ _ ing   3 It's w _ _ _ y   5 It's _ _ _ ny

2 It's s _ _ wing   4 It's _ _ ggy   6 It's cl _ _ _ y

Now talk about what the weather should be like for: a cycling holiday / a skiing holiday / a holiday on the beach / a sailing holiday / a murder mystery weekend. Do it like this: *Sunny weather, but not too hot, would be best for an Olympic weekend because people could do sports outside. It wouldn't be as much fun in the rain – and certainly not in the snow!*

8 Talking points

- What is important to you when you choose a hotel?
- What is the best / worst holiday you have ever had? Why was it so good / bad?
- How do you feel about flying? What do you like / dislike most?

Today's grammar

1 Adjectives and adverbs of manner

a) Adjectives → p. 136

- give information about a person or a thing: *The guest / The hotel was* ***nice***.

b) Adverbs of manner → p. 137

- give information about how someone does something: *They questioned the other guests* ***carefully***.
- usually end in 'ly'. Three irregular adverbs are: *He worked* ***hard*** */* ***well*** */* ***fast***.

Remember: These verbs are usually followed by an adjective, not an adverb because they give information about a person or a thing:

	is (be)	looks	sounds	
It / He	seems	smells	tastes	awful. (not awfully)
	feels			

2 Comparison of adverbs → p. 138

- are used to compare activities: *Sue ran faster than me.*
- ***More*** and ***most*** are normally used before adverbs with 'ly' on the end: *It rained even* ***more heavily*** *the next day.*
- Some irregular comparisons are: *He played* ***harder*** */* ***faster*** */* ***better*** */* ***worse*** *than me.*

A different kind of holiday

Homestudy

1 Adjectives and adverbs

The text below has twelve lines. Four of them are correct, but in the others there are incorrect adjectives or adverbs. Tick (✔) the lines that are correct. In the others, cross out the mistakes and write the correct form in the space below.

1 Anna has got a nicely weekend job at
2 the Swan Hotel. It's interesting, because
3 of the unusual theme weekends. She
4 worked very hardly at the Chocoholic
5 Weekend. The food tasted sweetly,
6 and some of the guests felt terribly.
7 She worked even harder at the Conservation
8 Weekend, when it snowed heavy. The chef
9 cooked good at the French Weekend, but
10 he spoke French very bad. The Murder
11 Weekend looked dangerously,
12 but in fact it was perfectly safe.

1 *nice*	7 ....
2	8 ....
3	9 ....
4	10 ....
5	11 ....
6	12 ....

2 Pronunciation

These verbs (in the simple present, third person singular) are all from Unit 10: *chooses, feels, forgets, looks, seems, smells, sounds, tastes, writes*. How should you pronounce the *-s* ending? Write each word in the correct place.

[z] as in *begins*	[s] as in *helps*	[iz] as in *changes*
....	....	....
....	....	
....	....	
....	....	

Now do the same thing with these plural nouns from Unit 10: *breaks, buildings, groups, phrases, rivers, sentences, students, sunglasses, walls*.

....	....	....
....	....	....
....	....	....

Now listen to the words.

3 Giving reasons

Listen to Anna talking about her weekend job, and write the name of the theme weekend under each picture. Then put *because, in order, so* or *that's why* into each sentence below. Circle T for true or F for false.

"The .... Weekend"

"The .... Weekend"

1 Anna wanted the job .... she could practise her English. T / F

2 Anna eats lots of chocolate .... to stay healthy. T / F

3 Some people had lots of antiques, ... they came in big lorries. T / F

4 There was a secret* sports class .... some people wanted a rest from being decadent. T / F

**secret = geheim*

4 Spelling

These adjectives are from Units 1-10. Form an adverb from each of them and write it under the correct spelling rule.

angry	comfortable	lucky
attractive	easy	noisy
automatic	enthusiastic	possible
beautiful	fantastic	safe
busy	happy	terrible

Add *-ly*:

....

Add *-ally*:

....

Change *y* to *i* and add *-ly*:

....

....

Change *-e* to *-y*:

....

CHECKPOINT 11

What you learn

Diese Unit behandelt das Thema Sport und Spiele. Sie wiederholen hier u.a.:

- die einfache Form und die Verlaufsform der Vergangenheit (*past simple and past progressive*)
- die Vergangenheit von Hilfverben (*modal verbs of permission and obligation in the past*): allowed to, could, had to
- Entschuldigungen aussprechen (*apologizing*)

Grammar 1: The past simple (*went*) and past progressive (*was / were going*)

1 Cross out the wrong verb form.

1 They *played / were playing* football when it started to rain, so they had to stop.
2 They *stopped / were stopping* the game when it started to rain heavily.
3 While he *ran / was running* to the clubhouse, he fell over and hurt his arm.
4 This time last Saturday all of us *drank / were drinking* champagne in the bar.

2 Winston "no sports" Churchill

Fill in the missing verb in the past simple or past progressive.

At Harrow, the famous public school, Winston Churchill (1 *must*) .... do a lot of sports. Winston (2 *not like*) .... most sports but he (3 *can*) .... swim very well. One day while he (4 *practise*) .... in the large school pool, he (5 *see*) .... a small boy at the side of the pool who (6 *not swim*) .... So, just for fun, Winston (7 *get*) .... out, and (8 *push*) .... the boy into the water from behind. But the "small" boy was three years older *and* the school's best footballer. When Winston saw that the boy (9 *swim*) .... angrily in his direction, he shouted, "I'm very sorry, I thought you were in my class. You're so small." The boy still (10 *not seem*) .... very much friendlier, so Winston said very quickly, "My father, who is a great man, is also small." This quick thinking saved his life!

3 When he arrived ...

1 ☐ They put on their sports clothes when he arrived.
2 ☐ They were putting on their sports clothes when he arrived.

Tick (✔) the sentence which means that the boys had already started to change their clothes before he arrived?

Grammar 2: allowed to, can, have to and need to

1 Put this passage into the past.

Winston must practise every day. He isn't allowed to go out in the afternoons and has to go to bed early so that he can play in the team on Saturday.

....

....

....

....

2 Translate these sentences into German.

1 They were not allowed to smoke in the club house.

....

2 Guests had to sign the visitors book.

....

3 Members didn't need to buy tickets.

....

How to say it: Apologising

Underline the two phrases you could use when someone says, "I'm sorry".

1 I'd rather not.
2 That's all right.
3 I don't mind.
4 It doesn't matter.

page 115

Language & Culture: page 110
If you have any problems with these exercises, ask your teacher in the next lesson.

Activities and sports

Unit 11

1 Starter: What were you doing? 1

Talk to your partner and write down what he / she was doing:

- at three o'clock last Saturday,
- at 11o'clock last Sunday morning,
- at two thirty on Sunday afternoon,
- at seven o'clock last night.

Tell the class if your partner was doing anything connected with sport, like this: *Marion was jogging in the park on Sunday at three.*

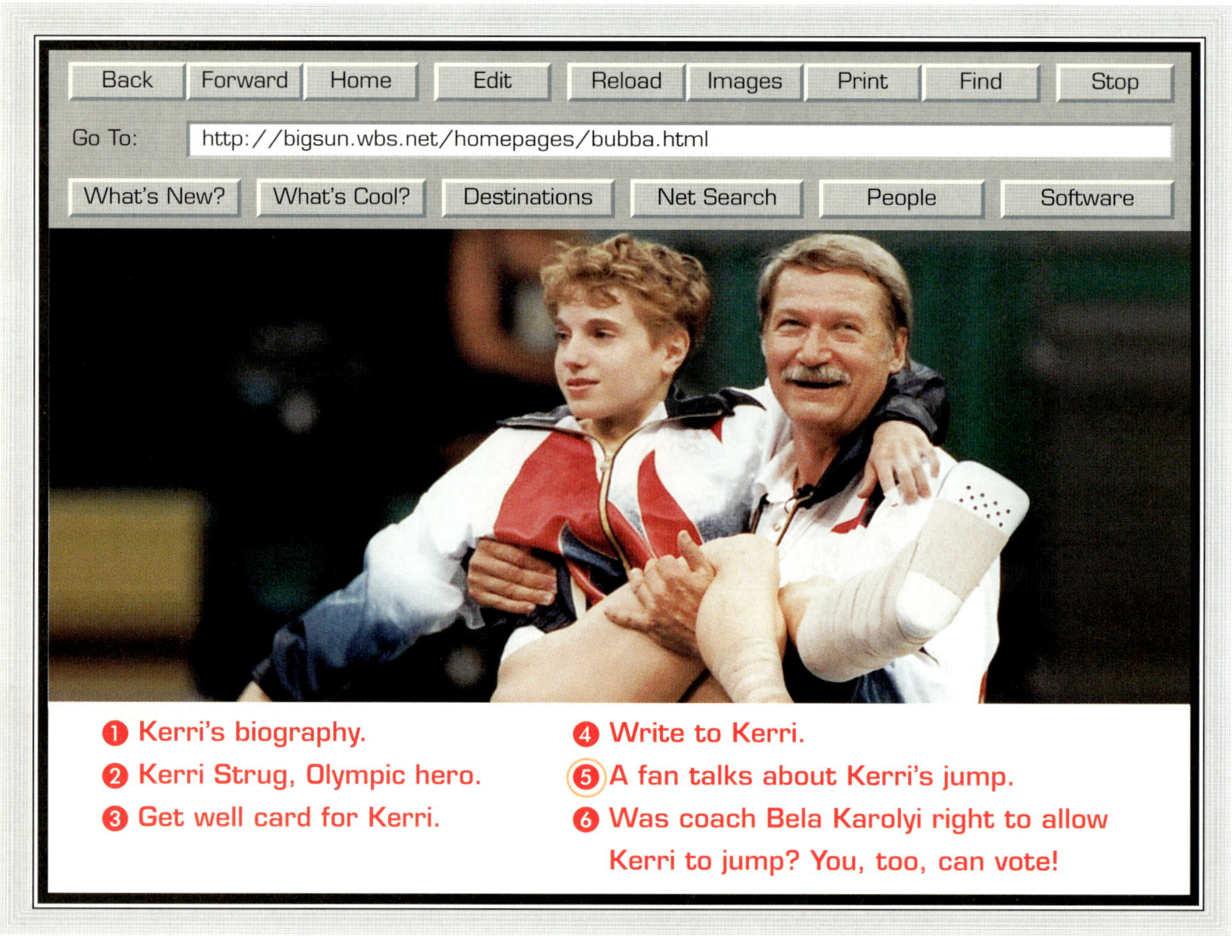

2 A dream come true

In Atlanta on 23rd July 1996, 18-year-old Kerri Strug won a gold medal for the American women's gymnastic team – the team's first Olympic gold in 60 years. Although she had just hurt her foot badly, her coach shouted to her to go on. Brave little Kerri made the last winning jump and she became America's new idol. Since then thousands of Kerri's fans have used the internet to find out all they can about her.

With a partner look at the page from the internet above. Choose two items that interest you. What do you think they could be about? Which one interests you most and why?

3 Exciting moments in sport 1

1 You are going to hear how a fan of Kerri's described that dramatic event. Write down what the fan was doing when Kerri made her first jump. What went wrong for Kerri and how did her coach Bela Karolyi react? Then compare your notes with a partner.

2 Now listen to someone talking about the marathon race in the 1908 Olympic Games in London. Write the answers to the questions and check them with a partner.

a) What was Conan Doyle doing when the runners came into the arena?

b) What did Conan Doyle do when Pietri fell for the fourth time?

4 A tennis drama

With a partner write these sentences in full, making any changes which are necessary.

1 Monika Seles / play / tennis match / Hamburg / 1993 / when / something terrible / happen
2 While / Monika and Magdalena Maleeva / change ends / a man / run / court / and / stab / Monika
3 The crowd / shout / and / everyone / be shocked
4 Monika's trainer / run / to help her
5 Luckily / she / be not badly hurt / but / she / have to / stop playing / over two years
6 1995 / she / win / comeback match / Martina Navratilova

5 Life was hard 2

You've heard stories about an athlete and a tennis player. These people had to do a lot of training. What do you think they had to do, weren't allowed to do, could and couldn't do before their sports events? Look at the list below and talk to a partner about what life was like for the athletes. Do it like this: *They had to train for hours every day. They couldn't go out in the evenings. They weren't allowed to go away on holiday.*

keep fit / sleep / alcohol and tobacco / food / weight / family life / relaxation

6 What about you? 1

Look at the pictures which show sporting accidents. Say what was happening and what happened.

Then write a sentence about an accident which happened to you. (You can make up a story if you like.) Give the pieces of paper to your teacher and he/she will read out some of the most dramatic events. Listen and say if you think the stories are true or not.

7 Vocabulary

➤ Idiom bank

There are a lot of expressions in English which come from sport. Match the expressions with the explanations.

1 The ball is in your court.	☐ a) They play well together.
2 That's not playing the game.	☐ b) He stops us having fun.
3 He's new to the game.	☐ c) It's your turn.
4 He's a spoilsport.	☐ d) That's not fair.
5 There's a good team spirit.	☐ e) He hasn't got a lot of experience.

8 How to say it: Apologising

Fill in the missing part of these conversations and read them with a partner. Look at the Checkpoint page for ideas.

9 Talking points

- What sports did you do at school and did you enjoy doing them? What sports do you like doing or enjoy watching nowadays and why?
- There is not enough time for a lot of sport at school. Should young people do more sports at school or should they do sport in their free time?

Today's grammar

1 The past progressive and the past simple

a) The past progressive → p. 132

- is used to describe an activity that was in progress at a particular point in time: *Yesterday afternoon at three o'clock they were playing football.*
- is used to describe the scene: *Monika was playing well.*

b) The past simple → p. 130

- is used to describe finished activities, one followed by another: *He got out and pushed him into the water.*

c) The past progressive and the past simple → p. 132

- are used together when something happened to interrupt an action in progress: *The players were changing ends when a man ran on to the court.*

2 Modal verbs of permission and obligation

→ p. 127

- ***Could*** is the past of *can* and is used to express permission: *We couldn't play in the team because we weren't good enough.*
- ***Was allowed to*** is the past of *is allowed to* and is used to express official permission: *We weren't allowed to leave the school without permission.*
- ***Had to*** is the past of *must* and is used to express obligation: *I had to show my membership card.* *Had to* is the past of *must, have to* and *have got to.*

Activities and sports

Homestudy

1 Spelling

Write the *-ing* forms of these verbs from Unit 11.

change	drink	play	stop
watch	do	jog	run
swim	win		

Just add *-ing*: ....

....

Double the last letter, then add *-ing*: ....

....

....

Leave off the final -*e*, then add *-ing*: ....

2 Past progressive

Write positive sentences (1&2), negative sentences (3&4) and questions (5&6).

1 What were they doing when you arrived?

....

2 What was she doing when you arrived?

....

3 Were they swimming when you arrived?

No, ...

4 Was he playing golf when you arrived?

No, ...

5 ....
when you arrived?

6 ....
when you arrived?

3 Past simple and past progressive

Which verb form is better? After each number, cross out the form you shouldn't use.

Last Sunday afternoon I (1) *jogged / was jogging* in the park. The sun (2) *shone / was shining* and some children (3) *played / were playing* football. I (4) *ran / was running* past the Park Café when I (5) *heard / was hearing* a terrible noise. I (6) *stopped / was stopping* and (7) *asked / was asking* what was wrong. A young man (8) *answered / was answering*: "Nothing's wrong. We (9) *played / were playing* some nice music, that's all."

4 Apologies

Each of the three dialogues has one apology and two reactions. Listen and write the number of the dialogue in the boxes by each apology or reaction that you hear.

Apologies	Reactions
☐ I do apologize.	☐ Don't worry about it.
☐ I'm so sorry.	☐ I don't mind.
☐ I'm awfully sorry …	☐ It doesn't matter.
☐ I'm terribly sorry.	☐ It can't be helped.
☐ Oh, I'm very sorry.	☐ Never mind.
☐ Please forgive me.	☐ That's all right.

5 Permission in the past

Look at this old list of company rules. Explain what the employees had to do or were / were not allowed to do in those days.

Company Rules

1 Arrive by 8.00 am.
2 Don't leave before 5.00 pm.
3 Don't eat in the office.
4 Smoking in the canteen only.
5 Men must wear suits and ties.

1 They ....

....

2 ....

....

3 ....

....

4 ....

.... in the canteen.

5 The ....

....

CHECKPOINT 12

What you learn

Diese Unit behandelt das Thema Einkaufen. Sie wiederholen hier u.a.:

- persönliche und besitzanzeigende Fürwörter (*personal and possessive pronouns*)
- zählbare und unzählbare Hauptwörter (*using countable and uncountable nouns*)
- Dank aussprechen (*thanking*)

Grammar 1: Personal and possessive pronouns

1 The church bazaar

Complete these sentences with: *her, his, mine, my, our, ours, their (2x), theirs, they, your, yours.*

When Mr and Mrs Lacey went for (1) .... usual Sunday walk, Mr Lacey suggested (2) .... should go to the church bazaar. For some reason Mrs Lacey didn't like the idea very much. They hadn't been there long when Mr Lacey called out, " Look Mary, those blue shirts look like (3) .... and that brown suit is just like (4) .... comfortable brown winter suit. And Mary, isn't that red dress like (5) .... " Mrs Lacey went bright red. "And isn't that lamp (6) ....? It's so much like the lamp we used to have in (7) .... bedroom." Mrs Lacey still didn't say anything. She knew it was (8) .... Mr Lacey said no more, bought the things and went home without saying a word but with (9) .... suit and shirts, (10) .... dress and (11) .... bedroom lamp.

2 It's or Its?

Which word is correct? Cross out the incorrect one.

It's / Its only a small shop but what I like about it best is *its / it's* friendly atmosphere.

Grammar 2: Using countable and uncountable nouns

1 *There is* or *there are*?

Which of these words can complete sentence 1 and which can complete sentence 2?

1 There is some ...   2 There are some ...

[*2*] biscuits	[ ] furniture	[ ] people
[*1*] bread	[ ] information	[ ] tea
[ ] change	[ ] news	[ ] vegetables
[ ] clothes		

2 How else can you say it?

Replace *a lot of* by *much* or *many*.

We can replace *a lot of* by *much* in sentences .... and ....

We can replace *a lot of* by *many* in sentences .... and ....

1 We didn't spend a lot of money.
2 Do a lot of your shop assistants work late on Thursdays?
3 There aren't a lot of people in the shop today.
4 There isn't a lot of tea left.

3 How much or how many? Only a little or only a few?

Cross out the wrong word(s).

A: How *much / many* miles is it to town?
B. Only *a little / a few*.
A: How *much / many* petrol have you got?
B: Only *a little / a few*.

How to say it: Thanking

Look at three different ways of thanking and reacting. Match these expressions with the situations.

Which is the most formal? ....

Which is the most informal? ....

1 A: Thanks very much.
  B: You're welcome, madam.
2 A: Thank you very much indeed.
  B: That's quite all right.
3 A: Thanks a lot.
  B: That's okay.

page 115

Language & Culture: page 110
If you have any problems with these exercises, ask your teacher in the next lesson.

Shopping in London

Unit 12

1 Starter: Food shopping

Look at this list of food: apples, bread, butter, cheese, cream, eggs, meat, oranges, potatoes, salt. Ask people in the class *how much* or *how many* of these things they've got in their kitchens. They will answer with: *quite a lot / only a little / only a few / none at all.*
Do it like this:

A: *How many biscuits have you got?* B: *Only a few.*
A: *How much milk have you got?* B: *Only a little.*

2 What's the answer?

Read about the chance to win a shopping weekend in London. Then ask your partner three questions to fill in the missing information in the competition. Begin with: *How much ...? How many ...?* Then decide how much you think the English money is in your currency.

3 The lucky winner

One of the lucky winners was Ingrid Miller from Bonn. She's going to stay in a hotel in Mayfair. Ingrid wants to buy some new clothes, have traditional English afternoon tea and take back a food hamper full of typical British specialities.

Look at this list of food. Ingrid wants to spend about £50 on food. With a partner choose the food for the hamper, like this:

A: *Shall we get some English cheddar cheese?*
B: *Yes, let's. How much shall we get?*
A: *Not too much, about a kilo. How much is it?*
B: *It's £5.95 for 400 grams, that makes about £12 for two packs.*

Food and Wine Selection

Scottish salmon (454g pack)	£16.75
Cheddar cheese (400g pack)	£5.95
Cumberland ham (125g pack)	£3.95
Breakfast tea (box of 60 teabags)	£3.95
Earl Grey tea (250g tin)	£3.35
Chocolate icy mints (250g box)	£6.60
Three fruit marmalade (340g jar)	£1.95
English shortbread biscuits (250g tin)	£2.75
Scottish (Macallan) whisky	£23.75
Medium dry sherry	£6.75

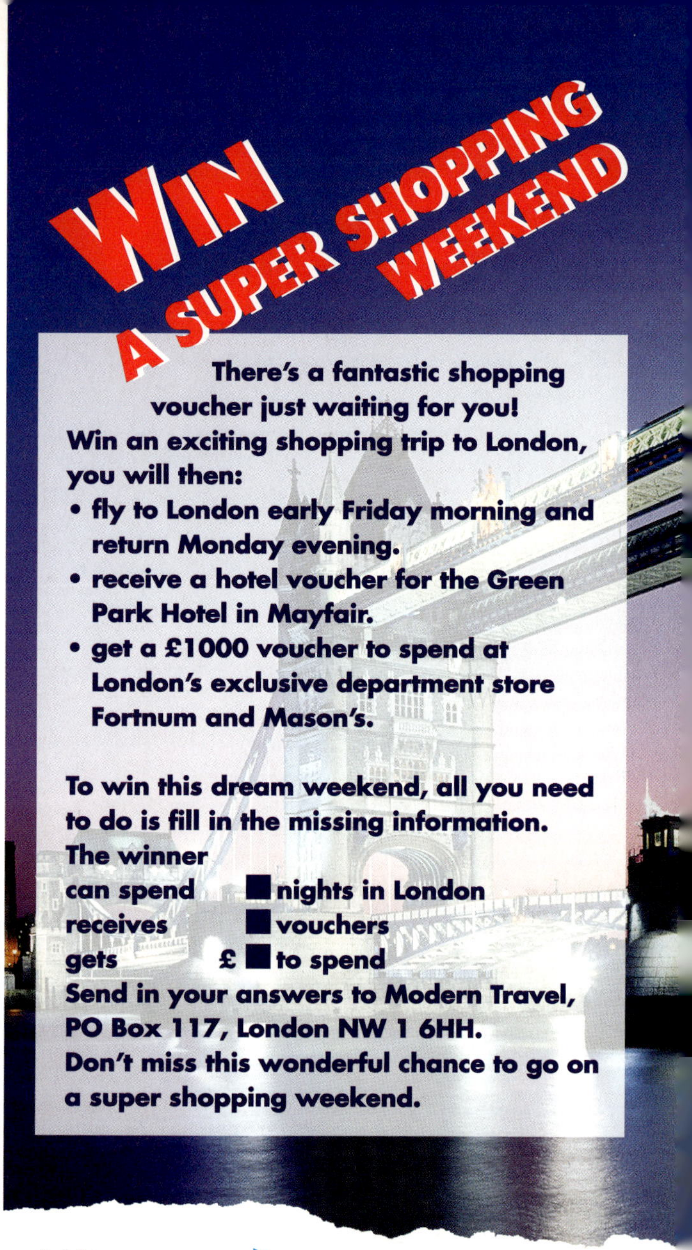

WIN A SUPER SHOPPING WEEKEND

There's a fantastic shopping voucher just waiting for you!
Win an exciting shopping trip to London, you will then:

- **fly to London early Friday morning and return Monday evening.**
- **receive a hotel voucher for the Green Park Hotel in Mayfair.**
- **get a £1000 voucher to spend at London's exclusive department store Fortnum and Mason's.**

To win this dream weekend, all you need to do is fill in the missing information.
The winner
can spend ■ nights in London
receives ■ vouchers
gets £ ■ to spend
Send in your answers to Modern Travel, PO Box 117, London NW 1 6HH.
Don't miss this wonderful chance to go on a super shopping weekend.

4 Afternoon tea

Afternoon tea can be almost a full meal with sandwiches, different kinds of cakes, and, of course, those famous British scones which you eat with butter, or thick cream and jam. With a partner take turns in offering each other some food. Do it like this:

A: Would you like some

butter	jam	sandwiches	tea-cakes
cake	lemon	sweetener	toast
cream	milk	sugar	

with your tea? / in your tea? / on your scone?

B: Yes, just one, please. or: Yes, just a little, please.
No, thank you.

5 How to say it: Thanking

Look at the different ways of thanking on the checkpoint page. Then practise with a partner what you would say in the following situations. Do it like this:

A: *Are these your gloves?*
B: *Oh, yes they are. Thank you very much indeed.*
A: *That's quite all right.*

1 A shop assistant realises that a customer has left her parcel on the counter.
2 A man offers his seat to an elderly lady on the bus.
3 A boy tells another youngster that the seat next to him is free.

6 Buying a dress

You are going to hear a conversation between Ingrid and a shop assistant in a fashion department. In which order did Ingrid use these six expressions when she asked the assistant for some help? Number them 1-6.

☐ Does this colour suit me?
☐ Where do I pay?
☐ Excuse me, can you help me please?
☐ Does it fit me?
☐ Thank you very much for your help.
☐ What size do I take?

Now listen again and write down the assistant's answers.

7 Vocabulary

➤ Word focus: *fit* or *suit*?
Put in the correct word.

1 These shoes don't .... me. They hurt my feet.

2 It doesn't .... him. He looks awful in it.

3 Will this really .... her? It looks much too big.

4 That blouse will .... me. It goes with my hair.

8 Whose is it? 1

In pairs or on your own, write down something which you would like to buy on a shopping trip in London. One student will collect all the pieces of paper and then ask: *Is this your Burberry raincoat? Are these your English books?* The others can answer: *Yes, it's mine. / No, they aren't ours, but perhaps they are his.*
The owner should then give the reason for buying the item/s, like this: *I'd like to buy a Burberry raincoat because it's so typically British.*

9 Talking points

- Many people say that the service in shops is very bad. What do you think?
- What kind of shops do you think should be open 24 hours a day?
- What are the advantages and disadvantages of tele-shopping or mail order shopping?

Today's grammar

1 Personal and possessive pronouns → p. 140

a) Personal pronouns

- ***I*** *hate tea: I, he, she, we* and *they* go **before** the verb.
- *Please help* ***me****: me, him, her, us* and *them* go **after** the verb.

b) Possessive pronouns

- *This is* ***my*** *bag: my, your, his, her, our, your, their* come **before** a noun.
- *This is* ***mine****: mine, yours, his, hers, ours, yours, theirs* are used **in place of** a noun.

2 Using countable and uncountable nouns → p. 138

- ***A lot of*** is used with countable and uncountable nouns: *There are* ***a lot of*** *shops. Has he got* ***a lot of*** *money? He hasn't got* ***a lot of*** *money.*
- ***Much*** is used with uncountable nouns in questions and negatives: *How* ***much*** *money have you got? I haven't got very* ***much*** *money.*
- ***Many*** is used with countable nouns in questions and negatives: *How* ***many*** *kilos do you want? I haven't got very* ***many*** *clothes.*
- ***A few*** is used with countable nouns: ***A few*** *customers came early.*
- ***A little*** is used with uncountable nouns: *I still have* ***a little*** *time for you.*

Shopping in London

Homestudy

1 A lot of, much and many

Put the words in the right order. In place of ****, use *a lot of* (2x), *much* (2x) or *many* (2x).

1 **** - blouses - bought - in - Ingrid - London

....

....

2 **** - at - department - money - she - spent - store - the

....

....

3 books - buy - didn't - **** - she

....

4 didn't - drink - Irish - **** - she - whiskey

....

....

5 did - eat - her - **** - scones - she - tea - with

....

....?

6 cream - did - her - in - **** - put - she - tea

....

....?

2 Choose the words

Write one of these words in each space: *few, fit, fits, her, hers, it's, its, little, many, much, suit, suited, suits, your, you're, yours.* Then draw circles around the words you didn't use.

It was (1) .... last day in London. Ingrid had already tried on a (2) .... dresses, but the colours hadn't (3) .... her. Then she saw a red dress in a shop window. "I haven't got (4) .... money left," she thought, "but why not?" She tried it on, but it was too big. "It doesn't (5) .... me very well," she said. "Yes, (6) .... right," said the assistant. "We haven't got (7) .... dresses left, I'm afraid. But wait a minute, why don't you try on this green one? (8) .... a lovely dress, and it might be (9) .... size."

3 Pronunciation

These words from Unit 12 all have an *a* in them. How should you pronounce the a? Put the right number in each box: 1 for [æ] as in c<u>a</u>t 3 for [ei] as in m<u>a</u>ke 2 for [a:] as in f<u>a</u>ther

☐ back	☐ conversation	☐ hate	☐ pay
☐ bad	☐ day	☐ jam	☐ sandwich
☐ cake	☐ department	☐ market	☐ take
☐ change	☐ fashion	☐ match	☐ thank

Now listen to the words.

4 Countable or uncountable?

Write *a, an* or *some* after each number.

I had (1) .... free time in London, so I decided to do (2) .... sightseeing. I had (3) .... luggage with me, but of course I didn't want to carry it around all day, so I left it at the station. Then I went to (4) .... tourist office and asked for (5) .... information. They gave me (6) .... map and (7) .... bus schedule. I went on (8) .... interesting tour of the city and then had (9) .... tea at (10) .... expensive tea room near the station.

There are five uncountable nouns in the text.

Write them here: ....

....

....

5 Thanking people and responding

In each of these three dialogue Ingrid thanks somebody for something. Listen and write down the other person's response.

Ingrid:	**The other person:**
1 *Thank you.*	....
2 *Thank you very much.*	....
3 *Thank you for your help.*	....

Lerntipp

Liebe Englisch-Expertin,

Lesen kann ich schon einigermaßen, aber wenn ich nur zuhöre, zum Beispiel vom Tonband, passiert es mir oft, dass ich abschalte und dann gar nichts mehr verstehe. Besonders, wenn die Leute eine schwierige Aussprache haben, Amerikaner oder so. Was kann ich machen?

Mit freundlichen Grüßen,
Marlene, Eisenach

Liebe Marlene,

Hörverständnis ist in der Tat eine der schwierigsten Fertigkeiten, die wir uns beim Sprachenlernen aneignen wollen. Diese Fertigkeit üben wir am besten ein, indem wir ganz viel und ganz systematisch zuhören. Wichtig ist dabei:

1) Entspannen Sie sich, denn das Verstehen lässt sich nicht forcieren. Wenn Sie etwa krampfhaft versuchen, jedes Wort auf Anhieb zu verstehen, werden Sie in der Tat abschalten müssen.
2) Setzen Sie sich kleine, realistische Lernziele. Wenn Sie wirklich meinen, „gar nichts" verstanden zu haben, hören Sie die Aufnahme noch einmal an mit dem Ziel, ein einziges Wort zu verstehen und aufzuschreiben. Und beim nächsten Mal zwei oder drei.
3) Überhaupt ist es vorteilhaft, jede Aufnahme mehrmals anzuhören. Sie werden jedes Mal etwas mehr verstehen.
4) Hören Sie nicht nur die English Network Refresher Cassetten, sondern auch Radio- und Fernsehsendungen auf Englisch. Leihen Sie sich englische Videos aus, oder sehen Sie sich englische Filme im Kino oder auf Kabelfernsehen an. So gewöhnen Sie sich an den Klang der Sprache und an die unterschiedlichen Akzente.

Viel Spaß und Erfolg beim Zuhören!

All the best,
Your English Expert

Wordfield

1 British and American spelling

Here are some words you know, as they are spelled in American English. Write the British spelling.

British	American.
1	center
2	color
3	license
4	neighbor
5	organization
6	pay by check
7	program
8	theater
9	traveling

2 British and American words

Match these British and American words. Write the correct number next to the American word.

British	American
1 car park	..... apartment
2 driving-licence	..... check (✔)
3 dustbin	..... driver's license
4 flat	..... garbage can
5 housing estate	..... housing development
6 lorry	..... line up
7 postal code	..... parking lot
8 queue (*verb*)	..... salesclerk
9 shop assistant	..... streetcar
10 telephone box	..... telephone booth
11 tick	..... transportation
12 tram	..... truck
13 transport	..... zip code

PANORAMA 3

USA: Time and money

1 American and British words

Match the American words with the British words.

USA	GB
1 automobile	☐ tyre
2 bill	☐ bank note
3 cart	☐ cinema
4 driver's license	☐ toilet
5 downtown	☐ trolley
6 elevator	☐ shop
7 gas	☐ city centre
8 restroom	☐ motorcar
9 mall	☐ petrol
10 movie theater	☐ lift
11 tire	☐ holiday
12 vacation	☐ shopping centre
13 store	☐ driving licence

2 Where time is money

Ithaca, in upstate New York, is just one of a number of small American towns which has its own money. And it's not against the law. The US Federal Reserve – the American central bank – allows Ithaca to make its own paper money, Ithaca Hours. In stores and businesses across the town you can see the sign "Ithaca Hours accepted here". More than 300 businesses take Ithaca Hours and even the bank accepts them. Small communities like Ithaca want to keep money in the town. They say the dollar bill – federal funny money – just "comes into town, shakes a few hands and then wanders out across the globe". Ithaca Hours stay in Ithaca. You can buy anything from books to food to services. You calculate what you pay for your goods or services in hours. So time is money. As in the LETS organisation, people agree about what they want to pay. But Ithaca has its own "real" money, which local businesses accept. And you can also borrow money. Stephanie Marx moved to Ithaca in 1993 to open a second-hand book store. At first she let customers pay up to 25% in Hours. Now she takes a 100% in Hours for the books. Stephanie Marx was one of the first people to borrow Hours to help her buy her store and the books. She didn't have to pay any interest on the money she borrowed. She just paid back what she had borrowed.

Ithaca is proud of its success with businesses. Paul Glover started the scheme in 1991 with 90 friends; today he sells a Money Starter Kit and Video for $40, and more than 30 other communities – from Hardwick, Vermont, to Santa Fe, are making their own money.

1 In which way is the Ithaca scheme the same as the LETS organisation described in Topics 1&2 and in which way is it different?
2 Which piece of information did you find the most interesting?

3 Who was behind it all?

Paul Glover wants to help his home town. He had an idea and it's a great success. He is just one of so many Americans who have spent their lives developing or marketing a good idea. Some died millionaires, others died without a penny, but their names live on.

Whose name do you connect with these things? Match the names to the things.

- ☐ Henry Ford
- ☐ Elisha Graves Otis
- ☐ Alexander Graham Bell
- ☐ Thomas Alva Edison
- ☐ Isaac Singer
- ☐ W. H. Hoover

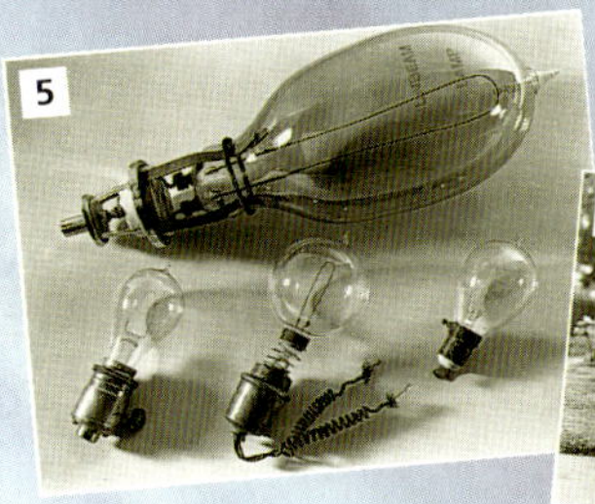

3 Some interesting facts

Read the information and say how three of these ideas helped to save time and / or make money.

- Mark Twain was the first person to write a book on a typewriter.
- In 1936 Sylvan Goldman put the first modern shopping carts in his store in Oklahoma City. But nobody wanted to use them so Goldman paid people to push the trolleys around. The trick worked; everybody started using them.
- Charles Birdseye thought of the idea of frozen food when he was out ice-fishing. The first frozen foods came on the market in 1930.
- The first escalators in the department stores were a sensation. Nurses used to stand at the top to help any customers who felt ill after the ride.
- It was H.G.Selfridge who had the idea of a basement with cheaper goods and who kept the shop window light on at night.
- The first mail-order service was in 1890. At that time most Americans lived in the country, so this service changed their lives.

4 Shopping in America

Read this text about the history of shopping in America and number the shops in the order you read about them. Then discuss with a partner where you do your food shopping and say why you prefer to do it there.

- ☐ supermarket
- ☐ department store
- ☐ shopping mall
- ☐ Mom and Pop store

It was as early as 1840 that an Irish immigrant, Alexander Stewart, opened the first (1). It changed shopping for millions of Americans. They could not only **buy** everything they wanted in one shop, but they could also **find** almost everything else they wanted, too. In time there was no end to the services the stores offered: *restaurants, post offices, libraries, hairdresser's, lost- and-found offices and even their own radio stations.* But for many years most Americans still did their food shopping at the local (2) shop where the atmosphere was very friendly and personal. But soon the (3) put the small family corner shop out of business. People wanted more fast food, and food which was cheap. They also wanted a lot of different kinds of food to choose from and here they could pick the food themselves from the shelves and fill the carts before paying at the check-out counter. But these stores, too, soon had their problems when the (4) was born in the suburbs of the towns. In the early 80s America had 20,000 of these shopping centres. By 1992 there were twice as many. In its first year of business more people went to see America's biggest shopping centre in Minneapolis with its 4,2 million square feet than went to the Grand Canyon!

5 Vocabulary

➤ Idiom bank: Time and money

"He spends money like water."
"He's in the money."
"He must have money to burn."
"He throws good money after bad."

Which two expressions mean: a) He's rich. b) He's not careful with his money.

Can you think of a situation where you could use one of the following expressions?
There's no time like the present.
We had the time of our lives.

6 Talking point

- We need money for the rent, for food, clothes, furniture, holidays and leisure time activities. What do you think is important to spend money on? What do you spend very little money on?

Test yourself

1 Test your tenses

Choose the form that fits best in each sentence. Mark your answers like this: (a)

1 Isolde Barr is an American orchestra conductor* who … up in a small town near Boston.
a has grown **b** grew **c** was growing

2 When she was four years old, her mother … to teach her to play the piano and violin.
a has started **b** started **c** was starting

3 When she was a college student, she … the violin in a symphony orchestra.
a has played **b** is playing **c** played

4 She … in Philadelphia when she met a famous conductor from Europe.
a has played **b** played **c** was playing

5 He … that she should become a conductor herself.
a has suggested **b** suggested **c** was suggesting

6 She … his assistant for several years, until he died.
a has been **b** was **c** was being

7 She … in Japan when she heard that he had died.
a has travelled **b** travelled **c** was travelling

8 By her 25th birthday, she … several famous orchestras.
a conducts **b** had conducted **c** was conducting

9 Now she usually … in New York with her husband.
a had lived **b** is living **c** lives

10 She already speaks French, and now she … German.
a had learnt **b** is learning **c** learns

11 This year she … at several German opera houses.
a conducts **b** had conducted **c** has conducted

12 Right now she … to Australia for the first time.
a flies **b** had flown **c** is flying

*conductor = *Dirigentin / Dirigent*; conduct = *dirigieren*

2 What's the right word?

After each number, cross out the word or expression that is wrong.

Isolde Barr and her husband both (13) *do / make* a lot of travelling for their work, so they don't have (14) *many / much* time to be together. They talk to (15) *each other / themselves* on the telephone almost every day, though, and they try to find a (16) *few / little* days to be together every month. They always enjoy (17) *herself / themselves* when they are together in a (18) *strange / strangely* city. Isolde (19) *is liking / likes* to go shopping with her husband, because he always knows which colours and styles (20) *fit / suit* her the best. And wherever they are, he always seems to know where there is a (21) *nice / nicely* little restaurant where they can sit (22) *quiet / quietly* and have a (23) *good / well* meal.

3 Adjectives and adverbs

Write a new sentence that means the same as the first one, like this:

It was easy for her to find the concert hall.
She found the concert hall easily.

24 The members of the orchestra were polite when they welcomed her.

The ……………………………………………………………………

25 Her conducting was energetic.

She……………………………………………………………………

26 The way the orchestra played was beautiful.

The ……………………………………………………………………

4 Test your spelling

Listen to the text and write in the missing words. Can you spell them correctly?

Isolde Barr says that (27) ……………………… she is very happy with her career as a conductor. There are some (28) ……………………… . She is always very (29) ………………………, so she and her husband are (30) ……………………… at home in their lovely New York apartment. They try to spend their (31) ……………………… time together but it's not always possible because of their heavy work (32) ……………………… .

MY SCORE OUT OF 32: ……..

CHECKPOINT 13

What you learn
Diese Unit behandelt das Thema Schule und Lernen.
Sie wiederholen hier u.a.:
- die Zukunft mit *going to* (*going to future*)
- die Verlaufsform der Gegenwart mit zukünftiger Bedeutung (*present progressive for future*)
- Briefe schreiben (*letter-writing*)

Grammar 1: The *going to* future

1 What is going to happen?
Look at these three pictures. Write a sentence about each picture.

phone

rain

crash

....

....

2 Future plans
Use *going to* to
- translate this question: *Was haben Sie vor?*

....

- re-write these sentences:

1 She is planning to look for a job in France.

....

2 Have her parents got plans to visit her?

....

3 I don't intend to visit her.

....

Grammar 2: The present progressive for future arrangements

Tick the two sentences which talk about the future.
☐ 1 She's taking a French exam.
☐ 2 She's going to take a French exam.
☐ 3 She's taking a French exam tomorrow.

Which tense is used in sentence 1? When is she taking the exam?...

Which tense is used in sentence 3? When is she taking the exam?...

To talk about definite arrangements in the future, you can use the *present progressive* in place of the *going to* future. Tick (✔) the two sentences where you can replace *going to* with the *present progressive.*
4 ☐ They are going to get married in June.
5 ☐ She's going to do her homework.
6 ☐ They are going to arrive here at 8 o'clock.
7 ☐ She's going to write to her friend.

Grammar 1& 2: The *going to* future and the present progressive for future arrangements

A child student
The youngest university student in the world is 7-year-old Michael Tan. He (1) *is studying* mathematics at a university in New Zealand and he (2) *is taking* his final exams at the end of this year. He says he (3) *is going* to be a mathematics professor when he has finished his studies!

Which phrase, 1, 2 or 3, tells you about ...
☐ a) a present activity?
☐ b) a plan for the future?
☐ c) a definite arrangement for the future?

How to say it: Writing letters

1 Where does it go?
When you write an English letter, where do you write:
- your address? On the *left / right* of the paper.
- the date? *Before / After* your address.
- your name? At the *beginning / end* of the letter.

2 The beginning and the end
Match these ways to start and finish a letter.

1	Dear Mum,	☐ a)	Best wishes,
2	Dear Mr Richards,	☐ b)	With love,
3	Dear Peter,	☐ c)	Yours sincerely,

page 115

Language & Culture: page 110
If you have any problems with these exercises, ask your teacher in the next lesson.

Classes and courses

Unit 13

1 Starter: Look what I'm going to do

Think of something that you are going to do. Tell the class the things you've got ready for this activity. They will try to guess what you are going to do. Do it like this:

A: *I've got my 'Network' English book and a pen.*
B: *Are you going to do your homework?*
A: *No, I'm not.*
C: *Are you going to *(go to) your English course?*
A: *Yes, I am.*

***Remember:** It sounds better to use the present progressive tense with the verb *to go*.

2 Karen's letter

Read Karen's letter. What differences can you see between the layout of an English letter and a German letter?

Now read the second paragraph again and write down:

1 one thing which Karen is doing now,
2 one thing which she plans to do in the future,
3 one thing which she has arranged to do in the future.

Compare your list with a partner.

What does *Ave.* mean? You might see these abbreviations in letters or on envelopes. What do they mean?
Mr. / Co. / Ltd. / P.S. / P.T.O. / Rd. / Sq. / and, the most important ... *XXX* !

97 Albert Ave.
Bramcote
Nottingham
NG 93LW
February, 13th, 19..

Ms M. Patterson
The English Bookshop
18 Rue le Trioulet
Marseille
France

Dear Ms Patterson,

After reading your advert in our school magazine for an assistant in the English bookshop during August and September of this year, I decided to write to you because I would like a job in France from the end of July to the middle of October.

I am eighteen years old and I am in my last year at Richmond Secondary School. I am studying very hard at the moment because I am taking my 'A'-level examinations in English, French and German in May. After that I am going to study French and German at University – if my exam results are good enough!

I would very much like to work in your bookshop because it would not only improve my French but it would give me more experience of the French way of life and I would also enjoy having contact with French students.
I am looking forward to hearing from you in the near future.

Yours sincerely,

Karen Lewis

3 The English school system

Listen to Karen, who is at an English secondary school, talking to Martine, a French exchange student, about English schools. Tick (✔) the things they talk about:

☐ homework	☐ school hours	☐ pupils' ages
☐ uniforms	☐ teachers	☐ private schools
☐ holidays	☐ exams	☐ lunchbreaks

Listen again and make notes about anything Karen says which is different from the school system in your country.

4 Letter-writing

With a partner, write a short letter to Karen telling her about the differences between schools in your country and schools in England. Start and end your letter like a typical English letter.

Remember: In a personal letter, you begin with your address but you don't need the address of the person you are writing to. Here is a sentence to start you off: *It was interesting to hear about English schools. The school system here is a bit different. For one thing, ...*

Now compare your letter with another pair of students. Did you tell Karen the same or different things?

5 Vocabulary

➤ Education

Cross out the wrong words and then check your answers with the rest of the class.

1 What *note / mark* did you *get / become* in the exam?

2 Our teacher *checked / controlled* our *homework / homeworks*.

3 The teacher *taught / learnt* us some *light / easy* words.

4 Sue always *does / makes* her homework and works *hardly / hard*.

5 I never come to school *late / too late* because I always *get up / stand up* early.

6 He's going to *take / make* an exam and I hope he doesn't *fail / fall*.

6 What are you going to do? 1

Work in small groups and talk about some of your plans. What are / aren't you going to do when ...

- you get home?
- your holiday starts?
- you retire?
- your teacher leaves the room?
- you can speak English really well?

7 What are you doing next week? 2

Now say one thing which you have **arranged** to do next week. (Look in your diary for ideas). Use verbs like: *drive / go / have / meet / play / see / take / visit / work*. The other people in your group will ask you for more details with question words like: *Why? / When? / What? / How? / Where? / Who?* Do it like this:

A: *I'm taking a French exam next week.*

B: *Where / When are you taking it?*

8 Plans or arrangements? 1 2

Put these verbs into the correct tense. When possible, use the present progressive tense (3x), or use the *going to* future (3x). Then compare your answers with a partner.

Karen says, "I (1 *play*) .... in the inter-schools tennis finals tomorrow. I (2 *play*) .... really hard and I (3 *win*) .... ! This evening I (4 *relax*) .... because I have to get up at 6 o'clock. All the players (5 *meet*) .... at the station at 6.30. and we (6 *catch*) .... the 6.45 train.

9 Talking points

- What do you think is better about the English school system and what is better about the one in your country?
- Do you know anything that is interesting or different about schools in other countries?
- At school, what were you good / bad at? Which subject did you enjoy most? Why? What didn't you like about school?

Today's grammar

1 The future with *going to* → p. 133

- is used to talk about personal plans and intentions: *I'm going to do my homework.*
- is used when we can 'see' what is going to happen: *Look at the clouds – it's going to rain.*

Remember: Try not to use *going to go to* because it sounds strange and try to avoid *going to come* – use the present progressive instead: *She's going to bed soon. She's coming on Tuesday.*

2 The present progressive for future arrangements (with a future time) → p. 133

- is used to talk about definite arrangements in the future: *She's taking an exam in June.*

Remember: We can use the *going to*-future, but when we use the present progressive tense, we have often bought a ticket, made an appointment, made a reservation, or made an arrangement with someone.

Classes and courses

Homestudy

1 The future with going to

Write the sentences. ? = make a question, - = make a negative sentence, + = make a positive sentence.

Next Tuesday Karen has to take an important exam.

1 + (Saturday) *She's going to study on Saturday.*

2 ? (study / Sunday / too) .... ?

3 + [short answer, 3 words] ....

4 - (study / Monday) ....

5 ? (What / do / Monday) .... ?

6 + (She and Paul / play tennis / Monday) ....

2 Pronunciation

These words are all from Unit 13. Underline the part of the word where the main stress comes.

ac<u>ti</u>vity	envelopes	progressive
arrangements	intentions	reservation
differences	interesting	secondary
education	mathematics	subject

Now listen and check your answers.

3 Spelling

These words from Unit 13 all have the sound /f/ in them, but they aren't all spelt the same way. Write in the missing letter(s) in each word.

a____ternoon	enou____	____otogra____y
de____inite	o____ten	pro____essor
di____erent	paragra____	uni____orms

4 The American school system

Karen and Martine are talking to Marc, an American college student, about American schools. Listen and fill in the answers.

1 The German word .... means something different in America.

2 "K-12" means ....

3 Number these years in the correct order (1-4):

☐ freshman ☐ junior ☐ senior ☐ sophomore

4 The American word .... means to fail.

Now listen again and fill in the missing information in the table:

	Ages	Grades
Nursery school		
Kindergarten		
Elementary school		
Junior high school		
High school		
College		

5 Write a postcard

Use these notes to write a postcard from Karen to Ms Patterson, the owner of the bookshop in Marseilles. Use the present perfect for something Karen has just done, the present progressive for something she has already arranged, and going to for intentions.

Thank / very much / nice letter
just bought / plane ticket
fly / London to Marseilles / August 2nd / 14:30
tomorrow / buy a map of the South of France
next weekend / read a book about Marseilles
looking forward / meeting you and working / bookshop

July 12

Dear Ms Patterson, ...

CHECKPOINT 14

What you learn

Medien stehen im Mittelpunkt dieser Unit. Sie wiederholen hier u.a.:

- die Zukunft mit *will* (*simple future: will / won't*)
- den Unterschied zwischen der Zukunft mit *will* und mit *going to* (*futures with will and going to*)
- Möglichkeit ausdrücken (*expressing possibility*)

Grammar 1: Simple future (*will*)

1 Future times

Cross out the words we can't use with the future tenses: *ago / in two weeks / last week / later / lately / next year / soon / tomorrow / yesterday.*

2 Will

Make a question and a negative sentence from this sentence: *He'll lend you his book.*

Question: ....

Negative: ....

3 The early days of the wireless (radio)

Read this conversation about the opening of the BBC in 1925.

"Gerald, read this article from this morning's newspaper. It's about the BBC."
"I can't ... . I haven't got my glasses with me."
"Then (1) **I'll read** it to you. Listen: 'Next month the British Broadcasting Corporation, the BBC, (2) **will begin** its regular broadcasts of news, information, music, weather reports, and entertainment.' I don't know about you, but I'm sure that people (3) **won't be interested** in the wireless ... they've got newspapers for information."
"Well, the wireless isn't *only* for information, it's also for entertainment. I think it's got a great future. I'm sure that, in a few years, most people (4) **will have** a wireless in their home."
"But look at the cost of it! It says that a BBC licence (5) '**will cost** only ten shillings a year' ... ten shillings*!"
"That's not expensive at all. I think (6) **I'll get** one!"

* *Before 1972, English money had pounds, shillings and pence. Today there are only pounds and pence.*

Now write down the numbers of the two phrases which tell you about ...

1 spontaneous decisions: ....

2 predictions: ....

3 future facts: ....

4 *Will* or *want to*?

What does it mean? Cross out the wrong word.

1 He will go later. = Er *will / wird* später gehen.
2 He wants to go later. = Er *will / wird* später gehen.

Grammar 2: *will* and *going to* future

1 I'm going to watch that American film later.
2 That's a good idea! I'll watch it, too.

Which sentence, 1 or 2, makes it clear that:

☐ the speaker has just at this moment decided to watch the film?
☐ the speaker decided some time ago to watch the film?

How to say it: Expressing possibilities

Put the underlined phrases into the negative.

1 I hope he <u>will read</u> it.	5 He <u>might read</u> it.
2 Perhaps we <u>will read</u> it.	6 I probably <u>will read</u> it.
3 I'<u>m</u> sure they will read it.	7 I <u>expect</u> he will read it.
4 I <u>think</u> she will read it.	8 He <u>may read</u> it.

1 ....

2 ....

3 ....

4 ....

5 ....

6 ....

7 ....

8 ....

page 116

Language & Culture: page 110
If you have any problems with these exercises, ask your teacher in the next lesson.

The media

Unit 14

1 Starter: Newspapers

Which articles or stories will probably be in the newspaper this week? Think about things like: international news, national news, sport, culture, personalities. Use phrases like:

Perhaps ...	*There'll probably be ...*
I don't think ...	*There may be ...*
I hope ...	*I expect...*

Do it like this: *I expect there'll be a report about the Wimbledon finals.*

2 In the future 1

The magazine article on the right is about televisions of the future. How have televisions and TV programmes changed over the last twenty years?

Now read the article and talk about how televisions will change over the next few years.

In small groups, write three or more sentences about one of the following headlines and then read them to the class. Begin like this: *Within the next few years, you'll probably be able to ... / Soon you won't have to .... / Before long ...*

The kitchen robot, tomorrow's answer to today's problems.

Virtual reality holidays in the 21st century.

Computerised cars – sit back and relax.

Multi-function PCs: your bank, boss, supermarket and teacher.

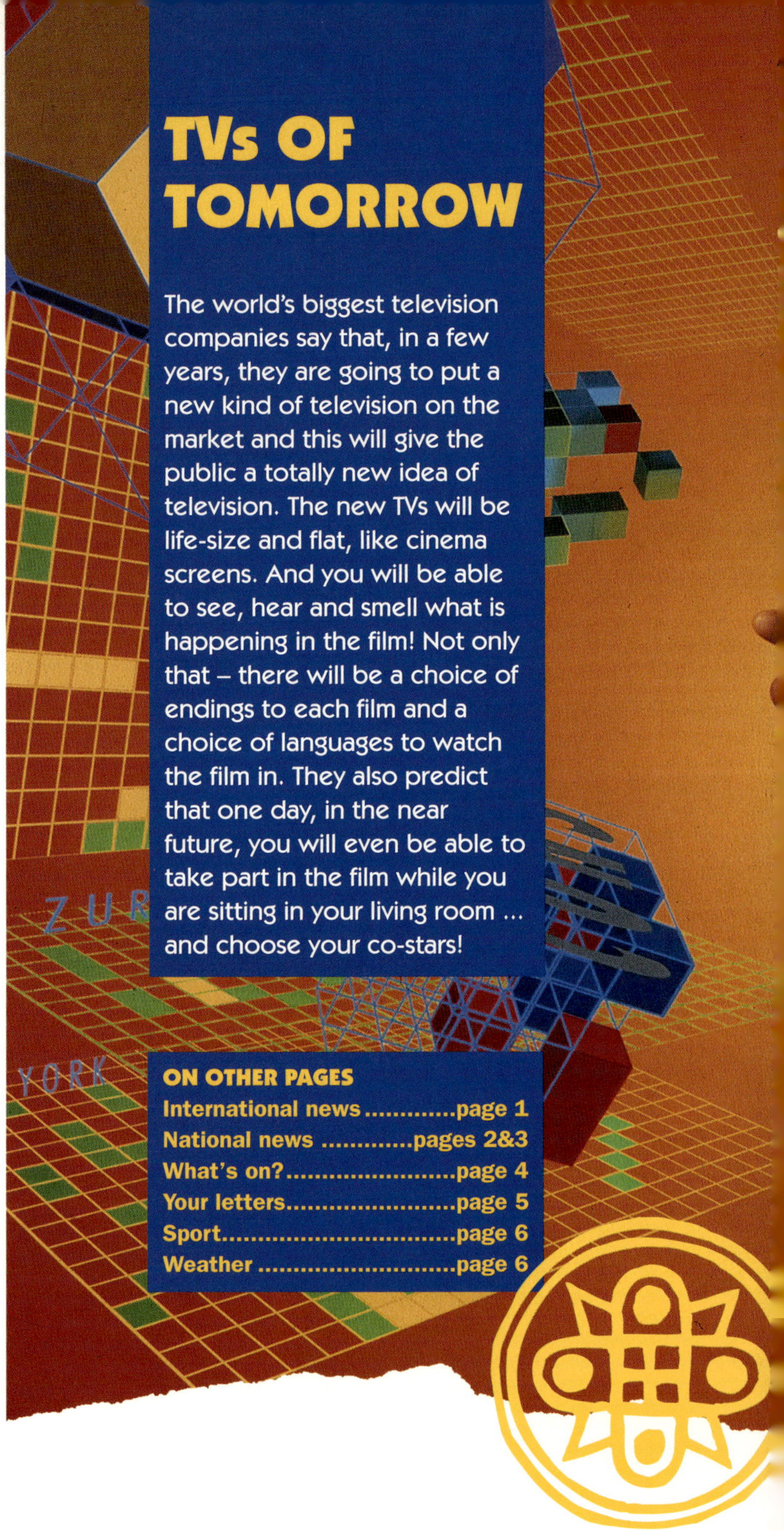

TVs OF TOMORROW

The world's biggest television companies say that, in a few years, they are going to put a new kind of television on the market and this will give the public a totally new idea of television. The new TVs will be life-size and flat, like cinema screens. And you will be able to see, hear and smell what is happening in the film! Not only that – there will be a choice of endings to each film and a choice of languages to watch the film in. They also predict that one day, in the near future, you will even be able to take part in the film while you are sitting in your living room ... and choose your co-stars!

ON OTHER PAGES

3 What's on?

Page 4 of your magazine is missing so you turn on your TV and change channels to see what's on. Number the programmes in the order in which you hear them and then compare your answers with a partner.

- ☐ soap opera
- ☐ the news
- ☐ comedy show
- ☐ documentary
- ☐ sports programme
- ☐ quiz

The documentary programme was about children and television. Choose one of the statements below and write down why you agree or disagree with it. In small groups, read out what you have written and discuss your opinions.

- Children shouldn't watch any TV.
- The TV should not be on during mealtimes.
- Children learn a lot from TV.
- Children shouldn't watch TV when they are alone.
- You can rent a video cassette instead of a babysitter!

7 *Going to* or *will*? 1 2

Which verb form, *going to* or *will*, is better in these situations?

1 I think I .... watch the news.

2 I .... watch my favourite programme at 8 o'clock.

3 The film .... last ninety minutes.

4 Look! She .... kiss him!

5 I'm sure you .... know him when you see him.

8 Talking points

- What do you think are the positive and negative things about TV?
- Do you ever prefer listening to the radio to watching TV? If so, when and why?
- TV and newspapers should be allowed to report about anything and anybody. What do you think?
- Which part of the newspaper do you read first? Why? Which parts do you never read? Why not?

5 Vocabulary

➤ Word focus: *turn*

How would you react in these situations? Match the phrases.

1 I want to watch TV.	☐ I'll turn it up.
2 The TV 's too loud.	☐ Yes, I'll turn it off.
3 I can't hear the TV clearly.	☐ Right, I'll turn it down.
4 This programme is boring.	☐ O.K. I'll turn it on.

6 What are you going to watch? 2

Tell a partner which kinds of programme you enjoy or don't enjoy. What's your favourite TV programme at the moment? Are you are going to watch TV this week? If so, what are you going to watch this evening? / tomorrow? / this week? / at the weekend?

Today's grammar

1 The simple future → p. 133

- is used for predictions: *In 2020 we'll all have life-size TVs.*
- is used for spontaneous decisions: *I'll answer the phone.*
- is used for facts: *The news will be on after the film.*

Remember: It is not used to talk about plans or intentions.

2 The *going to* future → p. 133

- is used for personal plans: *I'm going to buy 'Time' magazine tomorrow.*
- is used when you can see what is about to happen: *Look! The film's going to start.*

The media

Homestudy

1 Questions about the future

Use these words to write questions. The first word of each question is missing.

1 all / from / have / kitchen / now / robots / twenty / we / years

....

....?

2 comedy / going / on / show / stupid / that / to / TV watch / you

....

....?

3 change / in / much / next / television / ten / the / very / years

....

....?

4 daughter / going / to / tonight / TV / watch / your

....?

2 *Will* or *going to*?

Read this dialogue between Karen, who is English, and Martine, a French exchange student. Fill in each gap with *will* or *going to* and one of the words or expressions from each box.

do	look	spend
feel	move	stay
have	retire	

he	I	you
he	they	your parents
I	they	

K: What (1) .... next year, Martine, after you finish school?

M: Well, I've decided on one thing.

(2) .... a long holiday, and after that perhaps (3) .... for a job.

K: Has your brother made any plans?

(4) .... in Marseilles next year?

M: He hasn't decided yet, but personally I think

(5) .... to Paris.

K: How (6) .... about that?

M: Oh, they won't mind. They've got some plans, too.

(7) .... next year, and I expect

(8) .... part of the year in Paris themselves.

3 Plans, decisions and predictions

Listen to the four dialogues and write the number of the dialogue in the box next to each picture. The pictures show something that one of the people is planning to do or has just decided to do.

Now listen to the dialogues again and circle two of the numbers after each question. In which of the dialogues does somebody

- decide spontaneously to do something? 1 2 3 4
- talk about something already planned? 1 2 3 4
- make a prediction about the future? 1 2 3 4

4 Expressing possibility

Write one of these words in each of the gaps: *certain, expect, hope, may, maybe, might, perhaps, possibly, probably, sure, think.*

1 I'm .... / .... there will be something very interesting on TV this evening.

2 They .... / .... show a documentary programme at eight fifteen.

3 .... / .... / .... / .... there will be some important news from America.

4 I .... / .... / .... the news will be better today than it was yesterday.

5 Pronunciation

You heard these words in Unit 14. Do the underlined letters sound the same (✓) or different (✗)?

1 ☑ invented - television
2 ☐ airport - closed
3 ☐ prize - winner
4 ☐ sport - stop
5 ☐ time - will
6 ☐ child - children
7 ☐ must - sure
8 ☐ concentrate - chosen
9 ☐ safe - babies
10 ☐ not - alone

Now listen to the words.

What you learn

Diese Unit hat das Thema Essen und Trinken sowie Gesundheit und Wohlbefinden. Sie wiederholen hier u.a.:

- Nebensätze (*time clauses with: when, as soon as, before*)
- Bedingungssätze (*if-sentences: Conditional 1*)
- Vorlieben und Abneigung ausdrücken (*expressing likes and dislikes*)

CHECKPOINT 15

Grammar 1: Time clauses

1 When will she leave?

Read these sentences. Which one is correct? Cross out the incorrect one.

1 She'll leave Britain when she will finish her tour.
2 She'll leave Britain when she finishes her tour.

2 On tour with Madonna

Many stars have become health and fitness fanatics – Clint Eastwood has got a private fitness centre, Paul McCartney is a vegetarian and Michael Jackson often wears a mask over his mouth because the air is so dirty!

Look at these sentences about pop-star Madonna who is giving a concert in London next month. Use the word in brackets to make one long sentence from each pair of sentences. Make any changes which are necessary.

1 She'll arrive in London. Then she'll go jogging.

When ....

....

2 She'll sing in front of thousands of people. First she'll meditate.

Before ....

....

3 She'll get back to her hotel. She'll order a meal – but she won't eat any meat or drink any alcohol.

As soon as ....

....

Grammar 2: *If*-sentences (type 1)

Put the verb into the correct tense, present simple (*go/goes*) or simple future (*will go*), in these positive sentences.

1 If he (*drink*) .... too much, he (*have*) .... a headache tomorrow.

2 They (*lose*) .... weight if they .... (*eat*) less.

Now make sentence 2 negative so that the meaning stays the same.

....

....

Which sentence, a or b, tells you that he is sure he will see her?

a) ☐ He'll tell her *when* he sees her.
b) ☐ He'll tell her *if* he sees her.

How to say it: Likes and dislikes

Match these phrases with the faces.

1 🙂 2 😐 3 🙁

☐ I like ☐ I love ☐ I hate ☐ I don't mind
☐ I don't like ☐ I enjoy ☐ I dislike

Cross out the wrong words or phrases.

4 I enjoy *go / to go / going* to a restaurant.
5 They don't mind *cook / to cook / cooking* dinner.

Translate these sentences into German.

6 What do you like? ....

7 What would you like? ....

page 116

Language & Culture: page 110
If you have any problems with these exercises, ask your teacher in the next lesson.

Health and food

Unit 15

1 Starter: How soon will you do that? 1

Tell a partner when you will do some of these things:

- go home
- read this text
- go to bed
- have breakfast
- watch or listen to the news
- go to the dentist's next
- do your homework

Use the words: *as soon as / when / before*. Do it like this: *I'll do my homework as soon as I get home.*

2 Health quiz

Fill in the answers to the health quiz. Give your book to a partner, who will add up your score. You'll get 5 points for every A answer, 3 points for every B answer and no points if your answer is C! Then your partner will read out your result.

Did your partner answer any question with C? If so, warn him / her about the possible results, like this: *If you don't lose weight, you won't be very fit / you'll probably have health problems in a few years.*

3 What's the problem? 2

If you have a health problem, people will often make suggestions about what to do to make you feel better. Look at these suggestions and say what you think the problems are.

1 "If you take an aspirin and go for a walk in the fresh air, you'll feel better in no time."
2 "If you take these vitamin tablets every day, you'll soon feel like a twenty-year-old."
3 "If you smoke less in the future, it'll get a bit better."
4 "If you put a plaster on it, the bleeding will stop."
5 "If you stop eating sweets, you won't have as many problems."

Now work with a partner and make similar suggestions. Do it like this:

A: *How are you?*
B: *Not very well.*
A: *Why? What's the matter?*
B: *I can't sleep at night.*
   or: *I've got the flu and a high temperature.*
   or: *I've got backache.*
   or: *I've got a sore throat.*
A: *Well, if you ... .*

4 Enjoying life

Tell a partner about some *un*healthy things in your lifestyle (things you do or don't do and things you eat). Begin with: *I know it's unhealthy, but I really like / love / enjoy ...* or: *I know it's healthy, but I really dislike / don't like / hate ... .*

Your partner will then tell the class something about you, like this: *Sarah doesn't like vegetables very much and she really enjoys smoking a cigarette after meals.*

Remember: Use the *ing*-form of the verb when you talk about likes and dislikes: *He enjoys (playing) golf.*

How healthy are you?

Facts: 300,000 people die of heart disease in Britain every year – probably the result of fatty diets. 54% of British men say that they do no exercise. England and Ireland are the only European countries where the women drink as much as the men. Not very positive statistics! What about your lifestyle? Answer these questions and find out how (un?)healthy you are.

How many cigarettes do you smoke?

A ☐ None.
B ☐ Under 5 a day.
C ☐ Over 5 a day.

How often do you do any exercise?

A ☐ Regularly.
B ☐ Sometimes.
C ☐ Seldom.

Are you overweight?

A ☐ No.
B ☐ Yes, less than 10 kilos.
C ☐ Yes, more than 10 kilos.

5 Vocabulary

➤ Food and health

Read these phrases: *very well, very good, awful, great, not too bad, better, worse than before, fine, not very well, sweet, tired, salty, quite ill, nice.* You can use some of these phrases to answer the question *How are you?*, some to answer *What does it taste like?* and some to answer both questions. Write the two questions down and put the correct answers under the question.

Are you under stress at work?

A ☐ No.
B ☐ Not a lot.
C ☐ Yes.

How often do you eat vegetables and salads?

A ☐ Every day.
B ☐ A few times a week.
C ☐ Seldom.

How often do you drink alcohol?

A ☐ Occasionally or never.
B ☐ Once or twice a week.
C ☐ Every day.

How long do you sleep?

A ☐ 8 hours a night or more.
B ☐ Between 6 and 8 hours.
C ☐ Less than 6 hours.

0 - 14 Oh dear! You won't be able to enjoy your old age if you go on like this! Look at the C answers you had – if you change some of these habits, you'll feel better for it!
15 - 27 Your lifestyle is quite healthy but you'll have to change your lifestyle a little bit if you want to be fit and healthy in your old age. Try to find one habit you could improve.
28 - 35 Well done! If you continue like this, you'll live to be a hundred!

6 In a restaurant

Jeff and Nigel are in a restaurant. Jeff is a healthy eater and wants to order a healthy meal. Nigel loves food and orders lots of unhealthy things to eat and drink. The waiter recommends the most expensive things on the menu.
In pairs, try to guess who will speak about the following things. Write J for Jeff, N for Nigel and W for the waiter.

☐ baked potato	☐ chips	☐ mineral water
☐ beer	☐ coffee	☐ salad
☐ bread rolls	☐ cream	☐ salt
☐ butter	☐ fish	☐ soup
☐ caviar	☐ fruit	☐ steak
☐ champagne	☐ fruit juice	
☐ cheese	☐ ice-cream	

Now listen to the conversation and check your answers.

Listen again to the conversation and write down the phrases they use when:
1 Jeff wants to order.
2 The waiter wants them to order champagne.
3 Nigel wants a beer.
4 Jeff wants a tomato salad.
5 Nigel wants the salt.

Now look at these places to eat and drink: *a restaurant, a snack-bar, a tea room.* Decide what you would order in each of these places. What would you say?

7 Talking points

- What is the worst thing you have ever eaten? Where and *why* did you eat it?
- Do you think that you are a healthy eater? Why? / Why not? Some people are vegans and eat no meat or animal products. Do you think this is healthy? Why? / Why not? What meal would you cook for a vegan?
- What are the latest food and health scares?
- Why do people smoke cigarettes? How can smokers give up smoking?

Today's grammar

1 Time clauses → p. 134

- are used to say when something will happen:

Simple Future		Present simple
	as soon as	
She'll leave	***before***	*he telephones.*
	when	

2 *If*-sentences → p. 126 + 134

- are used to talk about a future possibility and its result:
  If you eat too much, you'll put on weight.

Remember: Don't use the future tense in the *if* half of the sentence: ***If plus will makes teachers ill!***

Remember: ***If*** is used for something which you think ***could*** happen. ***When*** is used for things which you are ***sure*** will happen.

Health and food

Homestudy

1 Time clauses

Read this postcard and write the present simple or the *will*-future of the verb in each space.

Dear Mother,

Don't worry! Everything (1 be) .... all right tomorrow. I (2 make) .... the tea before you (3 arrive) .... As soon as you (4 get) .... here, we (5 have) .... tea and then we (6 get) .... ready to go. I (7 call) .... a taxi as soon as we (8 be) .... ready. When we (9 get) .... to the station, I (10 buy) .... the tickets.

2 Conditional sentences

Use conditional sentences to answer the questions:

1 Shall we leave now? (we / arrive on time)

Yes, *if we leave now, we'll arrive on time.*

2 Should I eat a salad? (you / get some vitamins)

Yes, ...

3 Should he eat fish? (he / not put on weight)

Yes, ...

4 Should she go jogging every day? (she / keep fit)

Yes, ...

5 Shall we have drink? (we / not be thirsty later)

Yes, ...

6 Are you going out for a walk? (I / feel better)

Yes, ...

Now decide where to put in the word *will*. Tick (✔) one box in each sentence.

7 You ☐ feel ☐ better ☐ if ☐ you ☐ get ☐ some ☐ sleep.

8 If ☐ we ☐ ask ☐ them ☐ they ☐ tell ☐ us ☐ what ☐ happened.

9 They ☐ go ☐ swimming ☐ tomorrow ☐ if ☐ they ☐ have ☐ enough ☐ time.

3 Remember the words

Find fifteen more words about food and drink.

s	a	l	a	d	w	y	f	i	s	h	s
t	p	e	a	r	a	s	o	u	p	j	c
e	p	m	e	a	t	t	o	m	a	t	o
a	l	o	b	r	e	a	d	e	g	g	n
k	e	n	g	a	r	l	i	c	a	k	e

4 Likes and dislikes

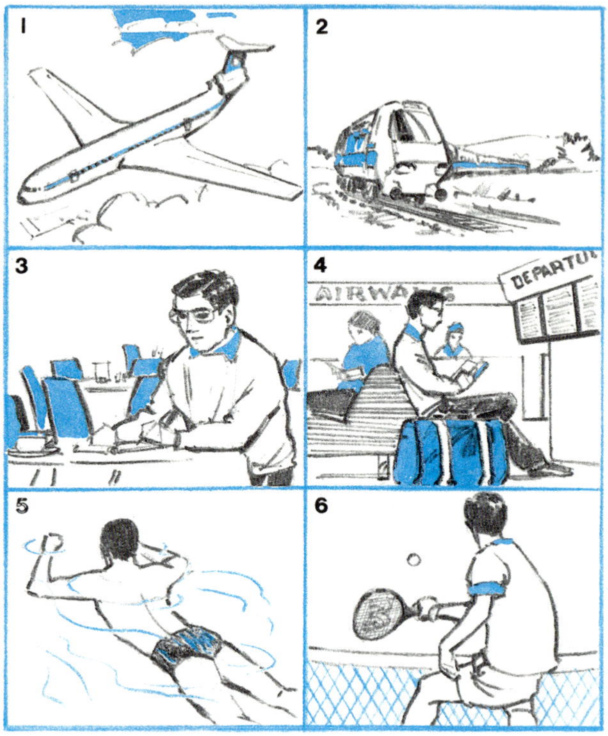

Clive, an Australian, is talking to Karen, who is English. Listen and circle two of the numbers after each question. Which pictures show things that Clive

- likes? 1 2 3 4 5 6
- dislikes? 1 2 3 4 5 6
- neither likes nor dislikes very much? 1 2 3 4 5 6

Now listen again and tick (✔) the boxes to show which of these expressions he used:

☐ I dislike ☐ I don't mind ☐ I like
☐ don't enjoy ☐ enjoy ☐ love
☐ don't like ☐ hate ☐ prefer

5 Pronunciation

These words from Unit 15 all have the letters ea in them. How should you pronounce the ea? Put the right number in each box: 1 for [e] as in bread 2 for [iː] as in eat 3 for [eɪ] as in break

☐ breakfast ☐ heavy
☐ cream ☐ leave
☐ each ☐ meal
☐ great ☐ meaning
☐ headache ☐ meat
☐ health ☐ steak

Now listen to the words.

CHECKPOINT 16

What you learn
Diese Unit beschäftigt sich mit anderen Ländern und deren Sitten und Gebräuche. Sie wiederholen hier u.a. :
- das Frageanhängsel „nicht wahr?" (*question tags*)
- Relativpronomen (*relative pronouns*: *who, which, that)*
- Meinungen ausdrücken (*expressing opinions*)

Grammar 1: Question-tags

Which question, a or b, expects the answer "Yes.".
a) It isn't very warm in here, is it?
b) It's very warm in here, isn't it?

Now cross out the incorrect question-tag at the end of these sentences and write the short answers to the questions, like: *Yes, it is. / No, it isn't.*

1 Tokyo has got a restaurant for dogs,
hasn't it? / has it?..

2 The Greeks drink the least coffee,
don't they? / aren't they?.......................................

3 It snowed in the Sahara for the first time in1979,
wasn't it? / didn't it?..

4 You can't see any clocks in the casinos of Las Vegas,
can you? / do you?..

5 Traditional aboriginees won't eat in public,
will they? / won't they?.......................................

Grammar 2: Relative pronouns

1 Did you know ...?
Put the word *who* or *which* into these sentences.

1 The man .... made the first tea-bag was an American.

2 The city .... has the biggest cathedral is New York.

Which other word can you use to replace *who* and *which* in the above sentences? ....

2 Which word ...?
Now write the correct relative pronoun, *who, which* or *that*, in the following sentences.

.... is used to talk about people.

.... is used to talk about things.

.... can be used for people and things.

3 Can you leave it out?

Read the following sentences and cross out the word *who, which* or *that* when it isn't necessary.
1 New York, the city *that* we visited next, has got more Irish people in it than Dublin!
2 The Irish are the people *who* drink the most tea.
3 Los Angeles is a city *which* has got more cars than people.
4 The town *which* I was telling you about has got more psychotherapists than postmen!

How to say it: Expressing opinions

1 Cross out the wrong words.
1 *Personal / Personally* speaking, I don't like it!
2 What's your *meaning / opinion*?
3 I'm sure he'll win – what do you *mean / think*?

2 Agreeing
Complete these sentences to agree with the opinions.

1 I liked the food.	So ....
2 I won't go there again.	Neither ....
3 I wasn't very pleased.	Neither ....
4 I'm really pleased with it.	So ....

Put in the word *too* or *either.*

5 So do I. = I do..

6 Neither do I. = I don't ....

page 116

Language & Culture: page 111
If you have any problems with these exercises, ask your teacher in the next lesson.

Different countries, different customs

Unit 16

1 Starter: People in your class 1

Write down three things you think you know about another student in your class, like this: *I think Karen learnt French at school.*

Then check your information with that person, using a question-tag, like this:
Karen, you learnt English at school, didn't you?
You haven't got any children, have you?
You're going on holiday in summer, aren't you?

2 Superstitions 2

Look at these pictures of English superstitions and say which ones mean something in *your* country.
Read the text and then, with a partner, complete these sentences with *who* or *which* and compare your answers with another pair.

1 A superstitious person is someone ...
2 In England a black cat, not a pig, is the animal ...
3 A chimney sweep is someone ...
4 Friday 13th is a day ...

Now think of other superstitions. What is lucky / unlucky in your country?

We know that different countries have different customs. When two Japanese people meet, they often bow; Eskimos rub noses, the French kiss, Germans shake hands and, in some parts of Tibet, they put out their tongues as a sign of respect! But different countries also have different superstitions. In most countries a broken mirror means seven years bad luck but did you know that it is unlucky to open an umbrella in the house in England? You shouldn't walk under a ladder in the street, either. And what do you do if you spill salt? Most people think that horseshoes are lucky and the English think it's lucky if a black cat crosses your path. Before an exam you must cross your fingers to bring you luck (you'll be even luckier if you see a chimney sweep on your way to the exam!) and don't forget to take a mascot with you – all these things will help you – if it's not Friday 13th!

3 What is polite? 1

Different cultures have got different ideas about politeness, too. What advice would you give to someone who is going to meet his / her partner's parents for the first time? You're going to hear Sue, an English woman, talking to Margit about what happened when she first met her husband's parents in Bavaria. Before you listen, read these sentences from the conversation and add the question-tags. Then listen and correct your answers.

1 It's terrible, ...?

2 Well, at least you weren't late, ...?

3 Oh, of course, you couldn't speak German then,

...............................?

4 Oh no, you left the paper on, ...?

5 You don't put your hand under the table in England,

...............................?

6 You hadn't forgotten to shake hands,

...............................?

7 You certainly won't make those mistakes again,

...............................?

Margit's voice sometimes went up at the end of the tag – that's because she wanted information and she was asking a **real question**. Sometimes her voice went down because she was just checking something she already knew. Listen again and write down the numbers of the sentences when she wanted information and asked a real question.

4 What do you think?

Talk about what is important to you when someone visits *your* home for the first time. Do it like this:

A: *Personally, I don't think it's necessary for people to bring a present when they come to dinner.*

B: *No, neither do I. / I don't, either. But I expect them to phone and thank me the next day.*

A: *Yes, so do I. / I do, too.*

Think about things like using first names, clothes, table manners, presents, conversation, thanking, when to leave ... . Do you expect a man to behave differently from a woman? If so, how? And what about children?

5 Vocabulary

➤ Countries and nationalities

How many different nationalities are there in your class? Now say what nationality people from these countries are: Belgium, France, Greece, Italy, The Netherlands, Portugal, Russia, Spain, Sweden, Switzerland.

6 Who was it? 1 2

In small groups, write down what nationality the following people were and why they became famous.

Alexander Graham Bell	Christopher Columbus
Amy Johnson	Agatha Christie
Charlie Chaplin	Guglielmo Marconi
Yuri Gagarin	Alfred Nobel

Then check your answers with another group, like this:
Who was John Logie Baird? He was the Scotsman who invented the television, wasn't he?
If no-one in the class is sure of the details, look at page 111.

Now *you* think of a famous person and ask the class what they know about him / her.

7 Talking points

Every country has got its own customs which other nationalities often find strange or interesting.

- In Thailand it's not polite to touch children's heads. Tell the class about any custom which surprised you in another country.
- In England a bride should have
  "Something old, something new,
  Something borrowed, something blue."
  What wedding customs are there in your country?
- In German there are two words for *you*. How would you explain to an English person when to use 'Du' and when to use 'Sie'?

Today's grammar

1 Question-tags → p. 124

- are often used to check facts: *Your name is Sue, isn't it?*
- When the sentence is positive, the tag is negative: *He broke a mirror, didn't he?*
- When the sentence is negative, the tag is positive: *You aren't superstitious, are you?*

Remember: When your voice goes down at the end of the tag, you aren't really asking a question, you just want the listener to agree with you.

2 Relative pronouns: which, who, that → p. 141

A clause is part of a sentence. A relative clause is used to say which person or thing we are talking about.

- ***Who*** or ***that*** is used for a person: *Marconi is the man* ***who / that*** *invented the radio.*
- ***Which*** or ***that*** is used for a thing: *A horseshoe is something* ***which / that*** *brings you luck.*
- When the second clause has a subject, we can leave out the relative pronoun: *The broken mirror is a superstition (which / that)* ***we*** *all know.*

Different countries, different customs

Homestudy

1 Superstitions

Write a question tag at the end of each sentence.

1 A broken mirror means bad luck, ...?

2 Black cats bring good luck, ...?

3 Friday 13th is an unlucky day, ...?

4 He's got a horseshoe for good luck, ...?

5 It will bring me luck if I cross my fingers, ...?

6 I shouldn't walk under a ladder, ...?

7 You won't forget your mascot, ...?

8 You don't really believe all this, ...?

2 Agreeing

Choose a response to agree with each statement, and write the number in the box.

1 I don't know Quentin.	a) ☐	Neither will I.
2 I like skiing.	b) ☐	Neither have I.
3 I won't do that again!	c) ☐	Neither am I.
4 I'll be 40 next year.	d) ☐	Neither do I.
5 I'm not hungry yet.	e) ☐	So will I.
6 I'm quite busy today.	f) ☐	So am I.
7 I've been to London.	g) ☐	So have I.
8 I've never met Karen.	h) ☐	So do I.

3 Opinions

Listen to five dialogues about children, and decide which sentence best describes each dialogue. Write the number of the dialogue in the box.

☐ She agrees with him.
☐ He agrees with her.
☐ She disagrees with him.
☐ He disagrees with her.
☐ She agrees with him, but she thinks something else is more important.

4 Relative pronouns

Complete sentences 1-4 with *who* or *which*.

1 I'm reading a book .... is very interesting.

2 It's about a man .... doesn't eat meat, eggs or fish.

3 He used to have a girlfriend .... ate steak three times a week.

4 But finally he married a woman .... is a vegan, just like he is.

Now read this paragraph and decide which of the numbered words (*that*, *who* and *which*) are not absolutely necessary. Cross them out.

Claire and Tony Smith are friends that (5) we have known for years. They are the people who (6) live in the big white house which (7) you can see at the end of our road. It's a house that (8) has been there since the seventeenth century. The dinner which (9) we had at their house last night was excellent. The wine that (10) they served was from a little town in France. It is a town which (11) they often visit on their summer holidays. They are the only English people that (12) I know who (13) speak very good French.

5 Write the sentences.

Use these words to write about Peter. Be careful to make your sentences fit the tag questions.
1 *grown a lot lately;* 2 *live next door;* 3 *very good at maths;* 4 *stay out too late;* 5 *be home by seven o'clock*

1 ...., hasn't he?

2 ...., doesn't he?

3 ...., is he?

4 ...., will he?

5 ...., won't he?

6 Pronunciation

Underline the part of each word where the main stress comes.

Italy - Italian	possible - possibility
nation - nationality	probably - probability
person - personality	reserve - reservation
photograph - photography	vegetable - vegetarian

Now listen to the words.

Lerntipp

Liebe Englisch-Expertin,

unsere Kursleiterin sagt uns immer wieder, die Grammatik sei nicht Ziel des Englischkurses, sondern nur ein Hilfsmittel, damit wir die Regelmäßigkeiten der Sprache schneller merken und verstehen. So weit, so gut. Mein Problem ist, daß ich dieses "Hilfsmittel" nur lästig und verwirrend finde. Warum können wir die Sprache nicht einfach durch Hören und Sprechen lernen, so wie kleine Kinder das machen, ohne uns mit Grammatikregeln aufzuhalten?

Mit freundlichen Grüßen
Anja, Winterthur

Liebe Anja,

viel Hören und viel Sprechen ist auf jeden Fall für den Spracherwerb in jedem Alter unerläßlich, insofern liegen Sie völlig richtig. Wir Erwachsene sollten uns nicht schämen, in bestimmten Lernphasen „wie kleine Kinder" vorzugehen und auch Spaß daran zu haben.

Andererseits haben kleine Kinder (von allen anderen Unterschieden einmal abgesehen) mehr Zeit als wir, sie sind sozusagen hauptberuflich mit dem Spracherwerb beschäftigt und wollen ganz dringend ihre erste Sprache erwerben. Erwachsene haben meistens auch anderes zu tun und sollten schon deswegen alle Möglichkeiten aufgreifen, um das Sprachenlernen zu beschleunigen und zu rationalisieren. Dazu gehören Lesen, Schreiben, das Benutzen von Nachschlagewerken – und eben auch Grammatikregeln. Hier ein paar Tipps dazu:
Prägen Sie sich die wichtigsten grammatischen Bezeichnungen auf Deutsch und Englisch ein, vor allem die Wortarten (noun, verb, usw.). und die Zeitformen des Verbs (past simple, present perfect, usw.) Diese Bezeichnungen werden Ihnen helfen, in Nachschlagewerken wie English Network Grammar die jeweils gewünschte Information schnell zu finden.

Wenn Ihnen eine Grammatikregel nicht sofort einleuchtet, lassen Sie sie erst einmal beiseite und kommen Sie darauf zurück, nachdem sie eine Weile die entsprechende Struktur geübt haben.

Haben Sie keine Angst, zur Grammatik Fragen zu stellen. Am besten schreiben Sie Ihre Fragen möglichst genau auf, und fragen Sie gleich in der nächsten Kursstunde Ihre Kursleiterin / Ihren Kursleiter. Wenn es Ihnen gelingt, eine präzise Frage zu stellen, haben Sie gute Chancen, eine präzise Antwort zu bekommen und diese auch zu verstehen.

Seien Sie nicht böse, wenn Grammatikregeln nicht 100% zutreffen. Die Sprache ist, wie sie ist, und die Regeln sind da, um die Sprache zu beschreiben, so gut es geht. Es gibt fast immer irgendwelche Ausnahmen, trotzdem können die Regeln sehr hilfreich sein, wenn sie die Mehrzahl der Fälle abdecken.

Yours sincerely,
Your English Expert

Wordfields

Education, health, the media

Put each of these words into one of the categories:advert, articles, backache, broadcasting, channel, disease, entertainment, exam, fitness, flu, headline, homework, lesson, marks, maths, news, overweight, primary, pupil, relaxation, screen, secondary, stress, vegetarian

Education	Health	The Media

1 Write longer words that mean the same as:

advert .... maths ....

exam ....

2 Write words that mean the opposite of:

healthy .... meat-eater ....

underweight ....

3 A-levels come at the end of .... school.

4 The BBC is the ....

5 Wireless is an old word for ....

6 *The Times* is a ....
(There's a new one every day.)

7 *Time* is a ....
(There's a new one every week.)

PANORAMA 4

Indian influences

1 Starter: What do you know?

The four pictures below are connected with India in some way. Tell the class anything you know about these connections.

2 About the pictures

Listen to these pieces of information about the pictures and write the numbers in the boxes in the order you hear them. Check your answers with a partner.

Now make four small groups. Listen to the information again and each group should make notes about one of the pictures. Then talk about your picture – what you know about it and what you heard about it. Each group should write 3 or 4 sentences about their picture and read them to the class.

3 Languages in India

Put these missing words into the text: *important / official / government / business / central / cultural.*

There are 12 main languages in India and about 850 other languages and dialects! Since 1947, when India became independent, Hindi has been the (1) .... language, with 240,000,000 speakers. But, because there are so many other languages, (2) .... officials, (3) .... people and the media usually use English to communicate. The only way the (4) .... government in the capital, New Delhi, can communicate with non-Hindi states in the south of India is in English. So the English language plays an (5) .... role in India's political, (6) .... and business life and, in a country of 840 million people, there are more English speakers in India than there are in England!

5 Indian influences in England

You can see the influence of India in many areas of British life – even the traditional English drink, tea, is from India. In literature, Salman Rushdie, writer of *The Satanic Verses* is just one of the many Indian or Anglo-Indian writers in Britain today; in medicine, a large number of doctors come from Indian families; in design, Indian fabrics are very popular; and the local Post Office or supermarket often has an Indian manager. But India's biggest influence on British life is ... the Indian restaurant. No town is complete without one! In Rusholme, a small area in Manchester, there are over 80 Indian restaurants – lots of streets full of restaurants selling their hot, spicy foods. The whole area smells wonderful. Curry (a mixture of different spices) with rice or Indian bread is the main dish and lassi, a milky drink, is often served with the meal to cool your mouth!

4 What a mix-up!

Fill in the question words.

As we know, speaking English is not always without problems! Years ago, when the ex-German President, Heinrich Lübke, welcomed the Indian leader to Germany, he planned to greet him with the words "................ are you?" In fact, he said, "................ are you?" Nehru replied coldly, "Sir, I am the Prime Minister of India!"

Which two words did Lübke mix up?
Are there any English words which *you* mix up? Which are they?

Here are some 'problem words' which you've already seen in this book:
mustn't / needn't; lend / borrow; make / do.
Write a sentence with each of these words and then compare them with a partner.

6 Foreign influences on language

Indian languages have influenced the English language. *Bungalow, pyjamas, jungle, curry, mango, shampoo, punch, dungarees, polo* and *catamaran* are all Indian words which we use in English. English has 'borrowed' words from many languages. We use the Portuguese words *marmalade* and *veranda*, the word *ketchup* is from Malaya and from German we have taken the words *kindergarten* and *rucksack*. Every language adopts foreign words. Think about German ... .
In small groups, you have got two minutes to make a list of any English words you can think of which are used in German, like *manager, pullover* or *cornflakes*. One student should read the list to the class. Read out any other words which are on your list.

7 False facts

Now you have read and heard a lot of information about India, try to corrrect these 'false facts'.

1 The Ganges is a mountain.
2 India became independent in 1945.
3 Hindi is a religion.
4 Bombay is the capital of India.
5 English is the official language of India.
6 *Veranda* is an Indian word.
7 Curry is grown in India.
8 Lassi is a kind of tea.

8 Talking points

- Have you ever been to India or any other country outside Europe? If so, tell the class what you thought was the most positive and the most negative thing about your journey.
- Which country would you like to go to? Why?
- Are there any Indian restaurants in your area? What other kinds of restaurants are there?

Test yourself

1 Questions and negatives

Make questions and negative sentences, like this:

+ They live in New York.
? Do they live in New York?
- They don't live in New York.

+ She's going to write the report tomorrow.

1 ? ....?

2 - ....

+ It'll be warmer tomorrow.

3 ? ....?

4 - ....

+ They're flying to London on Tuesday.

5 ? ....?

6 - ....

+ Their plane leaves at 9:35.

7 ? ....?

8 - ....

2 Test your spelling

Listen to the text and write in the missing words. Can you spell them correctly?

Three years ago Jeff was very dissatisfied with himself. He was (9) .... heavy and felt unfit. So he went to a doctor who (10) .... to his problems and then gave him some good (11) .... Now he gets plenty of (12) .... and he eats a lot more (13) .... and vegetables. He has lost some (14) .... and he is much healthier than he used to be.

3 Time clauses

Make one sentence out of two.

15 Jeff will get home. Then he'll make some tea.

When ....

....

16 He'll watch TV. First he'l go for a walk.

Before he ....

....

4 What's the right word?

After each number, cross out the word or expression that is wrong.

Gunter is a man in our intensive English class. He (17) *comes / is coming* from Salzburg, so I (18) *mean / think* he must be (19) *Australian / Austrian.* He (20) *wants to / will* improve his English so he can (21) *become / get* a better job. He (22) *is reading / reads* a (23) *daily / diary* newspaper in English every morning, and he always (24) *does / makes* his (25) *homework / homeworks.* He is going to (26) *make / take* an exam in England next summer. He is the (27) *only / single* one in our class who (28) *carries / wears* a suit and tie every day. His (29) *meaning / opinion* is that the rest of us should study more (30) *serious / seriously.*

5 Test your grammar

Choose the form that fits best in each sentence. For each sentence, mark your answer like this: **a**

31 You remember Anna, ...
a aren't you? **b** doesn't she? **c** don't you?

32 She is a Brazilian ... in England this year.
a which is living **b** who is living **c** who lives

33 She ... back to Brazil next month, but she hasn't bought her ticket yet.
a flies **b** is flying **c** is going to fly

34 She'll buy her ticket as soon as she ... the money from her job at the hotel.
a gets **b** is getting **c** will get

35 She'll say goodbye to all her friends before she ... England.
a leaves **b** is leaving **c** will leave

36 She wants to work in Brazil next year, ...
a doesn't she? **b** isn't she? **c** won't she?

37 If she ... a good job, she'll study for another year.
a doesn't get **b** isn't get **c** won't get

38 She'll be glad to see her parents, ...
a doesn't she? **b** will she? **c** won't she?

MY SCORE OUT OF 38: ....

CHECKPOINT 17

What you learn

Diese Unit hat die Jugend von heute und ihre Probleme zum Thema. Sie wiederholen hier u.a.:

- Bedingungssätze (*if-sentences: Conditional 2*)
- das Gerundium (*the gerund: verb + ing*)
- das Gerundium und Infinitivkonstruktionen (*gerunds and infinitives*)
- Ratschläge geben (*giving advice*)

Grammar 1: *If*-sentences (type 2)

1 What does it mean?

Are the statements about the sentence true (T) or false (F)?

Tim is intelligent but lazy. If he worked harder, he'd pass the exam.

1 ☐ he'd = he would
2 ☐ he'd = he had
3 ☐ The exams are sometime in the future.
4 ☐ The exams were sometime in the past.

2 If …

Put the verbs into the correct tense.

A woman was tired of hearing her neighbour's son complaining about his school.

3 Translation

1 Wenn ich Sie wäre, würde ich ihn einladen.

....

2 Würdest du zu der Party gehen, wenn er dich einladen würde?

....

....

3 Ich wäre nicht hier, wenn mein Englisch perfekt wäre.

....

....

Grammar 2: The gerund

1 Infinitive (*to do*) or gerund (*doing*)?

Complete these sentences with *going* or *to go*.

1 Is she allowed .... there?

2 I don't mind .... there.

3 She's not afraid of .... there.

4 He's never enjoyed .... there.

5 Would you like .... there?

6 We decided not .... there.

7 They're worried about .... there.

8 Are you interested in .... there?

9 He asked me .... there.

2 What is correct?

Cross out the wrong word.

After prepositions (*of, in, about*) we use the *gerund / infinitive*.

3 Be careful!

Here are some phrases which you often hear. Cross out the incorrect verb form.

1 I'm looking forward to *hear / hearing* from you.
2 He suggested to *tell / telling* her.
3 When we were children we used to *play / playing* there.

How to say it: Giving advice

Match the two halves of these sentences.

1 If I were you,	☐ a) going there?
2 What about	☐ b) I'd go there.
3 I don't think you	☐ c) go there?
4 Why don't you	☐ d) should go there.

page 117

Language & Culture: page 111
If you have any problems with these exercises, ask your teacher in the next lesson.

The early years

Unit 17

1 Starter: Daydreams

Are you a hundred per cent happy with yourself and your lifestyle? Most of us would like some things in our lives to be different in some way. Tell the class about your daydreams. Do it like this: *If I had more free time, I'd travel more.* Begin your sentence with *If I could / had / were …*

Crisis Line

Problems at school or at home?
Phone the Crisis Line for help.

- **You can phone us day or night.**
- **You don't have to give your name.**
- **The calls are free.**

Phone: 0800 3694

2 The happiest days of their lives?

- Look at the Crisis Line poster. What service does the Crisis Line offer?
- Why do you think some children might not want to give their names?
- What kind of problems do you think children and teenagers phone the Crisis Line about?

Now read what Susan Beveridge, who works for 'Pre-teens' magazine, says about how the magazine tries to help young people.

Why does Susan think that it's necessary for 'Pre-Teens' magazine to provide a Problem Page and a Crisis Line?

Adults like to think that children's lives are perfectly happy and carefree but kids have their problems too – and we adults don't always have the time to listen and we don't take their problems seriously enough either. Nowadays a lot of children just don't have anyone to talk to – parents are usually at work, grandmothers and aunts often live miles away and there aren't always brothers and sisters they can share their problems with. 'Pre-Teens' magazine has got a Problem Page that young people can write to and ask for help – and we've also started the Crisis Line phone service. Young people can phone up and talk about what's worrying them and we try to give them advice. They phone about all kinds of things – school problems, how long they should be allowed to stay out at night, fashions, problems between members of the family, smoking, boyfriend problems, pocket money – all kinds of things. We get about a dozen calls a day – even more at the weekend and during school holidays. Do you know, when pop-groups split up, we get hundreds of calls from kids who have no-one who understands what a tragedy this is for them! If only teachers and parents had a bit more time and showed a bit more understanding …

3 A call for help 2

Twelve-year-old Tim and his family have just moved from Birmingham to the south of England. Listen to Tim talking to Susan on the Crisis Line. What do you learn about Tim? Complete the sentences.

1 Tim doesn't want ....

2 He doesn't like ....

3 Tim used ....

4 Tim doesn't mind ....

5 He doesn't enjoy ....

6 Tim is good at ....

4 If ... 1

Tim would be happier if things were different. In small groups, write down a sentence about each of the following situations in Tim's life and then compare them with another group. Begin your sentences with *If ...* .
Do it like this: Tim is at a new school now.
If he were at his old school, he would still have his old friends.

1 Both his parents work full-time.
2 Tim hasn't got any friends.
3 Tim spends his weekends in his room.
4 There isn't a youth club in the area.
5 Tim isn't sporty.

5 Giving advice

Now listen to Tim and Susan again. Susan gives him some advice. Read the phrases below and tick (✔) the four phrases which she uses.

☐ Why don't you ...? If ...
☐ I suggest ...
☐ I really don't think you should ...
☐ You could ...
☐ I think you should ...
☐ What about ...?
☐ I were you, I'd ...

6 Problem page

There are Problem Pages not only in teenagers' magazines but also in magazines for adults. Many of the adults' letters are about their children. Talk about the kinds of difficulties which parents may have with teenage children. Then, with a partner, write a letter to a Problem Page (3 or 4 sentences) about one of these problems – from the parent's *or* the teenager's point of view. Give your letter to another pair of students and they will give you some advice using some of the phrases from the exercise above.

7 Vocabulary

➤ Things to read

Many young people read magazines like 'Pre-Teens'. In small groups, look at this puzzle and put a circle round all the names you can find of things to read. One has been done for you. When you have found ten things, try and add three more. Read your three words to the class and add any new ones which you hear to your list.

M	A	G	A	Z	I	N	E
E	H	A	R	A	S	E	P
S	E	D	T	X	T	W	O
S	A	V	I	Y	O	S	S
A	D	E	C	T	R	P	T
G	L	R	L	E	Y	A	C
E	I	T	E	X	W	P	A
Z	N	L	E	T	T	E	R
P	E	B	O	O	K	R	D

Now choose one of the words from the puzzle or from your list and define it, like this: *When you go on holiday, you can send one of these to a friend.* The other students will try to guess which word you have defined.

8 Talking points

- What problems do you think young people have today which their parents didn't have?
- What advantages do young people have which their parents didn't have?
- How do *you* feel about teenagers with nose-rings, tattoos or green hair?

Today's grammar

1 *If*-sentences (type 2) → *p. 126*

- are used when we imagine a situation which is not real: ***If** I **were** a child again, I**'d work** harder at school.*
  Remember! *If I **were** ...* is more formal English. In spoken English you often hear *If I **was** ...* .
- are used when we imagine a situation which is possible but not probable: ***If** I **won** £1,000,000 on the lottery, I **would stop** work.*
- are used to give advice: ***If** I **were** you, I**'d speak** to the teacher about it.*
  Remember! We don't usually put *would* in the *if* part of the sentence.

2 Gerunds → *p. 126*

- are used after prepositions: *He isn't interested **in** taking exams.*
- are used after certain verbs: *I **suggested** doing more homework.*
- are used after certain phrases: *He doesn't **mind** doing homework.*

The early years

Homestudy

1 Listening

A few months later Tim rang up the Crisis Line again. Listen and decide if each sentence is true (T) or false (F). Circle T or F.

1 Tim spoke to the same woman again. T / F
2 He said she'd given him some good advice. T / F
3 Tim's music teacher comes from London. T / F
4 There was already a music club at school. T / F
5 Tim isn't allowed to play music any more. T / F
6 School used to be harder in Birmingham. T / F
7 The music teacher speaks like Tim's dad. T / F

Now listen again. What did Susan say when she gave Tim advice? Match the beginning and end of each sentence, and write the right letter in the box.

8 I think you should	☐	a) asking your music teacher to talk to your dad?
9 If I were you I'd	☐	b) ask some of your new friends to help you?
10 Why don't you	☐	c) do your homework together sometimes.
11 Maybe you could	☐	d) talk to your dad about it again.
12 What about	☐	e) try to find some ways to get better marks in school.

2 Pronunciation

You heard these words in Unit 17. In each group of three there is one word in which the underlined letter(s) make a different sound. Which word is the different one?

1 boys	sports	weeks
2 club	lunchtime	music
3 factory	father	happy
4 football	good	school
5 got	job	work
6 great	speak	teacher
7 month	that	youth
8 swimming	Tim	time

Now listen to the words.

3 Conditional sentences

You are sure the people will not do these things. Use if-sentences (type 2) to answer the questions.

1 Do you think she'll go to London? (spend too much money) No, of course not.

If she *went to London she'd spend too much money.*

2 Do you think he'll take the bus? (be late for the meeting) No, of course not.

If ....

....

3 Do you think they'll drive all night? (be terribly tired tomorrow) No, of course not.

....

....

4 Do you think she'll buy a new car? (not have enough money for her holiday) No, of course not.

....

....

4 What does it mean?

What does the if-clause tell us? Write a sentence with *don't*, *isn't* or *might*.

1 If it rains, I'll take a taxi.

It might rain.

2 If John was here, I'd ask him.

....

3 If they lived nearby, we'd visit them.

....

4 If Mary calls, I'll ring her back tonight.

....

5 If I knew his address, I'd write him a letter.

....

6 If I see him tonight, I'll tell him.

....

7 If he was rich, she'd probably marry him.

....

5 Gerunds

Complete the second sentence so that it means the same as the first one.

1 She writes books and articles very well.

She's very good ....

2 Could you turn the TV down a bit, please?

Would you mind ....

3 I'm happy that I'm going to see you next week.

I'm looking ....

4 He thinks it's too dangerous to go out at night.

He's afraid of ....

5 I always have a good time when I travel by train.

I always enjoy ....

CHECKPOINT 18

What you learn
Diese Unit beschäftigt sich mit Festen und Geschenken zu einem besonderen Anlaß: der Volljährigkeit. Sie wiederholen hier u.a.:
- die Zukunft – ein Überblick (*the future – an overview*)
- den Genitiv (*genitive + possessive*)
- Einladungen aussprechen (*making, accepting and refusing invitations*)

Grammar 1: The future – an overview
In this unit you're going to look again at ways of talking about the future.

1 A party

1 What a good idea! I think I *'m going to have / 'll have* a fancy-dress party on my birthday, too.

2 I*'m going to have / 'll have* a party so I must write a shopping list.

3 Hi, Peter, I *'m having / 'll have* a fancy-dress party on Saturday and I'd like to invite you.

Write the number of the sentence which tells you about:
- ☐ a spontaneous idea (something she has just decided to do).
- ☐ a definite arrangement (something she has organised).
- ☐ a plan (something she hopes to do).

2 Present tenses to talk about the future
The present simple (*does*) and the present progressive (*is doing*) are sometimes used to talk about the future: *The film* ***starts*** *at 8.15 so we****'re meeting*** *outside the cinema at 8 o'clock but if you* ***come*** *late, we****'ll go*** *in without you!*
Use the same tenses to translate this sentence:
Am Dienstag fliegt sie um 9 Uhr nach Paris. Der Flughafenbus fährt um 7.15 Uhr ab. Wenn sie ihn verpasst, wird sie ein Taxi nehmen.

....

....

....

....

Grammar 2: The genitive

1 Whose are they?
Which sentence, 1 or 2, tells you that the tickets belong to one girl ☐ or to more than one girl ☐ ?
1 They're the girls' tickets. 2 They're the girl's tickets.

2 Which word?
Cross out one word in these sentences so that the meaning stays the same.
1 He is going to the baker's shop to buy cakes.
2 We're staying at my sister's house at Easter.

Now cross out the incorrect word in these sentences.
3 She's one of our friends. = He's a friend of *us / ours*.
4 He's one of Mary and Peter's colleagues. = She's a colleague of *them / theirs*.
5 He's one of my cousins = He's a cousin of *me / mine*.

How to say it: Invitations
Put in the correct verb form: *have / to have / having*.

1 Would you like .... dinner with me?

2 How about .... dinner together?

3 Shall we .... dinner together work?

Put in the correct word: *afraid / kind / love*.

4 Great, I'd .... to.

5 I'm .... I can't.

6 That's very .... of you.

To refuse an invitation, you can use sentence ....

To accept an invitation, you can use sentence ....

To thank someone for the invitation, use sentence ...., then you can go on to accept or refuse.

page 117

Language & Culture: page 111
If you have any problems with these exercises, ask your teacher in the next lesson.

An adult at last

Unit 18

1 Starter: A party 1

Your class decides to have a party. Everybody must decide quickly what to bring to the party and tell their partner, like this: *"I'll bring some cassettes."* When you've done that, tell the class what your partner is planning to bring, like this: *Doris is going to bring a cake.*

2 At last!!!

1 What do you think Paul is celebrating on July 23rd?
2 When does the party start ?
3 What will Paul be able to do after July 23rd?
4 How do you know that Paul wants you to reply to the invitation?
5 What present would *you* take to
… Paul's party?
… a colleague's housewarming party?
… your friend's Christmas party?
… your sister's dinner-party?
… your boss's leaving party?

3 Invitations

Invite your partner to a party next week. Give details about what kind of party it is, and say when and where it is. Your partner should accept the invitation – or refuse and give a reason.

4 A friend of mine 2

These two sentences express the same idea: *At the party I introduced him to* ***a friend of mine****. At the party I introduced him to* ***one of my friends****.*
Change these sentences in the same way. At the party …
1 I danced with a colleague of hers.
2 I spoke to one of their neighbours.
3 I met one of your cousins.
4 I saw an old teacher of his.
5 I talked to a good friend of ours.
6 I had a drink with a student of theirs.

5 A birthday present

Listen to Paul telling his sister Diane about the birthday present from his parents. Tick (✔) the four things he talks about. Then check your answers with a partner.

☐ 1 the ferry	☐ 4 meeting a friend
☐ 2 a hotel	☐ 5 tourist attractions
☐ 3 French food	☐ 6 Belgian drivers

Now listen again to what he says about the things which you ticked and complete these sentences.

1 .... at 9 o' clock.

2 If I can't ....

3 .... at his flat in Paris next Friday.

4 We .... visit all ....
....

Now compare your answers with the rest of the class and decide why the particular tense was used in each sentence.

6 Over to you

In small groups, talk about the next exciting thing which is going to happen in your life … in your job, in your home or family, something you're going to buy, a holiday, a celebration or something you're going to do in your leisure time. Do it like this: *My brother is getting married next month and our cousins are probably going to fly over from Australia so I'll meet members of the family that I've never seen before.*

7 Vocabulary

➤ The family

Diane and Paul are *brother* and *sister*. Here's a list of some male members of the family: *brother-in-law, son, husband, father, uncle, cousin, grandfather, nephew*. Write down the female members of the family, like this: *brother – sister.*
Now find out who has got the most brothers, sisters, sons, daughters, nephews and nieces in your class.

8 Who is it?

Write down the names of two members of your family and show them to a partner. Your partner will ask you how they are related to each other. Use ***'s*** in your answer, like this:
A: *How is Diane related to Paul?*
B: *Paul is Diane**'s** brother. / Diane is Paul**'s** sister.*
Remember: Not: He's the ~~X~~ brother of Diane.
But: He's Diane's brother.

Now make similar sentences about any famous people you know, like this: *Yoko Ono was John Lennon's wife. / William and Harry are Prince Charles's sons.*

See if you can find the answer to this puzzle.
A young man had a car accident and was taken to the doctor's. The doctor said, "That's my son!" But the young man's father had died years before. Can you explain why the doctor said that?

The doctor was the young man's mother.

9 Talking points

- Have you ever given money as a present? If so, who did you give it to and why?
- What age do you have to be in your country to: vote, get married, have a full-time job, buy alcohol, drive a car? Do you think these are the ideal ages to do these things? If not, what would you change?
- After finishing full-time education, what kind of things may happen in the next phase of life? Think about things like: family, jobs, finance, homes.

Today's grammar

1 The future – an overview

The simple future → p. 133

- can be used for future facts: *Paul **will be** 18 on the 23rd.*
- can be used for predictions: *I'm sure **we'll have** lots of fun.*
- can be used for spontaneous decisions: *"I**'ll bring** some cassettes."*

The *going to* future → p. 133

- can be used for personal plans: *She**'s going to have** a party next week.*

The present progressive + a future time → p. 133

- can be used for future arrangements: *She**'s taking** her driving test on Thursday.*

The present simple → p. 133

- can be used for timetables and schedules: *The party **starts** at 8 o'clock.*

The simple future + present simple → p. 134

- can be used in sentences with *if, when, before*: *She**'ll be** happy **if** you **phone**.*

2 Genitive and possessive → p. 134

Apostrophe + s

- can be used to talk about a person's home or place of work: *He went to the baker**'s** (shop).*
- **'s / s'** is normally used for people, animals and time expressions and **of** is normally used for things: *Diane**'s** cousin / the dog**'s** owner (one dog) / the dog**s'** owner (more than one dog) / the children**'s** books / yesterday**'s** newspaper / the roof **of** the house.*
- **Remember:** When we speak about one of a group, we can say: *It's **one of her cousins** or It's **a cousin of hers**.*

An adult at last

Homestudy

1 Diane's family tree

At Paul's birthday party, Diane is telling somebody about her family. Listen and write the people's first names in the boxes.

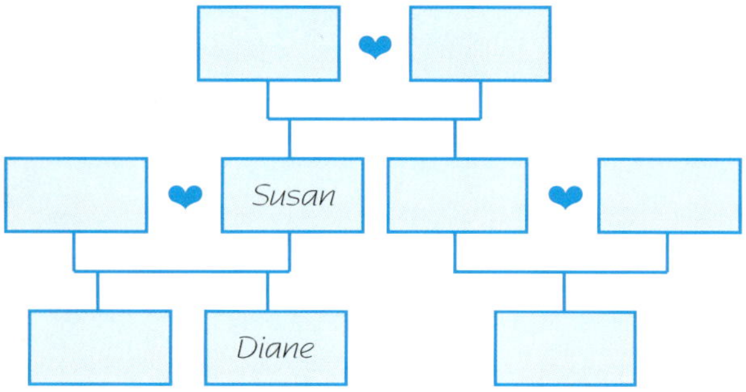

Check your answers before going on to exercise 2.

2 Remember the words

Look at Diane's family tree and write in the missing words. Can you spell them correctly?

Monica is Diane's (1) ...., and so Diane is Monica's (2) .... Paul is Monica's (3) .... Paul and Diane have got a (4) .... named David. Paul and David are Mary's (5) ...., and Diane is her (6) .... Jim is Susan's (7) ....

3 Pronunciation

Practice saying these genitives: 1 Chris's car, 2 his parents' house, 3 Mrs Monk's family, 4 Pop's dog, 5 Susan's bicycle, 6 Susan Beveridge's computer, 7 the baker's wife, 8 the boss's telephone, 9 the children's grandmother, 10 the dentist's holiday, 11 the waitress's uniform, 12 yesterday's newspaper. How should you pronounce the 's or s' ending? Write each number in the correct box.

[z] as in *begins*	[s] as in *helps*	[z] as in *changes*
5, ...	....	....

Now listen to the words.

4 Genitives

Make one sentence out of two, using a genitive.

1 The hotel has got a manager. He is angry.

The manager of the hotel is angry. ....

2 My grandfather has got a house. It is beautiful.

....

3 The boys have got a car. It isn't very clean.

....

4 Jim has got some colleagues. Tom is one of them.

....

5 The future

After each number, decide which of the two forms is better. Cross out the other one.

Diane has just decided what to do this summer: she (1) *is going to visit / will visit* some friends of hers in Germany. If she (2) *has / will have* enough time, she (3) *is travelling / will travel* by train. The timetable says that a Eurostar train (4) *is leaving / leaves* on Monday at 7.52 a.m. If she (5) *goes / will go* to a party the night before she (6) *is / will be* very tired. Maybe she (7) *is sleeping / will be able to sleep* on the train.

Now write down what Diane says:

8 Diane is predicting rain for this afternoon.

She says: "I think *it'll rain this afternoon.* ...."

9 She has arranged to drive into town with Paul.

She says: "..."

10 She intends to buy her ticket today.

She says: "I ...."

11 She suddenly realizes that she has forgotten to buy a map of Germany. She says to herself:

"I ....this afternoon."

6 Invitations

What could you say to invite somebody to a party? Use each of these words once: *about, come, coming, invite, like, like, my, my, my, party, party, party, to, to, to, to, to, you, you.*

1 Would ....

2 I'd ....

3 How ....

CHECKPOINT 19

What you learn
Diese Unit zeigt Personen, die in ihrer Lebensmitte ihren Lebenstil geändert haben. Sie wiederholen hier u.a.:
- die Gegenwart – ein Überblick (*the present – an overview*)
- die Satzstellung (*word order of time expressions*)
- Komplimente machen and darauf reagieren (*complimenting*)

Grammar 1: The present – an overview
In this unit you're going to look again at ways of talking about the present.

Making a change
Put the verbs into the correct tense: the present perfect (*has done*), the present progressive (*is doing*) or the present simple (*do*).

Ralph Young is a doctor who normally (1 *work*)

.... at a medical institute

in Sussex. He (2 *be*) .... now in his fifties but he (3 *only be*)

.... a doctor since 1989.

At the moment he (4 *not work*) .... in Sussex, but in a hospital for the poor in Ghana.

Dr Young (5 *feel*) .... that the people in Ghana really (6 *need*)

.... his help and so he

(7 *not mind*) .... giving up his holiday time to do this. He (8 *have*)

.... a very interesting life so

far. He (9 *work*) .... in a number of African countries and he (10 *already learn*)

.... a few of the local languages.

And now translate this information about Dr. Young.
Dr. Young ist seit ungefähr zehn Jahren Arzt. Er mag seine Arbeit und er arbeitet immer während seines Urlaubs. Er ist gerade nach Ghana geflogen und arbeitet zur Zeit in einem Krankenhaus dort.

....

....

....

....

....

Grammar 2: Word order

When?* and *How often?
Look at the position of the underlined words in the sentences below.
1 He often works hard.
2 He is often busy.
3 She has often worked overtime.
4 He will do it this year.
5 At this time tomorrow he'll be in London.

Now read the words and phrases below. Decide which of the underlined words they could replace in the above sentences. Put a ring round the number(s). The first one has been done for you.

a) seldom	(1)	(2)	(3)	4	5
b) in a week's time	1	2	3	4	5
c) always	1	2	3	4	5
d) at 9 o'clock	1	2	3	4	5
e) twice a year	1	2	3	4	5

How to say it: Making compliments
Here are some compliments and reactions. Put the words in the right order. In each sentence there is one word which is not necessary – cross this word out.

1 a / dress / How / pretty / What.

....

became / got / I / it / Thank / yesterday / you.

....

2 a / did / good / job / very / work / You.

....

It's / nice / of / say / so / tell / to / you.

....

page 117

Language & Culture: page 111
If you have any problems with these exercises, ask your teacher in the next lesson.

Changing lifestyles

Unit 19

1 Starter: Thanks for the compliment

Compliment someone in the class on how they look, on something which you know they can do well or on something which they have got with them. When someone compliments you, give a suitable answer. Do it like this:

A: *That's a lovely pen – is it new?*

B: *Yes, it is. It was a birthday present from my husband.*

2 A new start

The painting below is by one of Britain's most popular modern artists. If you saw this painting on a friend's wall, what would you say about it?

Now read about the artist, Beryl Cook, and then say what you think is unusual about Beryl.

Beryl Cook is a shy, mature woman who, although she hates publicity, has become one of the most popular and talked-about artists in Britain today.

Beryl's career started quite late in life. Years ago, she was showing her little son how to use paints and a paintbrush when she discovered her own love of painting – and a new hobby for herself! When she was in her late forties, some friends suggested showing her paintings at a local exhibition. She wasn't very happy about the idea but she agreed. That week her paintings appeared in The Sunday Times Magazine and she soon became famous!

Beryl usually gets her ideas from everyday situations and you can sometimes see her sketching people in the local pub. Nowadays Beryl is a successful artist and she and her husband can afford to have holidays all over the world and so her paintings have become more exotic – one shows tango-dancers in Buenos Aires and another shows sunbathers in a New York park. At the moment she's working on a painting of prostitutes in Barcelona!

Beryl's paintings are seldom serious – they simply show people who are having FUN! Because of this, and her primitive style of art, some critics say she isn't a 'real' artist at all – but she has brought art to people who have never before shown any interest in paintings. Up to now she has sold lots of paintings and you can see her work everywhere in Britain – on birthday cards, postcards, in art galleries – and even on postage stamps.

3 Beryl Cook ▶2

Here are three more sentences about Beryl. With a partner, put the words into the correct order.

1 always / are / Beryl's / exhibitions / very popular.

....

....

2 Beryl and her husband / in London / last year / to a club / went .

....

....

3 a neighbour / of theirs / a stripper in the show / saw / They / was / who !

....

....

4 for paintings / from / gets / like this / often / original ideas / She / situations.

....

....

4 Time expressions ▶1 + ▶2

Find the shaded word or phrase in the text which has a similar meaning to these words: *from time to time / normally / not often / now / so far / these days.*
Re-write the sentences in the text using the above words. Make any changes which are necessary.

Now make sentences about yourself with some of the shaded words and tell them to a partner. Do it like this: *I **sometimes** have to speak English on the telephone. **At the moment** I'm reading a book about travelling in Europe. I've done three English courses **up to now**.*

5 Making a change

You are going to hear how three middle-aged people, – Heather Clark, Steve Lord and Mrs Howell – have changed their lifestyles. Listen and then say *how* each of these people have changed their lifestyle.

Think of two things which Heather, Steve and Mr & Mrs Howell do every day in their new lives. What do you imagine they are probably doing at this moment in their new occupations?

Now listen to the three people again and say what you can remember about the family situations of each of them. (*Are they married? Have they got close family?*) How do you think their present family situations makes it possible to lead their new lives?

6 Over to you ▶1

In small groups, talk about any changes which you have made recently to improve your lifestyle. Think about skills you've learnt, habits you've changed, things you've bought, changes in your job or groups you've joined. Do it like this: *I've joined an aerobics class. I go there twice a week and I feel much fitter than I did before.*

7 Vocabulary

➤ Prefixes

Steve says that the local people are very kind. The opposite of *kind* is ***un**kind*. With a partner, make the opposites of the following words by putting ***un-***, ***im-***, ***dis-***, or ***in-*** before them:

advantage	*correct*	*employed*	*lucky*	*practical*
agree	*countable*	*formal*	*popular*	*probable*
appear	*definite*	*happy*	*possible*	*successful*

Add any others which you know and then check your answers with the rest of the class.

8 Talking points

- If *you* could make some changes in your life, what would you do? Think about things like: travel, sports, career, education, family situation.
- What kind of things could happen to make someone change his / her lifestyle?
- Many employers are not happy to give a job to someone over forty. Why is this? Do you agree with them? Why? / Why not?

Today's grammar

▶1 The present – an overview

The present simple → p. 128

- is used for habits and routines: *She **goes** on holiday every year.*

The present progressive → p. 132

- is used for activities which are happening now: *She'**s painting** at the moment.*

The present perfect → p. 129

- is used for things which have happened up to now: *She **has had** several exhibitions so far.*

▶2 Word order: Time expressions → p. 124

- Time expressions (*when? / how often? / how long?*) normally go after the *place* at the end of a sentence: *Beryl has lived in Plymouth **for years**.*

Remember: *Time (when?)* can also go at the beginning of a sentence to stress the time: ***At the moment** Beryl is in Barcelona.*

- Some time words (*always, often, sometimes, never, still, just, already*) usually go before the main verb: *Beryl **seldom** gives interviews and she doesn't **often** appear on TV.*

Remember: These time words usually go after the verb *to be*: *She's **never** late.*

Changing lifestyles

Homestudy

1 Pronunciation

Read the following text and decide how to pronounce the definite article the each time it appears. Is it the 'weak' pronunciation /ðə/, as in *the book*, or is it the 'strong' pronunciation /ði:/, as in *the apple*? Write each number in the correct box.

Dr Ralph Young is on holiday from (1) the institute where he usually works. Yesterday he gave a talk at (2) the university about (3) the important work that he does at (4) the hospital in Ghana. At (5) the moment he is at (6) the airport, getting ready to fly to Africa. (7) The hours on (8) the plane won't be boring, because he's going to use (9) the time to study one of (10) the African languages that he is learning.

/ðə/, as in "*the book*" /ði:/, as in "*the apple*"

Now listen to the text.

2 Word order

After each sentence there is a time expression in brackets. Tick (✓) one, two or three of the boxes to show where this time expression usually comes.

1 ☐ Ralph ☐ Young ☐ is ☐ in ☐ Ghana ☐. (*this month*)

2 ☐ He ☐ is ☐ going ☐ to ☐ stay ☐ here ☐. (*for three more weeks*)

3 ☐ He ☐ spends ☐ his ☐ holidays ☐ working ☐ in ☐ Africa ☐. (*always*)

4 ☐ He ☐ is ☐ ready ☐ to ☐ help. (*always*)

5 ☐ He ☐ treats* ☐ people ☐ who ☐ are ☐ terribly ☐ ill ☐. (*often*)

6 ☐ He ☐ has ☐ written ☐ a ☐ report ☐ about ☐ his ☐ work ☐. (*just*)

7 ☐ He'll ☐ be ☐ in ☐ Chicago ☐ for ☐ a ☐ convention* ☐. (*next month*)

*treat = (hier) behandeln; convention = Kongress

3 Prefixes

Make the opposite of each of these words by putting *dis-*, *im-*, *in-*, *ir-* or *un-* before it.

_____dependent	_____polite
_____expensive	_____regular
_____friendly	_____satisfied
_____healthy	_____usual

4 Questions about the present

Write questions about Ralph Young. Use the present simple (four times), the present progressive (once) and the present perfect (twice).

1 (live / in Sussex?) *Does he live in Sussex?*

2 (*how long / doctor?*) ....

....

3 (*now / in his fifties?*) ....

....

4 (*usually / work in Sussex?*) ....

....

5 (*now / work in Ghana?*) ....

....

6 (*speak / the local language?*) ....

....

7 (*How many / languages / learn / already?*) ....

....

5 Listening

Which means of transport has Ralph Young used lately? Listen to part of a radio interview and tick (✓) the right pictures.

a

b

c

d

e

f

g

h

What you learn
Diese Unit betrachtet die ältere Generation. Sie wiederholen hier u.a.:
- die Vergangenheit – ein Überblick (*the past – an overview*)
- etwas machen lassen (*to have something done*)
- soziale Konventionen (*social responses*)

CHECKPOINT 20

Grammar 1: The past – an overview
In this unit you're going to look again at ways of talking about the past.

1 85 mph at 86 years old!
Put the verbs in the text below into the correct past tense: the past simple (*did*), the past perfect (*had done*) or the past progressive (*was doing*).

Arthur Wellsted, 86, of Nottingham (1 *ride*) .... his motorbike in Devon yesterday when a police car (2 *stop*) .... him. The policeman (3 *say*) .... to Arthur, "Do you know that you (4 *ride*) .... at 85 mph* when I (5 *see*) .... you?" Arthur (6 *be*) .... proud that he (7 *reach*) .... such a high speed although he (8 *not realise*) .... it at the time! Then he (9 *start*) .... talking to the policeman and he (10 *tell*) .... him about his hobbies – which include bungee-jumping and hot-air ballooning! The policeman (11 *not arrest*) .... Arthur and he said later, "I (12 *have*) .... a motorbike myself when I (13 *be*) .... younger. It (14 *be*) .... a pleasure to meet such an active and interesting old gentleman."

**mph = miles per hour*

One of the above verbs can be replaced by *used to* + a verb. Write this sentence, using *used to*:

....

....

2 When exactly?
Match the two halves of these sentences.

1 He was making tea when his sister came
2 Years ago, he used to make tea when she came
3 He made tea when his sister came
4 He had made tea when his sister came

☐ a) because she said that she was thirsty.
☐ b) and it was on the table when she arrived.
☐ c) but nowadays they always drink coffee.
☐ d) so he put the teapot down and opened the door.

Grammar 2: to have something done

1 Who does the job?
1 He has his motorbike repaired.
2 He has repaired his motorbike.

Sentence number ...... tells you that he has repaired his motorbike himself and sentence number ...... tells you that someone does this for him.

Match these German translations to the English sentences and write the number in the box.

☐ a) Er hat sein Motorrad repariert.
☐ b) Er läßt sein Motorrad reparieren.

Now put the words into the right order to make a sentence.
did / his bike / repaired / have / he / When?

....

How to say it: Social responses
Match the sentences to the situations.

1 A friend has lost a tennis match.	☐ a) Cheers!
2 You warn someone about danger.	☐ b) Bad luck.
3 You're having a drink with someone.	☐ c) Bye for now.
4 You're leaving a friend but are meeting him again later.	☐ d) Be careful.

page 118

Language & Culture: page 111
If you have any problems with these exercises, ask your teacher in the next lesson.

The Ugly Model Agency

Senior citizens

Unit 20

1 Starter: What do they look like?

These words are useful when you are talking about people and clothes: *colourful / expensive / fair / fat / late forties / long / mid-twenties / modern / slim / straight / tall / teenager*.
Put three of these words under the correct heading to describe someone's *hair – age – body – clothes*.

Which famous models do you know? What do you think a typical model looks like? How has this changed over the years?

2 The Ugly Model Agency

- Read the text about The Ugly Model Agency. What is so unusual about this agency?
- Write down any word in the text which you don't understand. Can someone in the class explain it to you (in English!)?
- Look at the first sentence again. There are a lot of adjectives which describe models. With a partner, find the opposites of these words in the first sentence: *dark, fat, old, pale, ugly, weak*. Which word has got two opposites?

In 1969 two photographers decided that they were tired of photographing the same slim, blond, beautiful, young women and handsome, strong, suntanned men, so they advertised in the *Evening Standard* newspaper for people with 'interesting' faces and they started a modelling agency with a difference – The Ugly Model Agency. There are now over 900 models who work for this very successful London agency and the models are not necessarily ugly but they have ... character – as you can see from the photographs. Some models are tiny and some are tall – including Chris Greener, the tallest man in the UK (2,30 m); there's a Prince Charles look-alike and a Michael Jackson look-alike; a bald, tattooed woman; sets of twins; Sumo wrestlers; pierced people – and their oldest model is 92 years old! Oldies are 'in' this year and the Ugly Agency has had lots of calls for elderly models. Levi jeans is running a very successful advertising campaign at the moment, using male and female models between the ages of 60 and 86, and the Versace fashion house, has an elegant woman in her eighties modelling this year's autumn collection.

3 Ethel – a model with a difference 1

You're going to hear an interview with the model Ethel Shepherd, in which she talks about her modelling career. Listen to Ethel and say if she could be one of the models in the picture? Why? / Why not?

Listen to the interview again and then answer these questions.

1 What was Ethel doing when she saw the advert?
2 What did Ethel do when she saw the advert?
3 What did Ethel use to do when she was a girl?
4 What had Ethel been for years before she became a model?

4 Interviews

Read the notes below which the interviewer made about Ethel. With a partner, write down the questions you think he asked her to get this information and add two more questions which you would like to ask her.

Born: Summerseat, 1922.
Left school at 14.
Previous jobs: factory worker (8 years), housewife.
Married Tom in 1944. 1 son, Harold, 1945.
Widowed: 1987.
Model: for 5 years.

5 Over to you 1

Interview a partner about the oldest member of his / her family – how old the person is, what the relationship is to him / her, what he / she looks like, details about the life history of that person.

6 To have something done 2

Ethel says she can now afford a cleaning woman to help her in the house once a week. Read this note which Ethel left for her cleaning woman last week.

Dear Mrs Chapman,
Please could you do the following jobs for me today:
Clean the bedroom windows and make the bed. Iron my blouses. Hoover the carpets and wash the kitchen floor. Wash the dishes, polish the silver teapot and prepare supper. Oh yes ... dust the bookshelves (they need it!). And could you cut the grass this afternoon, please? Many thanks.
I'm at Harold's for the day and will be back at six. Your lunch is in the fridge. Thanks again. See you next week.
Ethel Shepherd.

What jobs did Ethel have done while she was out? Make ten sentences.

What jobs do you sometimes have done for you? Think about things like beauty treatment, repairs or housework. Make sentences like this: *I occasionally have my hair done.*

7 What do you say?

What would you say in the following situations?

1 Someone apologises to you.
2 You arrive late for the lesson.
3 You want to attract the teacher's attention.
4 You didn't hear what your partner said.
5 A friend is taking an exam tomorrow.
6 Someone sneezes.
7 A friend has passed an exam.
8 Someone says, "Thank you very much."

8 Vocabulary

Idiom bank

Look at these sayings connected with age and explain what you think they mean.

- You are as old as you feel.
- You can't teach an old dog new tricks.
- It's as old as the hills.

Can you think of any sayings in German which are connected with age?

9 Talking points

- In the early 1900s, less than 1% of the world's population was over 65. By the year 2050, the percentage will be 20%. What will be different because of this?
- What, do you think, is the ideal age to retire? Why?
- What do *you* think is the recipe for a happy and healthy old-age?
- Why would / wouldn't you like to live to be a hundred?

Today's grammar

1 The past – an overview

The past simple → p. 130

- is used to talk about things which happened in the past in chronological order: *She **left** school and then she **got** a job in a factory.*

The past progressive → p. 132

- is used to describe an activity which was already in progress when something happened: *She **was reading** a magazine when she saw the advert.*

The past perfect → p. 131

- is used to talk about what had happened before a situation in the past: *She **had worked** in a factory for years before she married Tom.*

Used to do → p. 130

- is used to talk about past habits and states: *She **used to live** in Summerseat and she **used to be** a housewife.*

2 To have something done (causative have) → p. 128

- is used when someone does a job for you: *I didn't repair the car myself, I took it to the garage and **I had it repaired**.*

Remember: The word order is important: *to have + object + participle.*

Senior citizens

Homestudy

1 Questions about the past

Use these words to write questions about Ethel Shepherd, a model who is in her seventies. The first word of each question is missing.

1 a / factory / in / she / to / use / work

....

....? ☐

2 at / home / phone / rang / she / the / waiting / when

....

....? ☐ + ☐

3 a / become / daughter-in-law / encourage / her / her / model / to

....

....? ☐

4 a / about / advert / before / becoming / ever / model / she / saw / she / that / thought

....

....? ☐ + ☐

Which tenses have you used in these questions? Write one letter in each box above: a) the past simple, b) the past progressive, c) the past perfect, d) the past simple with use to.

2 Social responses

What would you say in these situations? Write one letter on each line.

1 "Ah-ah-ah-ah-choo!" "B _ _ _ _ _ _ _!"

2 (The doorbell rings.) "C _ _ _ _ _!"

3 "Bill, this is Linda."

"N _ _ _ _ _ _ _ _ _ _ _ _ _, Linda."

4 "Linda has just found a great new job."

"Oh, c _ _ _ _ _ _ _ _ _ _ _ _ _ _ _, Linda!"

3 Have something done

After each number, cross out the incorrect words.

Yesterday Ethel (1) *had the windows cleaned / had cleaned the windows*, because she didn't feel like cleaning them herself. But nobody had to iron her dresses for her, because she (2) *had ironed them / had them ironed* herself the day before. She doesn't like washing the kitchen floor, so she's going to (3) *have it washed / have washed it* tomorrow.

4 Describing people

You've offered to pick up three women at the airport. Their names are Cynthia, Molly and Silke, and they are all arriving on different planes. You don't know what they look like, but they have left descriptions of themselves on your answering machine. Listen and write the numbers and names below three of the pictures.

Now listen again and answer the questions by writing the person's number in the box.

Which of these women says that she …

… could be a pilot if she wanted to? ☐

… doesn't look a day over forty? ☐

… hopes the plane won't be full of schoolgirls? ☐

… hopes she won't get on your nerves too much? ☐

… is sure you'll recognise her? ☐

… looks like a woman in a song? ☐

… never wears more than one ring? ☐

5 Pronunciation

Fourteen of these twenty words have the sound /ʃ/ as in *show* in them. Underline the letter(s) that are pronounced /ʃ/.

attractions	information	school	shy
brush	invitation	share	situation
chair	patient	she	stress
enthusiastic	professional	shop	student
exhibitions	professor	should	sure

Six of these words do not have the sound /ʃ/. Write them here:

....

....

Now listen to the words.

Lerntipp

Liebe Englisch-Expertin,

durch den Kurs habe ich meine alten halbvergessenen Englischkenntnisse wiederaufgefrischt. Jetzt geht es mir darum, nicht gleich wieder aus der Übung zu kommen. Eigentlich wollte ich in einem englischsprachigen Land Urlaub machen, aber aus verschiedenen Gründen werde ich das in diesem Jahr nicht hinkriegen. Was kann ich hier zu Hause tun, um mein Englisch weiterhin zu üben?

Mit freundlichen Grüßen,
Arthur, Linz

Lieber Arthur,

auch zu Hause können Sie vieles tun, damit Sie Ihr Englisch nicht wieder vergessen.

Hören: Vielleicht haben Sie Satelliten- oder Kabelfernsehen; wenn ja, schauen Sie, was es an englischsprachigen Filmen und Sendungen gibt. Oder Sie können englischsprachige Filme auf Video ausleihen; suchen Sie zum Beispiel einen Film aus, den Sie schon auf Deutsch gesehen haben, und schauen Sie ihn noch einmal auf Englisch an. Auch Lieder bieten eine gute Möglichkeit, sich mit der englischen Sprache zu beschäftigen. Achten Sie beim CD-Kauf darauf, dass die Texte in gedruckter Form dabei sind.

Sprechen: In Ihrem Englischkurs, der gerade zu Ende geht, gibt es vielleicht Leute, mit denen Sie sich gerne treffen würden. Setzen Sie sich regelmäßig zusammen und reden Sie eine halbe Stunde Englisch miteinander. Oder schauen Sie, ob es in Ihrer Nähe einen englischen Gesprächszirkel oder einen englischen Stammtisch gibt.

Lesen: Fangen Sie an, regelmäßig englische Bücher zu lesen, nicht unbedingt die allerdicksten und schwierigsten, sondern z.B. Lektüren, die auf Ihre Lernstufe abgestimmt sind, etwa aus den Reihen Longman Structural Readers oder Longman Classics. Außerdem können Sie in den Ferien ein Übungsheft durcharbeiten, z.B. English Network 3 Break.

Schreiben: Führen Sie in den Ferien ein Tagebuch auf Englisch. Sie brauchen nicht viel zu schreiben, aber regelmäßig.

Schließlich können Sie sich überlegen, ob Sie nicht nächstes Jahr wieder an einem Englischkurs teilnehmen möchten, am besten an einem Kurs mittleren Niveaus mit einem Lehrwerk wie English Network Plus 1. Auf jeden Fall wünsche ich Ihnen auch weiterhin viel Erfolg und Freude beim Englischlernen.

Yours sincerely,
Your English Expert

Wordfield

Synonyms and antonyms

1 Synonyms

Match words with the same meaning from the list 1–15 with words in the list a–o. Write the number in the box.

1 accept	9 recently	☐ a) boring	☐ i) say no
2 begin	10 refuse	☐ b) certain	☐ j) say yes
3 big	11 slim	☐ c) fair	☐ k) shut
4 blond	12 speak	☐ d) find out	☐ l) start
5 close	13 sure	☐ e) guest	☐ m) talk
6 difficult	14 uninteresting	☐ f) hard	☐ n) thin
7 discover	15 visitor	☐ g) large	☐ o) twelve
8 dozen		☐ h) lately	

2 Antonyms (opposites)

Write a word that means the opposite of each of these words. Some of them can be made by adding a prefix at the beginning of the word.

1 advantage ....
2 clean ....
3 correct ....
4 countable ....
5 difficult ....
6 employed ....
7 expensive ....
8 heavy ....
9 noisy ....
10 popular ....
11 possible ....
12 safe ....

PANORAMA 5

People and technology

1 Starter: Computer phobia

Psychologists at Strathclyde University have, surprisingly, found out that more young people are afraid of computers than older people. Young people feel that they must master lots of computer skills to get a job and they are under stress to keep up-to-date with all the new software. Older people often learn only the skills which are necessary for their job and they are happy that modern technology makes their work easier. What about you? Are you 'computer-literate'? If you have no idea what the following terms mean, ask the computer-fans in your class and they will try to explain these terms **simply**:
hardware / software / E-Mail / Internet / CD Rom / surfing / hard disk / floppy disk.

Do it like this:

A: *I've no idea what a CD Rom is.*

B: *It's a sort of CD for your computer. It can have music on it or travel information or a language course – or even an encyclopedia. You put it into your CD Rom player and you can see and hear the information on your computer screen.*

2 International communication

Most computer terminology is in English so that people can understand each other world-wide. Read this part of a newspaper article which shows how language and technology can bring people together.

On-line Romance
Yesterday in Aberdeen, Scotland, 42-year-old Adrian Philpott married his Internet girlfriend, Cindy, a 46-year-old widow from Connecticut, USA. Their computer-romance started three months ago when Cindy interrupted Adrian's on-screen discussion about the film 'Braveheart'. Four weeks later a message from Adrian appeared on Cindy's screen asking her to marry him and she agreed. They met face to face for the first time at Heathrow Airport only three days before the wedding. Adrian said, "I wasn't looking for a partner – it simply happened. And it's not a bad way to meet ... we know that we share at least one interest!" After the honeymoon Adrian is going to move to Connecticut to live with his new wife and her four children. Cindy's 23 year-old son said, ".......... ."

In pairs, write down what you think Cindy's son said. Then tell the rest of the class.

The two articles on the right were also in the newspaper. Make two groups. Each group should choose one of the headlines and put together the article about it from the mixed up information. The last sentence of each article is not finished. Complete the last sentence and then read the article to the class.

Singapore trains bi-lingual police dogs

A have trained their dogs in both Chinese and English. This is necessary because more than 30 % of the policemen who work with the dogs are not of Chinese origin so English is

B get a reply as Titan has temperatures of minus 180 degrees and a poisonous atmosphere. The idea of sending messages into Space is not new. In the 1970s NASA

Greetings from planet Earth

C In Singapore 80% of the population are of Chinese origin but the education system here is bi-lingual and students must

D be fluent in Chinese and English. And now, so must the police-dogs! Since the beginning of the year, dog-trainers in the Singapore police force

E In 1977 the Austrian Secretary-General of the United Nations, Kurt Waldheim, sent a message into Space on the spaceship Voyager 1: "I send greetings on behalf of the people of our planet … ." Now you too can send a message into Space. ESA, the European Space Agency, has

F made this possible. Under the Internet number "http://www.huygens.com", you can send a message to Titan, one of the moons of Saturn – but you probably won't

G the main language of communication. The dogs' bi-lingual training lasts about one month and then they are able to understand the basic commands. When the training is finished, these dogs and their handlers ……..

H sent information about the planet Earth into Space. This included a lot of photographs: an Italian motorway, an American supermarket, …………

3 English as a world language

As you saw in the newspaper article, even *dogs* must learn English nowadays! English is used in *so many* areas of international communication in the world today – it is the language of the United Nations, the Miss World Contest, the Olympic Games, space travel, the World Council of Churches – the list is endless. Here are some statistics about the English language. Take it in turns to read out a sentence.

1 In the days of Shakespeare, around 1600, English was the first language of about 6,000,000 Englishmen. Today it is the first language of about 350,000,000 people.
2 English is now the most widely spoken and written language in the world and there are 750,000,000 people who speak it.
3 Of all the world's languages, of which there are about 2,700, English has got the biggest vocabulary with its $^{1}/_{2}$ million words – and if we count technical terms, that's another 300,000 words!
4 German has got 185,000 words and French has 100,000 words – and that includes words like "le camping" and "le weekend"!
5 Don't worry – the average Briton, American or Australian only uses about 5,000 words in every day speach.
6 More than $^{1}/_{2}$ the world's technical and scientific journals are in English and 80 % of all information stored in computers is in English.
7 English is used in 50 % of all European business deals, and $^{3}/_{4}$ of the world's letters and faxes are written in English.
7 The five largest broadcasting companies in the world, including the BBC and NBC, broadcast in English to over 100,000,000 peolpe.

If you have problems with any of these numbers, write them down in words – it will help you to remember how to say them.

4 Talking points

- In which situations do you use *your* English?
- What about computers? Do you ever use one? If so, when? And what for?
- Do you think that computers have brought more advantages or disadvantages to children's lives?
- When someone is brought up with two languages, they are bi-lingual. Has anyone in your class experience of this? What do you think are the advantages and disadvantages of bringing up children bi-lingually?
- This course is nearly finished. What are your next plans for using or learning English?

Test yourself

1 Test your grammar

Choose the form that fits best in each sentence. For each sentence, mark your answer like this: (a)

1 This … a good company to work for if we had a different boss.
a were **b** will be **c** would be

2 I would look for a new job if I … younger.
a am **b** were **c** would be

3 I … here for ten years now.
a have worked **b** had worked **c** work

4 I … for two other companies before I came here.
a am working **b** had worked **c** work

5 Last Friday … our boss's birthday.
a has been **b** was **c** will be

6 My … wives all came to the birthday party.
a colleagues **b** colleague's **c** colleagues'

7 I … complaining about the boss when he walked into the room.
a am **b** was **c** were

8 If I … him on Monday I'll have to apologize to him, of course.
a see **b** will see **c** would see

2 Test your spelling

Listen to the text and write in the missing words. Can you spell them correctly?

Next (9) .... our company is going to start a new advertising (10) .... I think it's a good idea but I am a bit (11) .... about it. The boss has decided that his (12) .... and daughter-in-law should make all the arrangements. Unfortunately (13) .... of them has had any (14) .... in this sort of thing before.

3 What's the right word?

After each number, cross out the word or expression that is wrong.

When Arthur Wellsted was younger, a friend of (15) *him / his* took him out for a ride on a motorbike and (16) *learnt / taught* him how to ride it. Now he (17) *goes / is going* out for a ride almost every day. He (18) *often visits / visits often* his grandchildren. They are afraid he will have an accident if he (19) *rides / will ride* his motorbike too (20) *fast / fastly*, but he says he is always careful.

4 Write the questions

Use these words to write questions about Arthur Wellsted. The first <u>two</u> words of each question are missing. The answers to the questions are there to help you.

21 a / him / policeman / stop / yesterday

....

....?

Because he was going too fast.

22 at / he / his / motorbike / 85 mph / on / riding

....

....?

On a road in Devon.

23 be / he / next / September / will

....

....?

Eighty-seven.

24 about / Arthur / later / policeman / say / the

....

....?

He said it was a pleasure to meet sach an active and interesting old gentleman.

5 Having things done

Complete the questions and answers, like this:
Does he repair his motorbike <u>himself? No, he has it repaired</u> at the garage.

25 Do they cut their hair ....? ....
.... at the hairdresser's.

26 Did she wash the windows ....? ....
.... by the cleaning woman.

27 Is he going to type the letters ....? ....
.... at the office.

28 Does he clean the steps ....? ....
.... by the boy next door.

29 Are they going to paint the house ....? ...
....

MY SCORE OUT OF 29: ....

Extra 1

Spring: March, April, May

1 St. Patrick's Day, March 17th

Find the ten missing words in the puzzle below.

Saint (1) .... is the national (2) .... of (3) .... who was born in 389 and legend says that he cleared Ireland of (4) .... – even today there aren't any in Ireland! On St. Patrick's Day, (5) .... 17th, there are big celebrations not only in the Irish capital of (6) .... but also in other cities, like (7) ...., which have a large Irish population (there are more Irishmen there than in Dublin!). On St. Patrick's Day, Irishmen wear a shamrock and the colour (8) .... – and you can even drink green (9) .... in some Irish (10) ....!

I	P	D	U	B	L	I	N
R	S	N	A	K	E	S	E
E	B	E	E	R	Z	A	W
L	U	P	U	B	S	I	Y
A	X	G	R	E	E	N	O
N	M	A	R	C	H	T	R
D	P	A	T	R	I	C	K

- What street celebrations are there where you live?

2 April Fool's Day, April 1st

Put the right adjective into the space: *excited / exciting / free / local / serious / silly*.

This is the day when people play tricks on other people and try to make them look (1) .... It is celebrated internationally – in Scotland an April Fool is a *gowk*, in France it's an *April Fish*.

On one April 1st a (2) .... radio station in England played an April fool's trick on its listeners. They broadcast a report about something really new – not a tea-bag, but a beer-bag! In a (3) .... voice, the radio announcer told the listeners about this (4) .... new idea – a bag which contained condensed beer! You had to put the *beer*-bag into a glass of mineral water and you could make beer! The listeners could phone for a (5) .... sample – and say which kind of beer they wanted – bitter or lager. Thousands of people were so (6) .... by the idea that they forgot it was April 1st and telephoned to ask for their free beer-bags!

- Do you know any TV or radio programmes which play tricks on people? How would you feel if this happened to you?

➤ Word focus: *exciting* or *excited*?

The children were very .... because the race was so ....

Now put the ending, *-ing* or *-ed*, on these words.

1 Are you interest.......... in space travel? I don't find it very interest.......... .

2 The film was so bor.......... that all of us were bor.......... and we left before the end.

3 She spent a tir.......... day at the office and was very tir.......... when she got home.

4 The sketch wasn't very amus.......... and not many people were amus.......... .

3 And locally ...

Hundreds of people watch the International Festival of Worm Charming – an annual event in Blackawton, Devon, in May. The aim is to encourage as many worms as possible to come out of the earth. (The Guinness Book of Records says that the record-holder is Tom Shufflebottom, who collected 511 worms in half an hour in 1980.) Two methods of doing this are: dropping water or tea onto the ground so that the worms think it's raining – or simply singing to them. Animal rights activists (the International Worm Liberation Front) are there to see that the worms are treated with care and respect and returned to their tunnels at the end of the contest! And they protest every year about the name of one meal at the local pub – Worm Pie.

The word *watch* has got two meanings: *They* ***watch*** *this contest every year. / A* ***watch*** *is smaller than a clock.* Make two sentences to show the different meanings of these words.

book	hard	left	match	rest	room	sign
box	kind	lift	pound	right	second	type
change	land	light	present	ring	show	

Extra 2

Summer: June, July, August

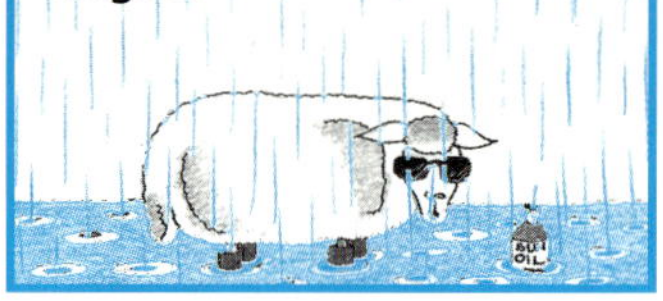

1 Independence Day, July 4th

Re-arrange the letters to make the missing words from the text: 1 dues, 2 nageb, 3 ttdaesr, 4 fghtou, 5 aousmf, 6 sayer, 7 bameec, 8 scnie.

America (1) _ _ _ _ to be a British colony. When the British (2) _ _ _ _ _ _ _ to tax American imports, the colonies (3) _ _ _ _ _ to protest. In 1775 the colonists, under the leadership of General Washington, (4) _ _ _ _ _ _ against the British and on July 4th, 1776, they issued the (5) _ _ _ _ _ _ 'Declaration of Independence'. After many (6) _ _ _ _ _ of fighting, the colonies (7) _ _ _ _ _ _ independent in 1783 – and (8) _ _ _ _ _ then Americans have celebrated July 4th as their national day.

- 1776 is one of the most important dates in American history. What do you think are the most important dates in your country's history? Why?
- What do you know about America?
  In small groups, write the answers to these questions in the boxes.

1 Elvis Presley was known as 'The ...' ☐☐☐☐
2 Famous for a 'Tea-Party' in 1773!
☐☐☐☐☐☐
3 The middle name of President John Kennedy.
☐☐☐☐☐☐☐☐☐☐
4 A waterfall on the border of the United States and Canada. ☐☐☐☐☐☐☐
5 The capital of America.
☐☐☐☐☐☐☐☐☐☐
6 The name of an American car-manufacturer and an American president. ☐☐☐☐
7 The most famous 'cowboy' actor, who died in 1979.
☐☐☐☐ ☐☐☐☐☐

Now write down the letters in the shaded boxes and re-arrange them to spell the name of one of America's largest cities.

....

2 Wimbledon, June/July

- What sports do you think of when you hear these place names? Wimbledon / Indianapolis / Wembley / Gleneagles / St Moritz / Isle of Man / Ascot
- What international sporting events have you heard of? If you could choose to go to one of them, which would it be?
- Now read the text and cross out the incorrect words.

Wimbledon is an area in South London – but (1) *everyone / anyone* thinks of tennis when they (2) *hear / listen* that name because (3) *it's / its* the home of the All England Lawn Tennis and Croquet Club. Although this club has got only 375 members, 360,000 people come every year to watch what is probably the most important tennis tournament in the world, (4) *which / what* takes place on the grass courts of Wimbledon each summer. If you are (5) *lucky / happy* enough to (6) *get / become* tickets for the Centre Court, you can watch some first-class tennis (and see a lot of celebrities in the audience!).

➤ Word focus: *see, watch* or *look at*?
Put the correct verb into these sentences.

1 Excuse me, could you sit down, please because I can't .... the game.

2 You can .... the TV programme to see when the match starts.

3 I'm going to .... the final again on TV this evening.

3 And locally ...

You're going to read about an unusual 'sport' involving animals. Which other animal sports have you seen or heard about? What do you think about these sports?

We've all heard about the 'animal' sports of bull-fighting and fox-hunting, but have you ever heard about the more humane sport of snail-racing? The annual World Snail Racing Championships take place in Congham, Norfolk, every July – and over 150 snails (and their owners) take part. The record-holder is a snail called Archie who took the title from a Canadian snail – the prize is a silver trophy, full of lettuce leaves.

- Archie is a strange name for a snail! Have you ever had a pet? If so, tell the class about it – and what its name was!

Extra 3

1 Guy Fawkes Night (or Bonfire Night), November 5th

With a partner put these verbs into the text below: *blow up / cook / dress / eat / have searched / kill / light / make / put / tried.*

On November 5th, 1605, Guy Fawkes (1) .... to (2) .... the Houses of Parliament and (3) .... King James the First of England. Guy Fawkes was later executed. And since then the guards in the Tower of London (4) .... the cellars of the Houses of Parliament on November 5th every year.

Children still (5) .... 'guys' – life-size figures of Guy Fawkes, which they usually (6) .... in their father's old clothes.

On Bonfire Night they (7) .... the guy on top of a large bonfire and burn him! Families (8) .... fireworks, (9) .... potatoes in the fire and (10) ....traditional sweets and cakes.

- How do you think children make a 'guy' ?
- Do you buy fireworks to celebrate anything? Why? / Why not?
- English people often look back on Bonfire Night with affection. Which celebrations did you enjoy most in your childhood? Why?

2 Thanksgiving, the last Thursday in November

Most American families try to get together for Thanksgiving celebrations. When do you get together with your family?

Now put these missing prepositions into the text: *at, for, for, from, in, in, of, on, on, to.*

In 1620, 102 'Pilgrim Fathers' sailed (1) .... England for the New World. The first Thanksgiving Day was (2) .... the autumn of 1621 when the English settlers invited the local American Indians to a celebration to thank them (3) .... their help and advice about farming and growing food. Thanksgiving is the biggest family celebration (4) .... America – and many families feel that it is more important to get together (5) .... Thanksgiving Day than (6) .... Christmas. It's the day when Americans thank God (7) .... the food which their land has produced. A lot (8) .... people go (9) .... church (10) .... this day and most Americans enjoy a dinner of turkey, corn, sweet potatoes and pumpkin pie.

- It's traditional for Americans to eat turkey and pumpkin pie at Thanksgiving. What traditional foods do you associate with celebrations where you live?
- The word *to* sounds the same as *too* or *two.* In small groups, write down words which sound like: *by / check / for / here / I / knows / meet / new / no / one / our / peace / pear / red / right / see / son / there / would.* Then compare them with other students.

3 And locally ...

The World Conker (Chestnut) Championships take place in Ashton, Peterborough in October and over 3,000 people come to watch this contest every year. To take part you must first find a hard conker, drill a hole in it and put a string through it. Then you hold the string so that your conker is in the air and an opponent tries to hit – and break – your conker with his. If he is not successful after three tries, you can try to break his conker in the same way. (Helmets must be worn!)

- Tell the class about any contest which you have taken part in.
- Has anyone in the class ever won a medal or a trophy? If so, what for?

Extra 4

1 New Year

Dinner for one

English people (and maybe some people in your class) don't know the sketch 'Dinner for One'. Tell them something about it before you read the text.

It's a German tradition on New Year's Eve to watch James, the butler, serving drinks to Miss Sophie's birthday guests. For over thirty years, TV audiences have planned their New Year celebrations around the English comedy sketch, 'Dinner for One', which you can see every year on December 31st. The sketch has gone into the 'Guinness Book of Records' as the world's most often repeated programme. You can see it in the USA, Denmark, South Africa, Italy, Belgium, Finland, Spain, Iceland, Holland, Australia, Bulgaria, Ireland – but not in England! English audiences have never seen this sketch! The NDR studios in Germany filmed the sketch in 1962. Although it was a big hit, James (the English actor, Freddie Frinton) only received a one-time payment of three thousand marks. He was also very disappointed that the programme never appeared on British TV – the BBC said that it wasn't good enough!

- German television broadcasts the sketch. Make similar sentences about the countries in the text which are highlighted.
- How do you celebrate New Year's Eve?

2 Valentine's Day

When is Valentine's Day and how is it celebrated? Read the text to find out more about Valentine's Day.

St. Valentine was a priest who lived in Rome in the third century. The Emperor had made a law which said that soldiers were not allowed to marry but Valentine continued to marry couples secretly. He was arrested and, while he was in prison, he fell in love with his guard's daughter. On the day of his execution he left her a letter, signed 'From your Valentine'. Nowadays on February 14th, Valentine's Day, romantic people send cards and flowers to their loved ones – often anonymously – and the personal columns of the newspapers are full of Valentine messages. The earliest Valentine card on record is from 1477. Margery Brews sent her boyfriend, John Paston, a message which was addressed to 'My right welbelovyd Voluntyne'.

- The abbreviation St. can mean saint or street. In small groups write down any other abbreviations which you know and ask other groups what they mean. Here are some to start you off: *P.S. / Prof. / Feb / m.p.h. / BBC / GB / cm / UN / Wed* .
- The English and Americans send more greeting cards than any other countries. Look at these messages from different greeting cards. On what occasion would you send each of these cards?

3 And locally ...

On Shrove Tuesday – or 'Pancake Tuesday' – there has been a a Pancake Race in Olney, Buckinghamshire every year since 1455. The rules say that all the competitors must be women who are wearing aprons and headscarves and they must run the race holding a frying-pan with a pancake in it!

- Shrove Tuesday is the same as *Faschingsdienstag*. How do people celebrate that day where you live?
- Have you ever worn a fancy-dress costume? If so, describe it to the class.

Story 1

The big match

It was Tuesday morning and Richard and his friend Paul were walking to work and talking about the big football match the following day. The local team had reached the final and everyone was very excited about it.

"I can't watch the match live because I'll be at work," said Paul, "but I'll either video it or watch it on TV in the evening."

"But watching a game when you already know the result just isn't the same as watching it live, is it? Do you know, my girlfriend has given me a ticket for the match – but what she *didn't* think about was that it's on a Wednesday afternoon and I'll be at work then, too."

"A ticket for the match! Wow! The atmosphere at the football ground will be fantastic. You *must* go. There must be some way of seeing the match. What can you do?"

"I don't know yet," said Richard. "I had thought I could phone my boss and say I was ill – but he'd never believe that. He knows that most of the people in the office would like to stay at home and watch the match, so he'd be very suspicious if I phoned and said I didn't feel well and I wasn't coming to work. But, don't worry, I'll think of something."

The rest of the day Richard couldn't concentrate on his work – he could only think about what he could do to go to the football match. Everyone in the office was talking about it. After work Richard went home, thinking only of the ticket in his pocket! Later on that evening, while he was making his dinner, he had an idea! He telephoned his sister and spoke to her for several minutes, smiled, put the phone down – and looked happier than he had done for days!

The next morning, the day of the match, Richard went to work as usual. At ten o'clock, while he was working, his boss came in and said, "Richard, could you come into my office for a moment, please?" Richard looked surprised but followed his boss into his office.

"Richard," he said, "your sister has just phoned. Bad news, I'm afraid. Your mother is ill and you should go to the hospital immediately to see her." Richard thanked his boss, left the office quickly and went to ... the football ground!

The match didn't start until three so he had plenty of time to get there. And his ticket was a good one – right at the front so he had a fantastic view of the game. The football match was really exciting and there were thousands of fans there. "Poor Paul," thought Richard, "he can only watch it on TV." The atmosphere was electric and the final score was 2-1 to the home team! The crowd cheered wildly at the end of the game as the local team collected the trophy.

On Thursday morning Richard went to work as usual. His colleagues looked at him strangely when he went into the office but they didn't speak to him. "I wonder why they haven't asked about my mother?" thought Richard. At ten o'clock his boss called him into his office. "Bad news again, I'm afraid, Richard. You see, I knew that most of your colleagues wanted to stay at home and watch the football match yesterday – but they didn't, they came to work. And as a reward I brought a TV into the office so that they wouldn't miss the match. But the football *game* wasn't the only thing we saw. We also saw a lot of *people* in the crowd. Tell me, Richard ... how is your mother?"

Story 2 The quiet young man

The doorbell rang and Mrs Black opened the front door. The young man who was standing there said, "Good afternoon. I'm looking for a room and I saw the notice in your window."
"Oh, yes. Come in. I'll show you the room," said Mrs Black pleasantly, "it's at the top of the house."
When the young man saw the room, he liked it very much and agreed to take it. As they were coming downstairs, a large man came out of a back room.
"Who's that?" the deep voice asked.
"This is Mr Thomas," said Mrs Black, "he's going to take the top room, dear." The large man looked at Mr Thomas but said nothing. "This is my husband, Mr Black, and he's ..." Mrs Black began.
"Tell him about my sleep," interrupted Mr Black.
"My husband is a fireman," explained Mrs Black, "and he often has to work at night and then he sleeps during the day."
"And," added Mr Black, "when I go to sleep, I want to *stay* asleep so I don't want any noise in the house. Is that clear?"
"Oh, yes, er... of course. I'll be very quiet."
"Good!" said Mr Black and went back into his room.
"Don't be afraid of him," said Mrs Black, "his bark is worse than his bite."
The days and weeks passed and Mr Thomas spent most of his free time in his room. He kept out of the big man's way, never came home late at night, and was always *very* quiet in the house!
One day he met Mr Black again on the stairs.
"Hello, Mr Black. Have you had a good day at work?" he asked.
"No!" replied Mr Black, "I have *not.* I'm on my way to bed now. To *sleep*, understand? I want a good night's sleep. And I'll get it – *if* there are no fire calls and *if* there's no noise in this house!"

Mr Thomas said goodnight and went quietly to his room. An hour later Mr Thomas called as quietly as he could from the top of the house, "Mrs Black – I'm sorry to trouble you, but do you think I could have a glass of water, please?"
"That's no trouble, dear, I'll get one from the kitchen," she answered.
A minute or two later, he called her again, "Sorry to ask you again, Mrs Black, but could I have another glass of water, please?"
She got another glass of water, gave it to him and went back to her room. Almost at once she heard him call again.
"Do you want *another* glass of water?" she asked.
"Two glasses, please, if I may."
"You *are* thirsty tonight," she said as she gave him the water.
"Oh, it's not for me," he said quietly.
"Well ... why do you want so much water?"
"I'll tell you if you like. But you must promise not to make a noise – and you mustn't tell Mr Black ... but my room is on fire!"

Story 3

The house on the hill

Barbara and Raymond Masters, a couple in their early thirties, were at the estate agent's.

"We have to live in this area," said Barbara, "because my husband has got a new job here. But we can't afford anything very expensive – £70,000 is about our limit."

The agent looked at his books. "Well, I have got *one* house for about that price – Hill House, a two-bedroomed country house with a garden, but it's been empty for several years so it needs a bit of renovating. It's a lovely place and only about ten kilometres from the town. I can't understand why nobody has bought it yet."

Barbara and Raymond thought that it sounded perfect. They had a car so going into town was no problem and Raymond was good at do-it-yourself so the renovations wouldn't be too expensive.

The estate agent gave them the keys and directions how to get there and the Masters went to have a look at the house.

As soon as they saw it, they fell in love with it. The outside of the house was a bit run-down and the garden was very untidy but inside the house everything was neat and clean.

"Let's go upstairs and look at the bedrooms," said Barbara.

As they were going upstairs, they heard a strange noise.

"What was that?"

"Oh, maybe a bedroom window is open and a bird has flown in," suggested Raymond.

"Good morning," said a man's voice behind them.

"Oh, you shocked me!" said Barbara. "Who are you?"

"My name's Bill. I come and tidy up the house every few weeks. Are you thinking of buying it?"

"I think we might," said Raymond. "It seems to be just what we're looking for."

"And the history of the house doesn't worry you?"

"The history of the house?"

"Ah, I see you're not from round here or you'd know the story. They say a man killed his wife here. In one of the bedrooms. They were a young couple, like you. But the police have never found her body. They say he buried her in the garden. And people say she comes back into the house and stands near the bed where ..."

"Oh, don't go on," said Barbara.

"Well, I don't believe the stories myself. And if you buy the house, I could come and do the gardening for you. Who knows? I might find what the police couldn't find ... "

"Oh, stop it! Raymond, let's go. I couldn't possibly live in a house like this."

Barbara ran out of the front door and Raymond followed her to the car.

Bill went up the stairs and unlocked a bedroom door. There were some old clothes on the floor, some food on a little table and a dog on a bed in the corner.

"They won't be back, Toby!" he said. "We've got the place to ourselves for another few months!"

Story 4

Japanese Red

Lenny had an antique shop full of beautiful old things. Some of the things were expensive but others were quite cheap so there was something for everyone in his shop.
One day a man came into the shop. He was wearing an old coat and he looked as though he hadn't got much money. He introduced himself – Arthur Spinks – and said he was looking for a birthday present for his granddaughter. He looked round the shop for a while and then picked up a little wooden box. "Oh," said Mr Spinks, "this would be perfect for my granddaughter – she could put her earrings in it." The box was Chinese and worth quite a lot of money but Lenny felt sorry for the old man and sold it to him cheaply.
Some weeks later Lenny told this story to Ron, a friend of his who was also in the antique business. "Arthur Spinks? *Poor* old man? Don't you believe it! He's got a huge house and it's full of antiques which he's bought cheaply from people like you. He's an expert on antiques."
Lenny was angry about this and decided to get his money back. The next time he saw Mr Spinks through the shop window, Lenny uncovered a glass bowl with an attractive red and gold fish in it. Mr Spinks came into the shop and this time his story was that he wanted something for his grandson. He looked at a lot of things in the shop but never directly at the glass bowl (which was hundreds of years old and worth a lot of money). Mr Spinks stopped at the table where the bowl was and looked at some old newspapers on the table – but his eyes were really on the beautiful Venetian bowl.
"Can I help you, sir?" asked Lenny.
"No, ... no, I don't think there's anything really suitable here for a little boy. But ... perhaps that fish ... that goldfish."
"Oh, I'm sorry, sir, that's a very rare fish, a Japanese Red, and rather expensive, I'm afraid. They're selling them in the High Street for £50."
"£50! That's an awful lot of money! But ... he *is* my favourite grandson so I'll take it," said Mr Spinks – with his eyes on the wonderful bowl!
"No, no, sir. I said they are selling them in the *High Street* for that price but I couldn't sell *this* fish. I've had him for years – he's like a friend."
"Well, how much *would* you sell it for?"
"Oh, no, I couldn't ... "
"Come on, how much do you want for it?"
"I wouldn't sell him for less than a hundred pounds!"
"A hundred pounds!"
"I *knew* it was too much for you, sir."
"No, no, I'll have it!"
"All right, sir, if you're really sure."
"Yes – here's the cash. I'll take it now."
" All right. Thank you, sir. The fish is yours. I'll just get another glass bowl."
"Don't trouble yourself. This one will be all right."
"Oh, no, sir, I couldn't give you this one."
"But I bought that bowl!"
"No, you didn't, sir – you bought the fish. Wait here, sir and I'll get you another bowl at once."
"Ron?" said Lenny on the telephone an hour later, "Spinks came in again today," Lenny laughed. "You were right! I got back the money for the Chinese box. Oh, and thanks for the bowl. You can have it back again tomorrow."

Language & Culture

Checkpoint 1: Queueing (p. 1)
The British *queue* and the Americans *stand in line*. In both countries people feel that life is much pleasanter if you wait your turn. So you should never *jump the queue* or *cut in line* (= *sich vordrängeln*). The British used to be famous for their queues at bus stops, but things have changed a bit. There are now lots of bus stops where a number of buses stop so you can't make a proper queue. Most people still don't push when their bus comes but they try to form a line to get on the bus. *Queueing* (or *queuing* spelt without the *e*) is still an important part of the British way of life.

Checkpoint 2: Meeting people (p. 5)
In Britain people usually only shake hands when they introduce themselves or when they are introduced. People shake hands on very formal occasions but when people meet privately, at parties or at friends' homes, they don't always shake hands even when they meet for the first time. When young people introduce themselves, they usually just say *Hi* or *Hello* without a handshake. When you meet friends, you give them a kiss or a hug (*jdn. umarmen*)

Checkpoint 3: Forms of address (p. 9)
American and British people seldom use their academic title in private life. If someone introduces him or herself as *Doctor*, he or she is probably a medical doctor. Even in professional life some specialists – a dentist, for example – just use Mr or Ms. *Ms* (pronounced miz) is used by professional women who do not think it is important or necessary to show if they are married (*Mrs*) or single (*Miss*). In business letters when you are writing to a woman you start your letter with for example: *Dear Ms Smith*, because you don't normally know if the person is married or not. It is becoming more and more common in less formal business letters to use both the first name and family name (*Dear Janet Smith*), ending with *Yours sincerely, Chris Poole*. Generally, both in business and in private life people start using first names much more quickly than they do in Germany. Even when British people are *on first name terms*, they are still very tactful when they don't agree with someone and use phrases like *I'm afraid I must disagree with you* or *I fully agree with you but … .*

Checkpoint 4: On the phone (p. 13)
In Britain when you answer the phone you usually say your telephone number or your name, but not just your family name as you do in Germany. You give your full name: *Eve Daniels*, or you can say: *This is Eve Daniels speaking*. When you give someone your number in the States you say: *You can get me **at** 212 840 4623*. In Britain you say: *You can get me **on** 220 1635*. When you say the numbers don't say: *two hundred and twenty, sixteen, thirty five*, but *two two oh, one six three five*. In Britain for 220 you can also say *double two oh*, and if the number is 222, you say *triple two*. In America 0 is *zero*, and in Britain 0 is *oh* or *zero*. Perhaps you didn't realise that the word *Handy* is not used in Britain or the United States for a phone which you can carry with you. The English word for *ein Handy* is a *mobile phone*. So you can hear people say: *You can get me on my mobile*.

Checkpoint 5: Neighbourhood watch (p. 21)
The organization Home or Neighbourhood Watch (American spelling, Neighborhood Watch) came to Britain from America in the 1980s. There are now over 5 million families in about 115,000 organizations. The idea is that people should keep an eye on each other's homes and ring the police if they see anything strange. People in the organizations say they feel much safer. The telephone number for the police is the same all over Britain, 999. In some areas local policemen work closely with the people and get to know them and their problems. This is called community policing.
If you want help from a policeman, you say: *Excuse me, Officer, can you help me?*

Checkpoint 6: House and home (p. 25)
Have you heard the expression *An Englishman's home is his castle*? Well, it is certainly true that in Britain most people want to live in a house. Sometimes the houses are very small and built in a long row (BrE: *terraced house*, AmE: *row house*) and they often haven't got a garden, but people think it's better to live in a house than in a *flat* (AmE:. *apartment*). These houses are not too expensive so that a lot of people can buy their own house when they get married. People who haven't got enough money to buy their own house can either rent a home privately or live in *council flats* or *houses* (*Sozialwohnungsbau*) and pay a low *rent* (*Miete*).

Checkpoint 7: *Some* or *any*? (p. 29)
You have just seen the rule for using *some* and *any* in English but there is a special use of *some*. If you ask someone to do something for you and you expect the answer *Yes*, you may also use *some* in the question form: *Excuse me, can you give me **some** information about the bus tours, please?* When you offer a person something, you also usually use *some*: *Would you like **some** brochures with information about the tours?*
But remember when you ask someone for something don't forget that little word *please*. Sometimes when you speak a foreign language, it is often difficult to get the tone quite right and you may sound a little impolite so a *please* and a smile makes all the difference!

Language & Culture

Checkpoint 8: Lifestyles (p. 33)
You learnt that the British and Americans like to live in their own houses but they are also quite happy to move house and in their lifetime they may live in a number of different houses in different parts of the country. A lot of people don't mind if strangers stay in their homes while they are away on holiday. So even if their home is their castle, they are willing to share it with other people. *Flat-sharing* (AmE: *apartment-sharing*) or *house-sharing* is also quite common among young professional people and students. Students often live in a *bedsit* or *bedsitting* room, which is one room used for eating and sleeping and is usually fairly cheap to rent.

Checkpoint 9: What's in a word? (p. 41)
You may have no problems enjoying your leisure time activities, but you may not be so sure how to spell or pronounce the word *leisure*. In British English it is pronounced /ˈleʒə/, but in American English /ˈliːʒr/. The word *hobby* also seems such an easy word because it is used in German. But be careful! There are expressions in German with *hobby*, which are quite different in English: Ein *Hobbykoch* is *a keen cook*, *ein Hobbygärtner* is *an amateur gardener*, *ein Hobbykeller* or *Hobbyraum* is *a workshop (in the cellar)*, although some people use it as *a party room*. Don't forget the plural of *hobby* is *hobbies*. The extra *e* in *whiskey* makes a difference, too! *Whisky* is made in Britain but *whisk**e**y* is either Irish or American.

Checkpoint 10: What's the difference? (p. 45)
Americans often use the word *vacation* instead of *holiday*: *They're on vacation for the next few weeks.*
In British English *vacation* is the university vacation, when the universities are closed. So the word *vacation* is used by students and people who work at the universities.
If you're on holiday in Britain or on vacation in the US, don't be surprised if you see traffic signs which tell you to *Drive slow*. Traffic signs don't always follow the rule of putting an *-ly* on the end of the adverb. You will also hear idiomatic expressions like *Take it easy* or: *Get rich quick*, where you don't put an *-ly* on the end, either.

Checkpoint 11: Public schools (p. 49)
Churchill went to Harrow, a famous *public school*, but the word *public* is rather complicated. The so-called public schools in Britain and especially England are expensive *private schools*, where pupils usually live as well as study, i.e. *boarding schools* (*Internate*). In the US and Scotland the so-called *public schools* are state schools, which are free. In the US there are also expensive private schools which, like the English public schools, prepare *pupils* (BrE) or *students* (AmE) for the elite universities and the top jobs. In these schools sport is very important because it is healthy and good for discipline but also because it teaches notions such a *team spirit* and *fair play*. Pupils who are good at sports have certain advantages when they apply for a place at an elite university.

Checkpoint 12: Teatime (p. 53)
Would you like some tea? could be an invitation to have a cup of tea or a pot of tea but it might also mean *afternoon tea*, which is in fact a light meal with sandwiches and cakes, which people sometimes have at about four o'clock in the afternoon. But these days, as most people are usually at work at this time of day, afternoon tea is something you have on a special occasion. The famous *cream tea*, which you can get in tea rooms or hotels, includes scones (small plain cakes) with delicious thick cream. An invitation to *supper* means that you will probably have an informal meal, but if you are invited to *dinner* you will expect it to be a formal *three-course meal* with wine.

Checkpoint 13: Studies (p. 61)
Students *take* an examination or *sit for* (BrE) an exam. They can either *pass* or *fail* the exam. In a letter giving information about their qualifications they should write: *I took my final examinations in 1996* and not *I passed my final examinations in 1996*. In English *Studium* is used in the plural: *I started my studies in 1996*.
In Britain the average student usually starts studying at the age of 18 and finishes at 21 or 22 – the age when the average German student starts his/her studies! Most students leave university after three or four years of *undergraduate studies* with a BA (Bachelor of Arts) or a BSc (Bachelor of Science). Some students continue their *graduate studies* and do an MA (Master of Arts) or MSc (Master of Science) or a PhD (Doctor of Philosophy). In the US, too, students leave university at a much younger age than in Germany.

Checkpoint 14: Standard English (p. 65)
BBC English is the kind of English which many people want to use when they speak English. Today, not everyone on the BBC speaks with this standard pronunciation but if you listen to the BBC World Service you certainly can improve your English. The *BBC World Service* broadcasts to countries all over the world. You can listen to the news, to current affairs programmes, plays, short stories, quizzes and many other interesting and entertaining programmes. You need a special radio, a World Receiver, and you get the best reception in many areas on AM 94 10.0, 120 95.0, and 61 95.0 depending on the time of day.

Checkpoint 15: Your health (p. 69)
In Britain when most people go to the doctor's or to hospital the treatment (*Behandlung*) is free. But working people do pay contributions (*Beiträge*) to the National Health Service. These are much lower than in Germany and so the Government also has to use taxes

Language & Culture

to run the very expensive system. In Britain people have to see their family doctor or *GP* (*General Practitioner*) in his *surgery* (*Praxis*) before they can see a specialist at the hospital. In the US there is no national health service but the government helps poor people through the *Medicaid* system and old people through the *Medicare* system. There you go to see your GP or *Internist* in his *office*, but you can also go straight to a specialist if you want to.

Checkpoint 16: Me, too (p. 73)

When you listen to British or American people talking they may agree with you and say: *Me, too* instead of *So do I* when you say *I love Paris*. You may also hear people answer *Me, neither* and not *Neither do I* when you say: *I didn't like the food*. This short form is sometimes used in everyday English and of course is easier if you have a problem finding the right auxiliary (*Hilfsverb*).

Question tags are very useful when you are trying to make conversation with strangers. They are used a lot, and it sounds less direct and friendlier to say: *You are a teacher, aren't you?* than *Are you a teacher?* Each country has a different idea about politeness and the British don't like to be asked too directly about certain subjects.

Checkpoint 17: Getting it right (p. 81)

You have seen that in conditional sentences there is usually no *would* in the *if* part of the sentence: *If I were you, I would go* and *I would do it if I had time*. Perhaps you have a problem with the comma in these sentences. There is a simple rule. If you look at the two examples above, you will see that when the *if* part of the sentence comes first, there is a comma. There is no comma when the *if* part of the sentence is second. In spoken English you can also say: *If I* ***was*** *you, I would go*. This is less formal than If *I* ***were*** *you*.

In German young people use lots of English words like *kids, party* and *image*. But there are German words in English too like *schadenfreude* and *kitsch*, and recently more people use words like *angst* or *Deutschmark*. Did you know that in America when you sneeze many people will say *gesundheit*? The German settlers in America have introduced German words into the language, especially food names like *schnitzel, schnapps* and *pretzel*.

Checkpoint 18: Ma or Pa (p. 85)

In Britain and America when children are small they call their parents *Mummy* and *Daddy* (AmE also *Mommy* and *Pop*). When they are adults they usually shorten it to *Mum* and *Dad* and if they are talking about their parents outside the family, they will often use the more formal *mother* and *father*: *My mother is at work but my father's at home*. Older people usually also prefer to address their parents with the more formal *Mother* and *Father*: *Mother, can you come over here, please*. If adults still use *Mummy* and *Daddy* it sounds a little affected. Grandfather is usually called *Grandpa* and grandmother *Gran, Granny* or *Nanny*.

Checkpoint 19: Art or arts? (p. 89)

If you are an *artist*, you have probably studied *art* at an art school and produce works of art such as drawings or paintings. If you are a *painter*, you could be an artist who paints pictures or a *decorator* – someone who paints houses and puts paper on the walls as their job. A student at the university who is taking an *arts* degree is studying subjects that are not scientific, like history or languages (*Geisteswissenschaften*).
In Britain the *Arts Council* is an organization which provides money to help the theatre, art, music and the cinema. But now money from the National Lottery is also used to support the arts.

Checkpoint 20: Political correctness (p. 93)

When you are speaking about people who are *old* it is politer to say *elderly* and not *old*: *A home for the elderly*. In the same way you should use *gentleman* and *lady* and not *man* and *woman* when speaking about people who are present: *This umbrella belongs to the elderly gentleman over there*. These *politically correct* words and expressions are used more and more in Britain and the US, for example, *OAPs* or *old-aged pensioners* (*Rentner*) are now called *senior citizens* (*Senioren*). Sometimes people feel that the use of political correctness is a little exaggerated and a *young girl* need not be called *a pre woman* just because the word *girl* is sometimes used in a negative context.

Information

Unit 16: Exercise 6: Who was it?

Alexander Graham Bell: Born in Edinburgh, Scotland in 1847. He invented the telephone in 1876 and died in Canada in 1922.
Amy Johnson: 1903-1941. English airwoman who flew solo to Australia in 1930.
Sir Charles Chaplin: 1889-1977. English comedian, composer and film-maker.
Yuri Gagarin: 1934-1968. Russian cosmonaut. He was the first man in Space (April, 1961).
Christopher Columbus: Born in Genoa, Italy in about 1541. He discovered America in 1492 and died in 1504.
Agatha Christie: 1890-1976. English detective story writer who created the character 'Miss Marple'.
Guglielmo Marconi: 1874-1937. Born in Italy. Inventor of the radio.
Alfred Nobel: 1833-1896. A Swede who invented dynamite, and gave his name to prizes for peace, literature, physics, chemistry and medicine.

Key

Checkpoint 1 (page 1)
→ Grammar (p. 128 + 137)
Grammar 1: 1 carries, catches, dances, does, flies, goes, has, washes
2 1 Does, 2 have, 3 helps, 4 don't, 5 need, 6 want, 7 rent, 8 has, 9 takes, 10 goes, 11 have, 12 is
3 1 He doesn't go to the theatre once month. 2 How often does he go to the theatre? 3 They don't book tickets by phone. 4 How do they book tickets?
Grammar 2: 1 always, 2 usually, 3 often, 4 sometimes, 5 seldom, 6 never
a) My neighbour *always / often / seldom / sometimes / usually / never* goes to the theatre.
b) He's *always / often / sometimes / usually* late for work on Monday mornings because of the heavy traffic.
c) Do you *always / often / sometimes / usually / never* take a taxi when it rains?
How to say it: Reihenfolge der Lösungen: 3, 1, 4, 2

Homestudy 1 (page 4)
1 2 She never goes to the dentist (or: to the dentist's). 3 They sometimes go shopping on Saturdays. 4 They don't usually travel by taxi. 5 He always travels by taxi.
6 He doesn't wash the (or: his) car on Sundays. 7 Does she go to the hairdresser (or: to the hairdresser's) every week? 8 How often does she clean the windows?
2 1 Let's, 2 Shall we, 3 We could, 4 What about, 5 Why don't you
3 cook, decide, do, drive, enjoy, find, fly, go, join, put, talk, think, try, walk, work, write

W	O	R	K	E	D	E	C	I	D	E	T
R	P	U	T	N	G	F	Z	T	R	W	H
I	F	L	Y	J	O	I	N	A	I	A	I
T	B	C	O	O	K	N	Q	L	V	L	N
E	H	T	R	Y	M	D	O	K	E	K	K

The four irregular 3rd person singular verb forms are: does, flies, goes, tries
4 2 ✗, 3 ✓, 4 ✓, 5 ✓, 6 ✗, 7 ✗, 8 ✓, 9 ✗, 10 ✓, 11 ✓, 12 ✓
5 1 F, 2 T, 3 F, 4 F, 5 T, 6 T, 7 T

Checkpoint 2 (page 5) → Grammar (p. 129 + 130)
Grammar 1: 1 been, bought, caught, fallen, felt, forgotten, got, known, shown, thought, worn
2 1 have you heard, 2 have closed, 3 have left, 4 has lived, 5 has got (or: has had), 6 has asked, 7 have not found, 8 have said, 9 have agreed
3 The correct answer is 2: I have known him for 20 years.
Grammar 2: 1 for 3 months, 2 **since** January. We use **for** to talk about a period of time. We use **since** to talk about a point of time. In German **since** and **for** is **seit**.
How to say it: 3a, 1b, 2c. 1b is the most formal situation. 3a is the least formal. a) Correct answer: "How do you do".

Homestudy 2 (page 8)
1 2 He hasn't mended Mary's garden-gate yet. 3 He has already done Mary's shopping. 4 He has already washed Len's milk-van. 5 He hasn't cleaned Sue's windows yet.
2 1 Mary has lived here all her life. (~~lives~~, ~~since~~) 2 She has been alone since her husband died in 1986. (~~for~~, ~~is~~) 3 She has been a member of LETS for two years. (~~is~~, ~~since~~) 4 We have known Mary for six months now. (~~know~~, ~~since~~) 5 We have known her since we joined LETS last December. (~~for~~, ~~know~~)
3 Pictures: A1, B4, C3, D2
Expressions: 1, 3, 3, 2, 4, 2, 1, 4
4 Add -*s* (regular): boys, Saturdays, taxis. Add -*es*: businesses, churches, classes, lunches. Change *y* to *i* and add -*es*: babies, communities, countries, dictionaries. Change *f* to *v* and add -*s* or -*es*: wives, yourselves. Irregular plurals: children, milkmen, women.

Checkpoint 3 (page 9) → Grammar (p. 130)
Grammar 1: 1 began, caught, checked, did, drank, ate, fell, felt, found, hired, lost, met, paid, put, recommended, saw, spent, told, thought, wore
2 1 started, 2 used, 3 was, 4 asked, 5 wear, 6 answered, 7 wear, 8 wore
Grammar 2: 1 One doctor used to have rollerblades. 2 He didn't use to wear skates. 3 Did he use to ride a bike at work?
a) He didn't use to ride a bike. *Used to* sounds strange in the other sentence because you normally say *used to* when you are talking about something which you did regularly in the past but you don't do any more.
How to say it: 1 I'm sorry but that's wrong. D 2 I'm sure you're right. A 3 Yes, that's very true. A 4 I'm afraid I must disagree with you. D 5 Look, you can't say that. D 6 You're quite right. A

Homestudy 3 (page 12)
1 1 was, 2 used to take, 3 drinks, 4 tells, 5 used to work, 6 didn't have, 7 could, 8 took, 9 learnt (AmE learned), 10 bought, 11 paid, 12 wore, 13 said, 14 didn't like, 15 didn't earn, 16 used to save, 17 decided, 18 drove, 19 spent, 20 rained, 21 flew
2 1 Did you use to travel (or: go) to work by underground? 2 How much money did you use to earn? 3 When did you use to start work? 4 What (kind of clothes) did you use to wear to work?
3 2, 3, 2, 1, 2, 2, 3, 2, 1. The man in the picture is probably saying "I think that's totally wrong!" or "That's not true at all."
4 appointment, assistant, coffee, colleagues, conversation, experience, important, modern, recommend, secretary, stewardess, technology

Checkpoint 4 (page 13) → Grammar (p. 131 + 134)
Grammar 1: 1 Sentence 2 tells us where Minh lives now.
2 1 He was born in Vietnam. 2 He left Vietnam in 1980. 3 He has had a lot of jobs so far / up to now.
3 1 has been, 2 was, 3 was, 4 fought, 5 came, 6 has lived, 7 went, 8 used to, 9 started, 10 gave, 11 made, 12 became
Grammar 2: 1 When Minh was a soldier, he wore a uniform. 2 He has travelled a lot in_Switzerland and in the U.S.A. 3 _Minh learnt to play the guitar when he was young. 4 He had_lunch an hour ago.
How to say it: More formal are: 1b, 2a, 3b, 4b, 5a, 6a.

Homestudy 4 (page 16)
1 1 left, 2 worked, 3 has had, 4 has decided, 5 rang, 6 hasn't sent, 7 didn't get, 8 Has ... heard, 9 Did ... learn, 10 Has ... taken

Message for Mr Leason. **From** Paul Quayle. **Tel. number** 001-416-555-3471. He has (or: He's) received your letter and has spoken to Mr Smith about it. Mr Smith seems very interested.
3 /d/ as in *called*: changed, enjoyed, happened, interviewed, lived, travelled. /t/ as in *asked*: checked, dressed, finished, talked, washed, worked. /id/ as in *needed*: decided, interested, started, wanted
4 1 ✗, 2 ✗, 3 a (or: the), 4 ✗, 5 an, 6 ✗, 7 ✗, 8 ✗, 9 a, 10 ✗, 11 a, 12 the, 13 the, 14 ✗, 15 ✗, 16 the, 17 a, 18 a, 19 the

Wordfield: Jobs (page 17)
1 policeman, 2 pilot, 3 milkman, 4 soldier, 5 secretary, 6 stewardess, 7 engineer, 8 nurse, 9 gardner, 10 assistant; Key word: colleagues.

Test yourself 1 (page 20)
1 Did she use to work as a secretary? 2 Has she ever taken a computer course? 3 Does she want to find a new job now? (or: Does she now want to find a new job?) 4 Was she late for her interview yesterday? 5 Do her parents often write to her? (Do her parents write to her often?) 6 Have they phoned today?
2 7 type, 8 know, 9 daughter, 10 enough, 11 appointment, 12 o'clock
3 13 b, 14 c, 15 c, 16 c, 17 b, 18 a, 19 c, 20 b, 21 a, 22 a, 23 b, 24 b
4 The **correct** word is: 25 for, 26 borrow, 27 boss, 28 by, 29 always, 30 a, 31 since, 32 an

Checkpoint 5 (page 21) → Grammar (p. 127 + 131)
Grammar 1: 1 1 F/S, 2 S/F, 3 S/F
2 In sentence 1.
3 1 phoned, 2 had seen, 3 did not catch, 4 had already driven, 5 arrived, 6 came, 7 found, 8 had written, 9 remembered, 10 had gone
Grammar 2: 1 Correct answer: 1 … and you have to leave your house empty, you needn't worry because …
2 Necessary: 2, 4, 5. Not necessary: 1, 3, 6.
3 1 Du darfst es nicht machen. 2 Du brauchst es nicht zu machen.
How to say it: 1 You can't leave the door open. 2 You shouldn't leave the door open. 3 Please don't leave the door open. 4 You mustn't leave the door open.
Sentence 4 is the strongest.

Homestudy 5 (page 24)
1 1 cleaned, 2 had cleaned, 3 hadn't (or: had not) painted, 4 didn't (or: did not) paint, 5 had/ bought, 6 did/buy
2 1 don't have to or: needn't, 2 mustn't, 3 have to, 4 don't have to or: needn't
3 1 g, 2 f, 3 j, 4 h, 5 b, 6 c, 7 d, 8 e, 9 a, 10 i
4 1 Mary was worried because there had been several break-ins in her neighbourhood. 2 Mary felt safer after she had joined Neighbourhood Watch. 3 Eileen organized a meeting after two children had died in accidents.
5 1 F, 2 T, 3 T, 4 T, 5 F, 6 F, 7 F, 8 T
6 could, mustn't, people, should, sign, walk, window, would

Checkpoint 6 (page 25) → Grammar (p. 128–131, 136)
Grammar 1: 1 1 lives, 2 has lived, 3 lived, 4 had lived
2 1 five times a week, 2 for years, 3 in 1985, 4 two years later, 5 since then, 6 before that 7 some years ago
Grammar 2: 1 a little - less - least, bad - worse - worst, big - bigger - biggest, boring - more boring - most boring, good - better - best, interesting - more interesting - most interesting, many - more - most, noisy - noisier - noisiest, small - smaller - smallest
2 Correct answer: 1 His garden is more attractive than mine. 2 Their house isn't as nice as mine. 3 Her car was as expensive as mine.
How to say it: Offers: 1 (F) Shall, 2 Let, 3 Can
Requests: 1 Can, 2 (F) could, 3 Would

Homestudy 6 (page 28)
1 1 bought, 2 enough, 3 school, 4 quiet, 5 want, 6 future, 7 work, 8 do
2 1 Shall I open the window for you? 2 Let me turn the radio on (or: turn on the radio) for you. 3 Can I get you something to drink? 4 Can I borrow your bicycle please? (or: Can I please borrow your bicycle?) 5 Do you think I could use your phone? 6 Would you send this fax for me please? (or: Would you please send this fax for me?)
3 1 youngest, 2 heavier, 3 as many, 4 most expensive, 5 shorter, 6 thinner, 7 as tall, 8 oldest, 9 more beautiful (or younger)
4 1 bought, 2 ✓, 3 decided, 4 ✓, 5 has been, 6 ✓, 7 stays, 8 talked, 9 were, 10 ✓

Checkpoint 7 (page 29) → Grammar (p. 127, 139 + 141)
Grammar 1: 1 1 into, 2 in. 3 *Before* is used with expressions of time; *in front of* is used with expressions of place. 4 We are driving to Rome, but no farther / further. 5 It must be ready by Friday. 6 They are staying until 6 o'clock. 7 By the time we arrived, we had seen everything.
2 1= at the weekend (BrE), at 6.30 a.m., at Christmas, at night, at Easter, at midnight. 2 = in 1967, in summer, in the morning, in January, in autumn, in two years, in the afternoon. 3 = on the weekend (AmE), on Monday, on January 3rd.
Grammar 2: 1 any, 2 anything, 3 any, 4 anywhere, 5 somebody, 6 something, 7 some, 8 anybody, 9 somewhere. You use *some* in positive sentences and *any* in negative sentences and questions.
Grammar 3: Don't park here.
How to say it: 1 Excuse me, can you tell me the way to the station, please? 2 Excuse me, could you tell me how to get to the station, please?

Homestudy 7 (page 32)
1 The correct words are: 1 any, 2 some, 3 anybody, 4 some, 5 anywhere, 6 some, 7 something, 8 any, 9 Some, 10 anybody
2 1 straight, 2 right, 3 second, 4 opposite, 5 cathedral, 6 left, 7 next, 8 next, 9 opera house. Mark found himself at the National History Museum. 10 Excuse me, could you tell me, how to get to the Bank Art Gallery, please?
3 1 off, 2 at, 3 to, 4 by, 5 at, 6 until, 7 into, 8 By, 9 for
4 1 birthdays, 2 boxes, 3 buses, 4 cities, 5 ✗, 6 lorries, 7 ✗, 8 timetables, 9 a, 10 some, 11 an
5 attraction, cathedral, direction, gallery, imperative, information, instruction, restaurant

Checkpoint 8 (page 33) → Grammar (p. 125 + 139)
Grammar 1: 1 2 What did he fall in love with? 3 Where did

he move them to? 4 What has Su Ning helped him with? 5 What are they now proud of?
2 1 Why, 2 Where, 3 Whose, 5 What, 5 How
3 a) Wer hat Ian geholfen? b) Wem hat Su geholfen? 1 Who told Ian about the house? Who did Mrs Bailey tell about the house?
Grammar 2: 1 all of them, 2 most of them, 3 a lot of them, 4 some of them, 5 a few of them, 6 both of them, 7 one of them, 8 none of them
How to say it: 1 wood, plastic, paper, cotton, wool, metal
2 1 high / low, 2 long / short, 3 thick / thin, 4 wide / narrow
3 Correct answer: A pen is for writing.

Homestudy 8 (page 36)
I I When could you come to New York? 2 Is it possible to go sailing there? 3 Have you got a car in New York? 4 Is your house in a quiet area? 5 You don't have any children, do you?
2 1 Who rang (you) up? 2 Who is she angry with? 3 Who came to look at it? (or: Who came to look at her flat?) 4 Who did she take with her?
3 1 All, 2 Most, 3) a lot, 4 None, 5 a few (or: some), 6 two, 7 both
4 1 What is she interested in? 2 How many houses has she looked at? 3 Who did she talk to yesterday?
5 1 A bungalow is a kind of house. 2 A lorry is bigger than a car. 3 A magazine is made of paper. 4 Cities are noisier than villages. 5 Coffee is something to drink. 6 Igloos are made of snow and ice. 7 Microwaves are for heating food.

Wordfield: Houses (page 37)

12 balcony	6 dishwasher
1 bathroom	10 door
1 bedroom	5 door-viewer
2 bungalow	14 downstairs
6 carpet	2 farmhouse
5 chain	19 fence
9 chimney	6 freezer
2 cottage	6 fridge
4 decorate	15 garage
1 dining room	16 gate
2 igloo	3 owner
5 key	4 paint
1 kitchen	4 re-build
3 landlord	4 repair
17 lawn	8 roof
18 lawn-mower	6 telephone
1 living room	1 toilet
6 microwave	13 upstairs
3 neighbour	11 window
7 next door	

Test yourself 2 (page 40)
1 1 lives (or: is living), 2 has lived, 3 organised, 4 had been, 5 had never had, 6 gave, 7 had written, 8 hadn't (or: had not) posted, 9 wanted (or: wants)
2 10 Where does she live?11 How long has she lived here? 12 Why was she so angry? 13 Who did she write a letter to? 14 What else did she decide to do?
3 The correct word or expression is: 15 in, 16 needn't, 17 difficult, 18 transport, 19 in front of, 20 than, 21 off, 22 some, 23 opposite.
4 24 swap, 25 couple, 26 Wednesday, 27 thought, 28 beautiful, 29 neighbours (in American English: neighbors)
5 30 a, 31 b, 32 b, 33 b, 34 b, 35 c, 36 c, 37 c

Checkpoint 9 (page 41) → Grammar (p. 128, 132 + 140)
Grammar 1: 1 *Know, like, love, want, understand* are not normally used in the progressive form. Is / are dancing, is / are dying, is / are giving, is / are going, is / are lying, is / are running, is / are winning
2 1 What are you doing? Are you working? 2 No, I'm not working at the moment – I'm watching television 3 Do you do your homework every week? 4 No, I never do my homework.
3 1 collect, 2 are, 3 has, 4 is travelling, 5 is looking, 6 likes, 7 hope
Grammar 2: 1 Correct answer: 1 They looked at each other. 2 They looked at themselves. 3 We can look after ourselves.
2 1 yourself, 2 herself, 3 myself, 4 himself, 5 themselves
How to say it: 3a, 1b, 4c, 2d, 5e

Homestudy 9 (page 44)
1 1 comes, 2 is (or: 's) staying, 3 know, 4 does she come, 5 is (or: 's) doing, 6 does, 7 Does she play, 8 doesn't play, 9 plays (or: does play), 10 tries, 11 is trying, 12 does she speak, 13 think, 14 is coming
2 They used 2, 4, 5, 6 and 8.
3 1 himself, 2 ✗, 3 ✗, 4 ✗, 5 herself, 6 ✗, 7 ✗, 8 themselves
4 2 The dog is sitting, not standing. 3 The man is reading a newspaper, not a magazine. 4 Only two people are swimming (in the river), not three. 5 He is eating an apple, not an ice-cream. 6 She is drinking from a bottle, not a glass. 7 She (the girl) isn't wearing shoes. 8 He (the man) isn't carrying (or: wearing) a rucksack.

Checkpoint 10 (page 45) → Grammar (p. 136–138)
Grammar 1: 1 bad - badly, careful - carefully, clear - clearly, fast - fast, good - well, happy - happily, hard - hard, terrible - terribly
2 1 wonderful, 2 unusual, 3 comfortable, 4 warm, 5 warmly, 6 friendly, 7 strange, 8 well, 9 hard, 10 quickly
3 Correct answer: 1 carefully, 2 interesting.
Sentence 1 gives information about the verb. Sentence 2 gives information about the noun. Sentence 1 needs an adverb. Sentence 2 needs an adjective. Sentence 4 tells us about her health.
Grammar 2: badly - worse - the worst, carefully - more - carefully - the most carefully, clearly - more clearly - the most clearly, fast - faster - the fastest, hard - harder - the hardest, well - better - the best
How to say it: 2a, 3b, 1c

Homestudy 10 (page 48)
1 2 ✓,3 ✓, 4 hard, 5 sweet, 6 terrible, 7 ✓, 8 heavily, 9 well, 10 badly, 11 dangerous, 12 ✓
2 Verbs ending in [z]: feels, seems, smells, sounds. Verbs ending in [s]: forgets, looks, tastes, writes. Verb ending in [iz]: chooses. Nouns ending in [z]: buildings, rivers, walls. Nouns ending in [s]: breaks, groups, students. Nouns ending in [iz]: phrases, sentences, sunglasses.
3 First picture: "The Chocoholic Weekend"

Key

Second picture: "The Unhealthy Weekend"
Sentences: 1 True/so, 2 False/in order, 3 True/that's why, 4 True/because
4 Add -ly: attractively, beautifully, safely. Add -ally: automatically, enthusiastically, fantastically. Change y to i and add -ly: angrily, busily, easily, happily, luckily, noisily. Change -e to -y: comfortably, possibly, terribly

Checkpoint 11 (page 49) → Grammar (p. 127, 130 + 132)
Grammar 1: 1 The correct sentences are: 1 They were playing football when it started to rain, so they had to stop. 2 They stopped the game when it started to rain heavily. 3 While he was running to the clubhouse, he fell over and hurt his arm. 4 This time last Saturday we were drinking champagne in the bar.
2 1 had to, 2 didn't (or: did not) like, 3 could, 4 was practising, 5 saw, 6 wasn't swimming, 7 got, 8 pushed, 9 was swimming, 10 didn't (or: did not) seem
3 Tick sentence 2: They were putting on their sports clothes when he arrived.
Grammar 2: 1 Winston had to practise every day. He wasn't allowed to go out in the afternoons and had to go to bed early so that he could play in the team on Saturday.
2 1 Sie durften im Clubhaus nicht rauchen. 2 Die Gäste mussten sich in das Gästebuch eintragen. 3 Die Mitglieder brauchten keine Karten zu kaufen.
How to say it: 2 That's all right. 4 It doesn't matter.

Homestudy 11 (page 52)
1 Just add *-ing*: doing, drinking, playing, watching
Double the last letter, then add *-ing*: jogging, running, stopping, swimming, winning
Leave off the final *-e*, then add *-ing*: changing
2 1 They were playing tennis when I arrived. 2 She was climbing a tree when I arrived. 3 No, they weren't (or: were not) swimming when I arrived. 4 No, he wasn't (or: was not) playing golf when I arrived. 5 Was she jogging (or: running) when you arrived? 6 Were they playing vollyball when you arrived?
3 The correct forms are: 1 was jogging, 2 was shining, 3 were playing, 4 was running, 5 heard, 6 stopped, 7 asked, 8 answered, 9 were playing
4 Dialogue 1. Apology: I'm awfully sorry … Reactions: That's all right. I don't mind. Dialogue 2. Apology: I'm terribly sorry. Reactions: Never mind. It can't be helped. Dialogue 3. Apology: I'm so sorry. Reactions: It doesn't matter. Don't worry about it. The other three apologies were not used in the dialogues.
5 1 They had to arrive by 8.00 am. (in the morning). 2 They weren't allowed to leave before 5.00 pm. (in the afternoon). 3 They weren't allowed to eat in the office. 4 They were allowed only to smoke in the canteen. 5 The men had to wear suits and ties.

Checkpoint 12 (page 53) → Grammar (p. 138 + 140)
Grammar 1: 1 1 their, 2 they, 3 mine, 4 my, 5 yours, 6 ours, 7 our, 8 theirs, 9 his, 10 her, 11 their
2 Correct answer: **It's** only a small shop but what I like about it best is **its** friendly atmosphere.
Grammar 2: 1 1 = bread, change, furniture, information, news, tea. 2 = biscuits, clothes, people, vegetables
2 1 much, 2 many, 3 many, 4 much
3 A: How many miles is it to the shopping centre?
B: Only a few.
A: How much petrol have you got?
B: Only a little.
How to say it: Order of pictures: 1, 3, 2. Situation 2 is the most formal and situation 3 the most informal.

Homestudy 12 (page 56)
1 Ingrid bought a lot of blouses in London. 2 She spent a lot of money at the department store. 3 She didn't buy many books. 4 She didn't drink much Irish whiskey. 5 Did she eat many scones with her tea? 6 Did she put much (or: a lot of) cream in her tea?
2 1 her, 2 few, 3 suited, 4 much, 5 fit, 6 you're, 7 many, 8 It's, 9 your. Words not needed: fits, hers, its, little, suit, suits, yours.
3 1 [æ] as in c<u>a</u>t: back, bad, fashion, jam, match, sandwich, thank. 2 [a:] as in f<u>a</u>ther: department, market. 3 [ei] as in m<u>a</u>ke: cake, change, conversation, day, hate, pay, take.
4 1 some, 2 some, 3 some, 4 a, 5 some, 6 a, 7 a, 8 an, 9 some, 10 an. The five uncountable nouns are: time, sightseeing, luggage, information, tea.
5 1 You're welcome. 2 That's quite all right. 3 Don't mention it.

Wordfield: British and American English (page 57)
1 1 centre, 2 colour, 3 licence, 4 neighbour, 5 organisation, 6 pay by cheque, 7 programme, 8 theatre, 9 travelling
2 1 car park / parking lot, 2 driving-licence / driver's license, 3 dustbin / garbage can, 4 flat / apartment, 5 housing estate / housing development, 6 lorry / truck, 7 postal code / zip code, 8 queue (verb) / line up, 9 shop assistant / salesclerk, 10 telephone box / telephone booth, 11 tick / check (✔), 12 tram / streetcar, 13 transport / transportation

Test yourself 3 (page 60)
1 1b, 2b, 3c, 4c, 5b, 6b, 7c, 8b, 9c, 10b, 11c, 12c
2 The <u>correct</u> words are: 13 do, 14 much, 15 each other, 16 few, 17 themselves, 18 strange, 19 likes, 20 suit, 21 nice, 22 quietly, 23 good
3 24 The (members of the) orchestra welcomed her politely. 25 She conducted energetically. 26 The orchestra played beautifully.
4 27 although, 28 disadvantages, 29 busy, 30 seldom, 31 leisure, 32 schedules

Checkpoint 13 (page 61) → Grammar (p. 133)
Grammar 1: 1 1 She's (or: is) going to phone. 2 It's going to rain. 3 They're (or: are) going to crash.
2 What are you going to do? 1 She is going to look for a job in France. 2 Are her parents going to visit her? 3 I'm not going to visit her.
Grammar 2: Sentences 2 and 3 are talking about the future. The *present progressive* is used in sentence 1: She is taking the exam *now*. The *present progressive* is used in sentence 3: She is taking the exam *tomorrow*.
You can use the *present progressive* in sentence 4 (*They are getting married tomorrow)* and sentence 6 (*They are arriving here at 8 o'clock*).
Grammar 1 & 2: 1a) a present activity, 3b) a plan for the future, 2c) a definite arrangement for the future.
How to say it: 1 On the right of the paper. After the address. At the end of the letter.
2 1b, 2c, 3a

Key

Homestudy 13 (page 64)

1 2 Is she going to study on Sunday, too? 3 Yes, she is. 4 She isn't going to study on Monday. (or: On Monday she isn't going to study.) 5 What is she going to do on Monday? 6 She and Paul are going to play tennis on Monday. (or: On Monday she and Paul are going to play tennis.)

2 activity, arrangements, differences, education, envelopes, intentions, interesting, mathematics, progressive, reservation, secondary, subject.

3 afternoon, definite, different, enough, often, paragraph, photography, professor, uniforms.

4 Answers to the questions: 1 Kindergarten; 2 all the grades from kindergarten to the end of high school; 3 the correct order: *1 freshman, 2 sophomore, 3 junior, 4 senior;* 4 flunk. Nursery school, age 3-4; kindergarten, age 5, grade K; elementary school, age 6-11, grades 1-6; junior high school, age 12-13, grades 7-8; high school, age 14-17, grades 9-12; college, age 18-21.

5 Dear Ms Patterson,
Thank you very much for your nice letter. I have (or: I've) just bought my (or: a/the) plane ticket.
I am (or: I'm) flying from London to Marseilles on August 2nd at 14:30 (or: at 2.30 p.m., or: at half past two in the afternoon). Tomorrow I am (or: I'm) going to buy a map of the South of France. Next weekend I am (or: I'm) going to read a book about Marseilles. I am (or: I'm) looking forward to meeting you and working in your (or: the) bookshop.
Yours sincerely, Karen Lewis

Checkpoint 14 (page 65) → Grammar (p. 133)

Grammar 1: 1 *Ago, last week, lately, yesterday* cannot be used with the *future tense*.

2 Question: Will he lend you his book? Negative: He won't lend you his book.

3 1 spontaneous decision: 1, 6. 2 predictions: 3, 4. 3 future facts: 2, 5.

4 Correct answers: 1 He will go later. = Er wird später gehen. 2 He wants to go later. = Er will später gehen.

Grammar 2: Sentence 2 makes it clear that he has just at this moment decided to watch the film. Sentence 1 makes it clear that the speaker decided some time ago to watch the film.

How to say it: 1 I hope he won't read it. 2 Perhaps he won't read it. 3 I'm not sure they will read it. 4 I don't think she will read it. 5 He mightn't read it. 6 I probably won't read it. 7 I don't expect he will read it. 8 He may not read it.

Homestudy 14 (page 68)

1 1 Will we all have kitchen robots twenty years from now? 2 Are you going to watch that stupid comedy show on TV? 3 Will television change very much in the next ten years? 4 Is your daughter going to watch TV tonight?

2 1 are you going to do, 2 I'm going to have, 3 I'll look, 4 Is he going to stay, 5 he'll move, 6 will your parents feel, 7 They're going to retire, 8 they'll spend.

3 1c, 2b, 3d, 4a. There are spontaneous decisions in dialogues 1 and 4, plans already made in 2 and 3, predictions in 2 and 4.

4 1 certain, sure; 2 may, might; 3 maybe, perhaps, probably, possibly; 4 expect, hope, think.

5 2 ✗, 3 ✗, 4 ✓, 5 ✗, 6 ✗, 7 ✗, 8 ✗, 9 ✓, 10 ✗.

Checkpoint 15 (page 69) → Grammar (p. 126 + 134)

Grammar 1: 1 The correct sentence is 2: She'll leave Britain when she finishes her tour.

2 1 When she arrives in London, she'll go jogging. 2 Before she sings in front of thousands of people, she'll meditate. 3 As soon as she gets back to her hotel, she'll order a meal … .

Grammar 2: 1 If he drinks too much, he'll have a headache tomorrow. 2 They'll lose weight if they eat less. They won't lose weight, if they don't eat less.
Sentence **a** tells us that he is sure he will see her.

How to say it: 1 like, love, enjoy. 2 I don't mind. 3 I hate, I don't like, I dislike. 4 I enjoy going to a restaurant. 5 They don't mind cooking dinner. 6 Was mögen Sie? / Was haben Sie gern? 7 Was möchten Sie?

Homestudy 15 (page 72)

1 1 will be, 2 'll (or: will or: shall) make, 3 arrive, 4 get, 5 'll (or: will or: shall) have, 6 'll (or: will or: shall) get, 7 'll (or: will or: shall) call, 8 are, 9 get, 10 'll (or: will or: shall) buy.

2 2 Yes, if you eat a salad, you'll get some vitamins. 3 Yes, if he eats fish, he won't put on weight. 4 Yes, if she goes jogging every day, she'll keep fit. 5 Yes, if we have a drink, we won't be thirsty later. 6 Yes, if I go out for a walk, I'll feel better. 7 You will feel better if you get some sleep. 8 If we ask them, they will tell us what happened. 9 They will go swimming tomorrow if they have time.

3 salad, fish, pear, soup, meat, tomato, bread, egg, garlic, cake; steak, apple, lemon, water, food, scone.

4 Clive likes 2 and 5. He dislikes 3 and 4. The ones he neither likes nor dislikes very much are 1 and 6. He used six of the nine expressions: I dislike, I don't mind, I enjoy, I hate, I love, I prefer.

5 1 [e] as in bread: breakfast, headache, health, heavy. 2 [i:] as in eat: cream, each, leave, meal, meaning, meat. 3 [ei] as in break: great, steak.

Checkpoint 16 (page 73) → Grammar (p. 124 + 141)

Grammar 1: In question b you expect the answer *yes*.
Correct question tags: 1 hasn't it? 2 don't they? 3 didn't it? 4 can you? 5 will they?

Grammar 2: 1 1 who, 2 which. **That** can replace **who** and **which** in the above sentences.

2 Who is used to talk about people. **Which** is used to talk about things. **That** is used for people and things.

3 1 New York, the city we visited next, has got more Irish people in it than Dublin. 2 The Irish are the people **who** drink the most tea. 3 Los Angeles is a city **which** has got more cars than people. 4 The town I was telling you about has got more psychotherapists than postmen.

How to say it: 1 Correct answers: 1 Personally speaking …, 2 What's your opinion? 3 … – what do you think?

2 1 So did I. 2 Neither will I. 3 Neither was I. 4 So am I. 5 I do too. 6 I don't either.

Homestudy 16 (page 76)

1 1 doesn't it? 2 don't they? 3 isn't it? 4 hasn't he? 5 won't I? 6 should I? 7 will you? 8 do you?

2 1d, 2h, 3a, 4e, 5c, 6f, 7g, 8b.

3 5, 1, 4, 2, 3.

4 1 which, 2 who, 3 who, 4 who. The words numbered 5, 7, 9, 10, 11 and 12 can be left out.

5 1 Peter (or: He) has (or: 's) grown a lot lately, hasn't he?

Key

2 He lives next door, doesn't he? 3 He isn't very good at maths, is he? 4 He won't stay out too late, will he? 5 He'll be home by seven o'clock, won't he?
6 Italy – Italian; nation – nationality; person – personality; photograph – photography; possible – possibility; probably – probability; reserve – reservation; vegetable – vegetarian.

Wordfields 4: Education, health, the media (page 77)
Education: exam, homework, lesson, marks, maths, primary, pupil, secondary.
Health: backache, disease, fitness, flu, overweight, relaxation, stress, vegetarian.
The Media: advert, articles, broadcasting, channel, entertainment, headline, news, screen.

1 advertisement, examination, mathematics;
2 unhealthy, vegetarian, overweight; 3 secondary;
4 British Broadcasting Corporation; 5 radio; 6 daily newspaper;
7 weekly magazine

Test yourself 4 (page 80)
1 1 Is she going to write the report tomorrow? 2 She's not (or: She isn't) going to write the report tomorrow. 3 Will it be warmer tomorrow? 4 It won't be warmer tomorrow. 5 Are they flying to London on Tuesday? 6 They aren't (or: They're not) flying to London on Tuesday. 7 Does their plane leave at 9:35? 8 Their plane doesn't leave at 9:35.
2 9 too, 10 listened, 11 advice, 12 exercise, 13 fruit, 14 weight
3 15 When Jeff gets home, he'll (or: he will) make some tea. 16 Before he watches TV, he'll (or: he will) go for a walk.
4 The correct words are: 17 comes, 18 think, 19 Austrian, 20 wants to, 21 get, 22 reads, 23 daily, 24 does, 25 homework, 26 take, 27 only, 28 wears, 29 opinion, 30 seriously.
5 31 c, 32 b, 33 c, 34 a, 35 a, 36 a, 37 a, 38 c

Checkpoint 17 (page 81) → Grammar (p. 126)
Grammar 1: 1 1 true, 2 false, 3 true, 4 false
2 1 were, 2 would send, 3 were, 4 would be
3 1 If I were you, I would invite him. 2 Would you go to the party if he invited you? 3 I wouldn't be here if my English were (or: was) perfect.
Grammar 2: 1 1 to go, 2 going, 3 going, 4 going, 5 to go, 6 to go, 7 going, 8 going, 9 to go
2 After prepositions (of, in, about) we use the gerund.
3 1 I'm looking forward to hearing from you. 2 He suggested telling her. 3 When we were children we used to play there.
How to say it: 2a, 1b, 4c, 3d

Homestudy 17 (page 84)
1 1 T, 2 T, 3 F, 4 F, 5 T, 6 F, 7 T, 8 d, 9 e, 10 b, 11 c, 12 a.
2 1 boys, 2 music, 3 father, 4 school, 5 work, 6 great, 7 that, 8 time
3 2 If he took the bus he'd (or: he would) be late for the meeting. 3 If they drove all night they'd be terribly tired tomorrow. 4 If she bought a new car she wouldn't (or: would not) have enough money for her holiday.
4 2 John isn't here. 3 They don't live nearby. 4 Mary might call. 5 I don't know his address. 6 I might see him tonight. 7 He isn't rich.
5 1 She's very good at writing books and articles. 2 Would you mind turning the TV down (or: turning down the TV) a bit (please)? 3 I'm looking forward to seeing you next week. 4 He's afraid of going out at night. 5 I always enjoy travelling by train.

Checkpoint 18 (page 85) → Grammar (p. 133 + 134)
Grammar 1: 1 1 What a good idea! I think I'll have a fancy-dress party on my birthday, too. 2 I'm going to have a party so I must write a shopping list. 3 Hi, Peter, I'm having a party on Saturday and I'd like to invite you.
1 = a spontaneous idea, 3 = a definite arrangement, 2 = a plan.
2 On Tuesday (at 9 o'clock) she is flying to Paris at 9 o'clock (on Tuesday). The airport bus leaves at 7.15 a.m. If she misses it, she'll take a taxi.
Grammar 2: 1 Sentence 2 tells you the tickets belong to one girl. Sentence 1 tells you the tickets belong to more than one girl.
2 1 He's going to the baker's to buy cakes. 2 We're staying at my sister's at Easter. 3 He's a friend of ours. 4 She's a colleague of theirs. 5 He's a cousin of mine.
How to say it: 1 to have, 2 having, 3 have, 4 love, 5 afraid, 6 kind.
To refuse an invitation you can use sentence 5. To accept an invitation you can use sentence 4. To thank someone for the invitation, use sentence 6.

Homestudy 18 (page 88)
1
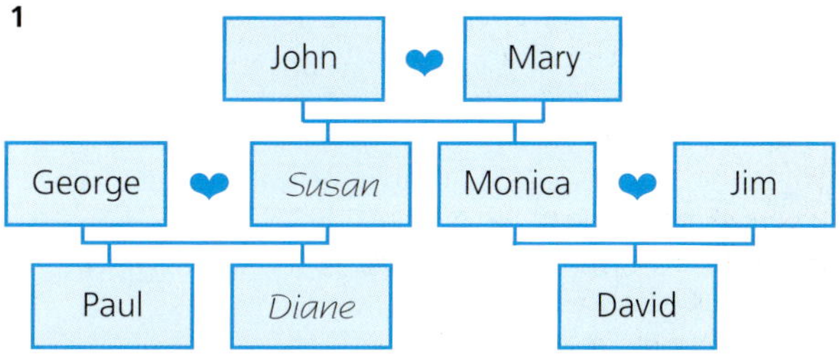

2 1 aunt, 2 niece, 3 nephew, 4 cousin, 5 grandsons, 6 granddaughter, 7 brother-in-law.
3 [z] as in *begins*: 5, 7, 9, 12.
[s] as in *helps*: 2, 3, 4, 10.
[z] as in *changes*: 1, 6, 8, 11.
4 2 My grandfather's house is beautiful. 3 The boys' car isn't very clean. 4 Tom is a colleague of Jim's. (or: Tom is one of Jim's colleagues.)
5 The correct forms are: 1 is going to visit, 2 has, 3 will travel, 4 leaves, 5 goes, 6 will be, 7 will be able to sleep. Diane says: 9 I'm (or: I am) driving into town with Paul. 10 I'm (or: I am) going to buy my ticket today. 11 I'll (or: I will) buy one (or: buy a map of Germany) this afternoon.
6 1 Would you like to come to my party? 2 I'd like to invite you to my party. 3 How about coming to my party?

Checkpoint 19 (page 89) → Grammar (p. 124, 128–129, 132)
Grammar 1: 1 works, 2 is, 3 has only been, 4 is not working, 5 feels, 6 need, 7 doesn't mind, 8 has had, 9 has worked, 10 has already learnt
Dr Young has been a doctor for about ten years. He likes his work and he always works during his holidays. He has just flown to Ghana and at the moment he is working in a hospital there.
Grammar 2: b) 4, 5; c) 1, 2, 3; d) 4, 5; e) 4, 5
How to say it: 1 What a pretty dress. Thank you. I got it yesterday. 2 You did a very good job. It's nice of you to say so.

Homestudy 19 (page 92)

1 /ðə/, as in *the book*: 2, 4, 5, 8, 9; /ði:/, as in *the apple*: 1, 3, 6, 7, 10

2 1 This month Ralph Young is in Ghana. or: Ralph Young is in Ghana this month. 2 He is going to stay here for three more weeks. 3 He always spends his holidays working in Africa. 4 He is always ready to help. 5 Often he treats people who are terribly ill. or: He often treats people who are terribly ill. or: He treats people who are often terribly ill. 6 He has just written a report about his work. 7 Next month he'll be in Chicago for a convention. or: He'll be in Chicago next month for a convention. or: He'll be in Chicago for a convention next month.

3 independent, inexpensive, unfriendly, unhealthy, impolite, irregular, dissatisfied, unusual.

4 2 How long has he been a doctor? 3 Is he now in his fifties? or: Is he in his fifties now? 4 Does he usually work in Sussex? 5 Is he now working in Ghana? or: Is he working in Ghana now? 6 Does (or: can) he speak the local language? 7 How many languages has he already learnt? or: How many languages has he learnt already?

5 b, d, e, f.

Checkpoint 20 (page 93) → Grammar (p. 128, 130–132)

Grammar 1: 1 1 was riding, 2 stopped, 3 said, 4 were riding, 5 saw, 6 was, 7 had reached, 8 had not realised / did not realise, 9 started, 10 told, 11 did not arrest, 12 had, 13 was, 14 was

I used to have a motor bike myself when I was younger.

2 3a, 4b, 2c, 1d

Grammar 2: 1 Sentence number 2 tells you that he has repaired his motorbike himself and sentence number 1 tells you that someone does this for him.

Match these German translations: 2a, 1b.

When did he have his bike repaired?

How to say it: 3a, 1b, 4c, 2d

Homestudy 20 (page 96)

1 1 Did she use to work in a factory? 2 Was she waiting at home when the phone rang? 3 Did her daughter-in-law encourage her to become a model?

4 Had she ever thought about becoming a model before she saw that advert?

Tenses: 1 d, 2 b+a, 3 a, 4 c+a

2 1 Bless you. 2 Come in. 3 Nice to meet you. 4 Congratulations.

3 The correct expressions are: 1 had the windows cleaned, 2 had ironed them, 3 have it washed.

4 The pictures: b 2 Molly, e 3 Silke, f 1 Cynthia.

The answers to the questions: 1, 2, 1, 2, 3, 2, 3.

5 The fourteen words that have the sound /ʃ/ in them are: attractions, brush, exhibitions, information, invitation, patient, professional, share, she, shop, should, shy, situation, sure.

The six words that do not have the sound /ʃ/ in them are: chair, enthusiastic, professor, school, stress, student.

Wordfields 5: Synonyms and antonyms (page 97)

1 1j, 2k, 3g, 4c, 5k, 6f, 7d, 8o, 9h, 10i, 11n, 12m, 13b, 14a, 15e

2 1 disadvantage, 2 dirty (or: unclean), 3 incorrect or: wrong, 4 uncountable, 5 easy, 6 unemployed or: out of work, 7 inexpensive or: cheap, 8 light, 9 quiet, 10 unpopular, 11 impossible, 12 dangerous or: unsafe

Test yourself 5 (page 100)

1 1 c, 2 b, 3 a, 4 b, 5 b, 6 c, 7 b, 8 a

2 9 autumn, 10 campaign, 11 worried, 12 nephew, 13 neither, 14 experience

3 The correct words and expressions are: 15 his, 16 taught, 17 goes, 18 often visits, 19 rides, 20 fast

4 21 Why did a policeman stop him yesterday? 22 Where was he riding at 85 mph on his motorbike (or: on his motorbike at 85 mph)? 23 How old will he be next September? 24 What did the policeman later say about Arthur (or: What did the police man say later about Arthur? or: What did the policeman say about Arthur later?)

5 25 Do they cut their hair themselves? No, they have it cut at the hairdresser's. 26 Did she wash the windows herself? No, she had them washed by the cleaning woman. 27 Is he going to type the letters himself? No, he's (or: : he is) going to have them typed at the office. 28 Does he clean the steps himself? No, he has them cleaned by the boy next door. 29 Are they going to paint the house them selves? No, they 're (or: they are) going to have them painted.

Tapescripts Homestudy

Unit 1: Exercise 5 (page 4)

- Hans, what does LETS mean, again?
- I don't remember. The, the S is for System, I think.
- Oh, here it is, on page 2. LETS means Local Exchange Trading System.
- You haven't got anything like that in France, have you?
- Yes, of course we have. They're called SEL. In the south of France, where I come from, there are over a hundred groups like that.
- Sell? Is that the English word sell, as in buy and sell?
- No, no. The English word sell is spelled with two Ls, S-E-double-L, but our French word SEL only has one L, S-E-L. It really means salt, like you put on your food …
- Like salt and pepper?
- Yes, but the groups, the organisations with the name SEL call themselves *"Système d'échange local"*, that means System of Local Exchange.
- That sounds just like LETS. Do they pay in bobbins, too?
- Well, it's the same idea, but in France they aren't called bobbins, they're called grains de sel. That would be in English grains – grains of salt.
- Grains of salt?
- Yes, those are very small, you know, little round pieces of salt.
- Ah, yes, in German that would be *Salzkörner*.
- That sounds funny. Do you have any groups like that in Germany, you know, organisations like LETS or SEL?
- Yes, we do. They're often called *Tauschringe*, that means trading rings or trading circles. There are about 200 of them in Germany, but not everybody knows about them.
- Do they have bobbins, too?
- In Kassel, where I come from, there's a group called the *Zeitbörse*, that means "time exchange," and instead of bobbin they call it *Talent*. A *Talent* is what you get for three minutes of work, so if you work for an hour you get twenty talents for it.
- So in England they use bobbins, in France *grains of salt* and in Germany *Talents*.
- Yes, but bobbins are only in Manchester. In other parts of England they have other names.
- Who told you that?
- Our teacher. In the break. And some of the German groups have other names, too. Some of them say *Kreuzer*, and some of them use an English word, peanuts.
- That's funny. You do lots of work and you get paid peanuts for it …
- What's so funny about that? I think peanuts are, you know, little salty things to eat, like in German *Erdnüsse*.
- Well, I don't know about in German, but yes, peanuts are little things to eat, like when you drink a glass of wine with some friends, but in English they also say peanuts for a very small amount of money, you know, not very much money. I heard this one American say that: 'Aww, that's only peanuts.'
- Ah, yes, of course, you're right. In Germany we have lots of big banks, you know, and our bankers say that sometimes, too. One German banker said that – I heard it on television. His bank lost millions of marks somehow, and he said it was only 'peanuts'.

Unit 2: Exercise 3 (page 8)

Dialogue 1

- Hello, my name's Cartwright, Len Cartwright. I deliver milk in this area for the local dairy.
- Pleased to meet you, Mr Cartwright. I'm Jim Rogers and I've just moved here from Chicago. In the States nobody delivers milk any more, at least not in my neighborhood.

Dialogue 2

- Mary, I'd like you to meet a new neighbour, Jim Rogers. Mr Rogers is American. He's just moved here from Chicago. Mr Rogers, this is Mary Duckworth.
- Nice to meet you, Mrs Duckworth.
- Welcome, Mr Rogers. I've lived here all my life, and we've never had an American neighbour before.

Dialogue 3

- Mr Rogers, I would like to introduce you to our local bank manager, Mr Williams.
- How do you do?
- How do you do, Mr Rogers.

Dialogue 4

- Mr Rogers, this is Lin Wang. Lin lives just down the street, and he's the man to ask if you need any repairs or odd jobs.
- Hello, Lin, I'm happy to meet you. You can call me Jim.

Unit 4: Exercise 2 (page 16)

- Good afternoon, Leason Industries, Manchester. Can I help you?
- Good morning, this is Paul Quayle calling from Toronto, Canada. I'd like to speak to Mr Leason, please.
- Could you hold on a moment, please, I'll see if he's in his office.
- Sure enough.
- Please hold the line while we'll try and connect you.
- I'm sorry, Mr Leason isn't at his desk at the moment, he's out in the factory. Would you like to leave a message?
- Yes, please. Tell him Paul Quayle called from Toronto, he met me at the trade fair last year.
- Is that Q-U-A-I-L?
- No, it's a Y, not an I. Q-U-A-Y-L-E, Paul Quayle.
- Has he got your telephone number, Mr Quayle?
- I think so, but please take it down again just to make sure. It's 001-416-555-3471.
- That's 001 for North America, area code 416, telephone number 555-3471.
- That's right. Tell him I've received his letter and I've spoken to Mr Smith about it. Mr Smith seems very interested.
- All right. You've received his letter and you've spoken to Mr Smith about it. Mr Smith seems very interested.
- That's right. Thank you.
- Thank you for ringing, Mr Quayle. Have a nice day. Goodbye.
- Goodbye.

Unit 5: Exercise 5 (page 24)

- Hello, everybody. It's eight o'clock, so let's get started, shall we? I'm sorry not everybody has got a seat. The room's really too small for so many people, isn't it? We've never had a meeting like this before, and I had no idea so many of you would come. Well, as you all know, we've got a serious problem with the dangerous traffic in our street, and we have to do something about it before more of our children are killed or injured. I've written a letter to the council, but I haven't sent it yet. I've made some copies so you can all read

it, and, if you agree, we can all sign it and send it to the council.
- I don't know if that'll do any good, Eileen. The council doesn't usually pay much attention to people like us.
- That's true, but we mustn't give up. We'll have to make them pay attention.
- Right. Let's paint some big signs and put them up at the corners.
- That's a good idea. We could even go to a council meeting and take some signs with us.
- Does anybody know a council member, by any chance? I don't, but I've looked up their names and telephone numbers. I haven't talked to any of them yet, though.
- Why don't we ring them all up? Each of us could take one name and number. If we explain the problem politely, maybe they'll understand how important it is.
- Good idea. And I'll ring up the newspaper, if nobody's done that yet.
- No, nobody has. Ask them to come round with a photographer. If we all work together, we can make the council do something for our children ...

Unit 7: Exercise 2 (page 32)
- Ahh, M'am. Excuse me, could you tell me how to get to the Bank Art Gallery, please?
- The Bank Art Gallery, of course, that's one of the most interesting art galleries in the whole city. Everybody here knows where that is. Just walk up to the next corner, young man, you see where the traffic lights are, by the bus stop, and turn left into Green Street. Go along Green Street until you come to Victoria Square. You'll see a large white building there, that's the opera house. And the art gallery is next to the opera house. You can't miss it.
- Thank you very much.
- That's quite all right, young man. I hope you'll enjoy it.

Unit 8: Exercise 1 (page 36)
- Hello.
- Hello, my name is Klaus Schmeder. I'm calling from Germany, and I'd like to speak to Don Ryan, please.
- Speaking.
- Yes, Mr Ryan, I got your letter from the Homeswapping magazine. You said you might be interested in swapping your apartment in New York for our house in Bavaria for a few weeks in September.
- That's right, I could get away from the first to the twentieth of September, and I'd like to do something a bit different. When could you come to New York?
- The beginning of September would be fine. My wife and I can only stay till the sixteenth, but our friends could stay until the twentieth.
- It says here that your house is near a lake, and I love water sports. Is it possible to go sailing there?
- Yes, you can rent a boat by the day or week. It's only a ten-minute-walk to the lake, but you can also use our car while you're here. Have you got a car in New York?
- No, I don't have a car here, I'm afraid, but otherwise the apartment has everything, including a fantastic view of the city. It's on the 39th floor, so it's very quiet up here. Is your house in a quiet area?
- Yes, it is.
- Good. That all sounds fine. I just have one more question. You don't have any children, do you?
- No, we don't.
- Good. I don't have anything against kids, but this apartment just isn't the right place for them, that's all.

Unit 9: Exercise 2 (page 44)
- Hello, Anna, how are you?
- Oh, hi, Len. I'm fine, thanks. And you?
- I'm fine, too. Anna, this is Robin. Robin, this is Anna, from Brazil.
- Hello, Robin. Don't I know you? Haven't we met before?
- Yes, we met at a party about two weeks ago.
- Who's that woman you were just talking to?
- That's Claire. We go to school together.
- Well, I must be off. Bye, Robin, see you later.
- Goodbye, have a nice day.

Unit 10: Exercise 3 (page 48)
- How did you get your weekend job, Anna?
- I just went in and asked for it. I was mainly looking for an opportunity to practise my English. I saw the hotel brochure, and as I don't have enough money to go there as a guest, I decided I wanted to work there. I got the job because of the Chocoholic Weekend. They thought as I'm Brazilian I must know all about chocolate. In fact I've never even seen a cacao tree, and I never eat chocolate because it wouldn't be good for my skin or my figure, but I didn't tell them any of that, I just said, oh yes, we Brazilians know all about chocolate, we all grow it in our gardens; we eat it for breakfast, lunch, tea and supper and drink it in the pub. I don't think they really believed me, but they laughed and gave me the job as the local chocolate expert. I even lead the tour of the chocolate factory, which smells wonderful and exciting but looks just like any regular dirty old factory. And in the evening I just talk to the guests and help them up to their rooms when they feel sick from eating too much chocolate.
- And what do you do for the other theme weekends?
- Oh, they always find something for me to do. At the last Antique Weekend I just worked at reception, there was so much to do. You should have seen all the antiques, people came with big lorries full of them. And at the Unhealthy Weekend my job was to lead a secret sports class.
- A secret sports class?
- Yes, a secret sports class, for those who wanted a rest from being decadent. We went jogging and did aerobics. It's all a bit crazy, but everybody has a good time on these weekends, and if they don't, I have to find out what's wrong and try to fix it.
- It sounds like the ideal job for you.
- It is, but when I tell my Brazilian friends about it, they don't believe me, they think the English are so stiff and formal and serious. The best thing about the job is that I get to speak English all the time, except for the French weekend, when I have to go around speaking French to everybody, even if they don't understand a word I'm saying. To make them feel like they're in France.

Unit 11: Exercise 4 (page 52)
Dialogue 1
- Oh, good, you're still here. I'm awfully sorry I kept you waiting.
- That's all right. I don't mind.

Dialogue 2
- Oh, my goodness. I'm terribly sorry. I seem to have broken something.
- Never mind. It can't be helped.

Dialogue 3
- Ouch!
- Oh, I stepped on your foot. I'm so sorry.
- It doesn't matter. Don't worry about it.

Unit 12: Exercise 5 (page 56)

Dialogue 1
- Here's your tea and your cakes.
- Thank you.
- You're welcome.

Dialogue 2
- Excuse me. I seem to have lost a bag full of things I'd bought. Is it here, by any chance?
- Well, I'll have a look. What colour is the bag?
- It's green.
- Well then, this must be your bag here.
- Yes, that one is mine. Thank you very much.
- That's quite all right.

Dialogue 3
- Excuse me, could you tell me if there are any flights to Frankfurt on Monday morning?
- Yes, there's a flight at 10.45 and another one at 11.50. Would you like a timetable?
- Oh yes, please. Thank you for your help.
- Don't mention it. Next please.

Unit 13: Exercise 4 (page 64)

- What's it like in America, Marc? How old are children when they start school?
- Well, when they're three or four years old they can go to nursery school if they want to.
- Or if their parents want them to.
- Yes, but when they're five years old they all have to go to kindergarten.
- They have to?
- Yes, they all have to go to kindergarten when they're five. They're not allowed to stay home any more.
- 'Kindergarten' is actually a German word, I think.
- Yes, but in German it means something different. Their kindergarten is like our nursery school.
- So in the States you have nursery school for the three- and four-year-old childen, and all the five-year-olds have to go to kindergarten.
- Right. Kindergarten in America is actually part of the school system, grade K they call it sometimes. My mother is a K to 12 teacher, that means she can teach in any grade from kindergarten to the end of high school.
- And what comes after kindergarten?
- After kindergarten the children go to the first grade, that's the beginning of elementary school.
- So the first grade is when the children are six years old?
- Yes, from 6 to 11 they go to elementary school, that's grades 1 to 6, and after that comes junior high school.
- That's something we haven't got in England. The American 'junior high school' is just for two years, isn't it, Marc?
- Usually, yes, in most places in the States junior high school is just the seventh and eighth grades, when the kids are 12 and 13 years old.
- And then they have to change schools again. I don't think I'd like that.
- Why not? After junior high school comes high school, which is usually four years. They're called the freshman, sophomore, junior and senior years.
- So a 'freshman' is actually a fourteen-year-old boy …
- … or girl …
- … in his, or her, first year of high school.
- Yes, that's right, but a freshman can also be an eighteen-year-old in his, or her, first year of college. First you're a freshman, sophomore, junior and senior in high school …
- … that's grades 9, 10, 11 and 12.
- Yes, and then if you go to college you start over again and you're a freshman, sophomore, junior and senior in college.
- The strange thing to me is that 'junior' is the third year, not the first.
- Oh, I'd never thought of that.
- So a senior in high school is about 17 and a senior in college is 21.
- Well, usually, yes. I mean, if you don't flunk out or anything.
- Flunk out?
- Flunk is American, Martine. F-L-U-N-K. It means to fail. When you don't pass.
- Un-huh.
- Which will happen to me if I don't get back to my lessons.

Unit 14: Exercise 3 (page 68)

Dialogue 1
- How do you like this one?
- Well, it's just my size. It fits me perfectly, but I'm not really sure the colour suits me. Have you got any others?
- Yes, of course. Here's a red one that's very nice. And here's a black one that might suit you.
- Mmmm. Well, yes, I'll try it on.

Dialogue 2
- You look excited.
- Me? I'm not excited.
- Come on, I know you better than that. You're all red in the face, and you're smiling from ear to ear.
- Well, I do smile sometimes, just for no reason. I'm a fairly happy person, I think.
- Yes, but not like that. There must be something new.
- Well, there is one little thing.
- What?
- Well, I didn't want to tell anybody yet, but – don't tell anybody else, okay? Bob and I are going to get married.
- Oh that's marvellous. I'm sure you'll be very happy together.

Dialogue 3
- What are you going to do this summer, Marc? Are you going back to the States?
- No, not yet. I'm going to stay in England and travel around the Lake District by bicycle. I love cycling, and I can borrow a good bicycle from a friend of mine in London.
- Oh. Well, that sounds … different, anyway.

Dialogue 4
- Hi, Karen.
- Hi, Paul.
- Karen, what are you doing this afternoon?
- I don't know. I can't decide. It's such a lovely day …
- Well, I have a suggestion. Why don't we go swimming together?
- I'd love to go swimming, but I haven't got the time. I've got

a big exam coming up next week, so I really should stay at home and study.
- When is your exam exactly?
- On Tuesday. Tuesday morning.
- Oh, well, today's only Saturday. And you really should get some exercise.
- Well, I don't know.
- Come on, decide.
- All right, I will go swimming with you. Wait for me downstairs. I'll get my things and meet you in five minutes.
- Okay. And don't worry about your exam. You'll do very well, I'm sure.

Unit 15: Exercise 4 (page 72)

- How long are you going to stay here in Europe, Clive?
- Well, I'll be in Europe for another six months or so. I have to be back in Australia in November.
- November, that's spring in Australia, isn't it?
- Yes, it is. Almost summer, actually. I love swimming, so I'm looking forward to having summer twice this year, once in Europe and once in Australia.
- Do you play tennis?
- Well, sometimes. Tennis isn't bad, I suppose, but I prefer swimming.
- Did you fly here from Australia?
- Yes, the flight took about twenty hours.
- Wasn't that boring?
- Well, yes and no. I don't mind flying. I just sleep and eat all the time. But what I really dislike is waiting at the airport.
- And what are you doing here in Europe?
- Well, I'm travelling a lot, by train mostly. I enjoy travelling by train, and I've been all over England and France already. There are some great new trains here in Europe these days.
- Yes, that's right. What are you going to do tomorrow?
- Tomorrow I'm going to do something terrible, write letters. I hate writing letters, but tomorrow I really have to, and I haven't even got my computer with me. I'll have to write them all by hand, of all things …

Unit 16: Exercise 3 (page 76)

Dialogue 1
- In my opinion, children should all learn to say please and thank you. Table manners can wait till later, perhaps, but basic politeness is really important.
- I think so, too. All they really need are those two little words to get them started.

Dialogue 2
- Personally, I think children would be more polite to adults if adults were more polite to them.
- Do you really think so?
- Yes, adults should set a good example.
- Well I don't think it would make much difference. I think adults have enough problems without trying to be polite to a lot of stupid little children.

Dialogue 3
- In my opinion, the first thing children have to learn nowadays is how to be safe in traffic. Nothing else we teach them will make any difference if they get run over by cars and don't even live long enough to grow up.
- Well, you're right that traffic is very dangerous for children, and they should learn to be careful, but just teaching the children isn't the answer. We have to teach drivers to drive more slowly and be more careful, and we have to change the streets so they can't drive so fast. That's what we have to do.

Dialogue 4
- I think television is really bad for children. They shouldn't watch it at all.
- Oh, I wouldn't say that. I watched a lot of TV when I was a child, and I don't think it hurt me. I was the youngest child in our family, and I was born the year my parents got their first television. They always called me their television child, because I grew up with it, much more than my older brother and sister.

Dialogue 5
- I don't think it's necessary for children to put on their best clothes every time their parents have visitors.
- Neither do I.

Unit 17: Exercise 1 (page 84)

- Hello, Pre-Teens Magazine. This is the Crisis Line, Susan speaking.
- Hello, ahh, this is Tim again. I phoned a couple of months ago, and …
- Tim?
- Yeah, Tim, in Essex. Are you the same person I talked to last time, or are you somebody different?
- Well, there are several of us who take turns here on the telephone, but let me see, Tim, from Birmingham?
- Yes.
- I remember now, you'd moved from Birmingham to Essex, and you were unhappy because you hadn't made any new friends.
- Yeah, that's me, and you gave me some good advice, and the best advice was when you said I should talk to my music teacher.
- So have you spoken to him or her?
- Yes, but I had to wait a while. My music teacher wasn't there. He'd gone to London for a few days, but when he got back I talked to him, and do you know what? He's from Birmingham, too. Well not exactly from Birmingham, but near by. And the main thing is that he liked the idea of starting a music club very much.
- Oh, that's good.
- And so we started a popmusic club at lunchtime. There were only a few members at first. But we made a lot of noise and then some more kids started coming round, there's even one who can play the drums.
- That sounds great, Tim. Fantastic.
- Yeah, it is. Or it was.
- It was?
- Yeah, it was. You see, my dad won't let me play music any more. He says I'm playing too much music and not doing enough school work.
- Are your marks going down?
- Well, yes, they haven't been too good since I moved here. I used to get better marks in Birmingham, but everything was easier there, it's not only because of the music.
- Well, Tim, I think you should talk to your dad about it again. – Maybe when your mum's there, too. And another thing: If I were you, I'd try to find some ways to get better marks in school.
- Well, sure, but – that's not so easy.

- Why don't you ask some of your new friends to help you?
- Well, I could ask, I suppose.
- Maybe you could do your homework together sometimes. If you show your dad that you're really trying to get better marks, perhaps he'll change his mind.
- That would be good.
- And if all that doesn't work: What about asking your music teacher to talk to your dad? If he's from the Birmingham area, too, just like your dad, maybe that would make a difference.
- Well, I'll think about that. They do have the same accent and everything. Oh, I've got to go now, there's someone at the door. Thanks a lot for the advice, bye.

Unit 18: Exercise 1 (page 88)

- Hello. I'm Diane.
- Hi, I'm Fred. I think I know you. You're Paul's sister, aren't you?
- That's right, Paul's my brother, and he's finally turned eighteen.
- I think my parents know your parents. Is your father's name George?
- That's right, George Brown. And my mother's name is Susan.
- Yes, they're the ones. George and Susan Brown, my parents often talk about them. Hasn't your mother got a sister?
- Yes, she has. Her name's Monica, Monica Robson, she's married to Jim Robson.
- Sure, I know them. Monica and Jim Robson are neighbours of ours. Their son David is about our age, isn't he?
- That's right. In fact, I think David's coming to the party tonight. Paul invited him, I'm sure. He's our cousin, after all.
- Isn't there a famous actor in your family?
- You must mean my grandfather, John Benson.
- John Benson, that's the one.
- Well, he's not terribly famous, but he is an actor. Or used to be, he's retired now. And my grandmother's an actress. Mary Benson. She's still an actress, you can see her on television sometimes.
- Mary Benson, yes, I've seen her. She plays the role of the grandmother in one of those soap operas, doesn't she?

Unit 19: Exercise 5 (page 92)

- With me in the studio today here in Chicago is Dr Ralph Young, a British doctor who spends his vacations working at a clinic in a small village in Africa. Dr Young, welcome to Chicago.
- Thank you, it's a pleasure to be here.
- Dr Young, you've come to Chicago to raise money for your clinic in Ghana, haven't you?
- Well, it's not my clinic, I just work there sometimes when I'm on holiday, as do a number of doctors from Britain, France, Germany and several other countries. And I'm actually in Chicago for a convention, but since I'm here I would in fact like to tell your listeners about our work in Africa.
- You've worked in several African countries, haven't you? Do you always fly to Africa from Britain, or do you sometimes go by boat?
- Oh, no, I always fly. Going by sea would take too long. And I fly within Africa sometimes, too, in little one-engined planes, to get to clinics that are far out in the bush.
- So you don't ride on elephants or anything like that?
- No, in fact I've never even seen an elephant, except in the zoo. I sometimes go round by bicycle in Africa, though, when I'm working in one of the larger towns.
  A bicycle can be quite practical for short distances, especially in the dry season. And in Ghana we sometimes travel to the clinic by river boat. The clinic is right on the river, so that's a good way to get there.
- I'll ask you some more about your work in the clinic in just a few minutes, but first here's some music and a word from our sponsor.

Unit 20: Exercise 4 (page 96)

1: Cynthia.

- Hello, this is Cynthia Green. I've heard you're going to pick me up at the airport, and that's very kind of you. That'll save a lot of time and I certainly appreciate it. I've heard a lot about you from my mother, and I'm looking forward to meeting you. You've already got my arrival time and the flight number, so I'll just have to tell you what I look like. Well, I'm fairly small, five foot three, and I look quite young, I'm afraid. I'm actually almost thirty, but you wouldn't know it from looking at me. I usually wear a suit, and put my hair up, and wear glasses. I don't even need glasses, I could be a pilot if I wanted to, but the glasses make me look a bit older, I think, and in my job that's fairly important.
  I hope the plane won't be full of schoolgirls, because I don't want to look like one of them. Anyway, I'll see you at the airport. Goodbye.

2: Molly.

- Hi, this is Molly, and I'm supposed to tell you what I look like so you can pick me up at the airport. Well, I'm American, of course, and I'm fairly, you know, ahh, large, sort of. What I look like is, in fact – I don't know if you ever hear country songs over there, but my friends say I look just like a woman in an old country song. The song was called "fair, fat and forty", and it went like this: "She may be short / she may be tall / but the gal who's best of all / is fair, fat and forty." And that's sort of what I look like. Well actually, I'm forty-two, but I don't look a day over forty, and I'm certainly fair, you know, blond hair, and light skin and that sort of thing, but I'm not really fat, that's not true at all, I mean I'm not terribly overweight or anything like that, it's just that there's a lot of me, there's a lot to hold onto, so to speak. And I talk quite a lot, as you may have noticed.
  I hope I won't get on your nerves too much. I'll try not to. Anyway, I'm glad you don't have a time limit on your answering machine, otherwise it would have cut me off a long time ago. Okay, so long, see you at the airport.

3: Silke

- Hello, my name is Silke, and I'm sure you'll recognise me. I've got long dark hair. And dark eyes. And I'm tall and thin, and wear dark shiny dresses, usually, and dark glasses and long dark earrings. And sandals. I always wear sandals, except in the winter. And I always wear a gold watch and a little bit of jewelry, one necklace, maybe, and one bracelet, and one ring, but no more. I'll see you at the airport. Goodbye for now.

Einführung
In der folgenden Grammatikdarstellung sind die Strukturen, die in den Units auftreten, in systematischer Form aufgeführt. Neben der Überschrift finden Sie einen Rückverweis auf die Unit, in der das betreffende Phänomen behandelt wird, sowie einen Hinweis auf eine weitere Übung, die Sie zur Festigung der Grammatik noch machen können. Diese Grammatikübungen finden Sie gleich im Anschluss an die systematische Grammatikdarstellung.

1 Wortstellung und Satzarten / Word order and different types of sentences

1.1 Bestätigungsfragen (mit nicht wahr?-Anhängsel) / Question tags → Unit 16, → Exercise 1

Subjekt	Hilfsverb oder *be*	Vollverb		Hilfsverb oder *be*	Subjekt
He	**is**		a teacher,	**isn't**	he?
Paul	**is**		friendly,	**isn't**	he?
You		like	golf,	**don't**	you?
You		enjoyed	the match,	**didn't**	you?
The students	**will**	arrive	soon,	**won't**	they?

An einen **bejahten** Aussagesatz wird ein **verneintes**, an einen **verneinten** Aussagesatz ein **bejahtes** Frageanhängsel gehängt.

In dieser Satzart werden **Hilfsverb** oder eine Form von ***be*** und das **Subjekt** des vorangegangenen Aussagesatzes wieder aufgenommen.

Enthält der Aussagesatz **kein** Hilfsverb, treten **do**, **does** oder **did** ein.

Das Subjekt wird in der Form des Personalpronomens wieder aufgenommen.

1.2 Kurzsätze mit *so / neither / nor* / Short sentences with *so / neither / nor* → Unit 16, → Exercise 2

He is ill.	– So **am** I.
I love San Francisco.	– So **does** my wife.
I met him in London.	– So **did** we.
We will be late.	– So **will** they.
He isn't an expert.	– **Neither/Nor** am I.
I don't like jazz.	– **Neither/Nor** do we.
They didn't meet her.	– **Neither/Nor** did he.
We can't swim.	– **Neither/Nor** can I.

Zustimmende Kurzsätze („Ich auch …") greifen die **be**-Form oder das **Hilfsverb** des vorangegangenen Aussagesatzes wieder auf. Enthält dieser nur ein Vollverb, wird in dem Kurzsatz eine Form von **do** benutzt.

Kurzsätze mit **neither/nor** entsprechen deutschen Kurzantworten mit „auch nicht". Die Verneinung des vorangegangenen Aussagesatzes wird in der Verbform **nicht** wieder aufgegriffen.

1.3 Aussagesätze mit Zeitangaben / Statements or positive sentences with time expressions → Unit 19, → Exercise 3

I read the newspaper	**in the evening.**
We played soccer	**last week.**
We played soccer in Chester	**last week.**
She has lived in London	**for years.**
At the moment Paul is in Berlin.	
Tomorrow we are having a meeting.	
The film star **seldom** gave interviews and **never** appeared on TV.	
She didn't **often** talk about her problems.	
He's **always** late. / They **are never** ill.	

Zeitangaben finden sich in der Regel am Ende von Aussagesätzen. Anders als im Deutschen werden sie Ortsangaben **nach**gestellt.

Am Satzanfang wird die Zeitangabe besonders hervorgehoben und betont.

Already, always, just, never, often, seldom, sometimes und **still** werden in der Regel vor das **Vollverb** gestellt.

Diese Zeitangaben werden ***be*** **nach**gestellt.

1.4 Fragesätze / Questions → Unit 8, → Exercise 4

Wir unterscheiden grundsätzlich zwei Typen:

(a) die **Entscheidungsfrage,** bei der die Frage auf eine Antwort vom Typ *JA* oder *NEIN* zielt:

Did he write the letter yesterday? – Yes, he did. / – No, he didn't.

(b) die **Ergänzungsfrage,** die durch ein Fragewort eingeleitet wird. Die Antwort ist meist kurz:

What did you do yesterday? – Nothing special.

1.4.1 Entscheidungsfragen / Yes- and No-Questions

Shall I help you with your bag? **Can** you do me a favour, please? **Has** he tried it out?
Do you want me to help you? **Does** she speak Spanish? **Did** they go to the party yesterday?
Is she in? **Were** they ill last week?

Entscheidungsfragen werden immer durch ein Hilfsverb eingeleitet.

Ist im entsprechenden Aussagesatz nur ein Vollverb vorhanden, tritt **do**, **does** oder **did** an den Anfang des Fragesatzes.

Eine Ausnahme bildet das Verb **be**.

1.4.2 Ergänzungsfragen / Wh-Questions

Es müssen zwei Arten von Fragen mit Fragewörtern unterschieden werden:

1. Das Fragewort ist nicht Subjekt oder Teil des Subjekts des Fragesatzes:

Where do you live? **What did you do last night?**

2. Das Fragewort ist Subjekt oder Teil des Subjekts des Fragesatzes:

Who works for a travel agency? **Who told you?**

who als Subjekt	**who** als Objekt
Who is he? **Who** talked about the subject?	**Who** do you love? **Who** did you take to the cinema?

Wird **who?** im Sinne von **wer?** gebraucht, tritt keine Umschreibung ein. Fragen mit **who?** im Sinne von **wen?** + Vollverb werden grundsätzlich umschrieben.

! Wie **who?** wird auch **what?** (= was?) behandelt: **What** makes her so fit? **What** does she do to keep so fit?

1.4.3 Präpositionen in Fragesätzen / Prepositions in questions

Who are you talking **about**? What do you need the money **for**? Which bus are you waiting **for**?	**Von wem** sprichst du? **Für was** brauchst du das Geld? **Auf welchen** Bus warten Sie / wartest du?

Anders als im Deutschen werden Präpositionen in der Regel **nicht** vor das Fragewort gestellt, sondern finden sich überwiegend am Ende des Fragesatzes. Diese Wortstellung ist für deutsche Lerner gewöhnungsbedürftig.

1.5 Bedingungssätze / *If*-clauses → Units 15 + 17, → Exercises 5 and 6

	Nebensatz *(present simple)*	Hauptsatz *(will)*
If	I **take** this medicine, you **eat** too much, they **don't eat** less,	I **'ll** certainly **feel** better. you **will put** on weight. they **won't lose** weight.

Typ 1: Oft hängt von einer Bedingung ab, ob ein zukünftiges Geschehen eintritt. Im *if*-Satz wird die **einfache Gegenwart** verwendet, wenn man die Erfüllung der Bedingung für möglich hält. Im Hauptsatz tritt dann in der Regel **will / won't** auf, um eine Folge oder Konsequenz auszudrücken.

	Nebensatz *(past simple)*	Hauptsatz *(conditional = would/wouldn't)*
If	father **had** a holiday we **lost** the game things **were** different I **were / was** you he **weren't / wasn't** ill it **weren't** raining they **didn't** work hard	we **would** go to the seaside. we **would** be very sorry. I **would** be happier. I **would / wouldn't** do that. he **would** come. the match **would** start. they **would** earn less money.

Typ 2: Ist die Verwirklichung der Bedingung **unwahrscheinlich** oder **unmöglich**, so steht im Nebensatz die einfache Vergangenheit und im Hauptsatz das **Konditional**.

! Für die 1. und 3. Person von ***be*** wird die alte Konjunktivform ***were*** gebraucht, umgangssprachlich immer häufiger ***was***.

Bedingungssätze werden auch verwendet, um **Ratschläge** zu erteilen: "If I **were / was** you, I **would** / I'**d** talk to the boss."

2 Das Zeitwort / The verb

2.1 Die *ing*-Form / The *ing*-form → Unit 15, → Exercise 7

2.1.1 Form / Form

ing-Formen (auch Gerundium / *Gerund* genannt) können von allen Verben außer von den modalen Hilfsverben gebildet werden. Beim Anfügen der *ing*-Endung ist zu beachten, dass

1. to put → pu**tt**ing	to swim → swi**mm**ing
2. to shine → shining	to write → writing
3. to die → d**y**ing	to lie → l**y**ing

1. der Endkonsonant nach kurzem, betontem Vokal **verdoppelt** wird,
2. dass ein stummes End-e entfällt und
3. dass *-ie* zu *-y* wird.

Eine *ing*-Form kann entweder direkt oder mit Hilfe einer Präposition (indirekt) an das Verb angeschlossen werden. Als Grundregel gilt: Ein **direkter Anschluß** erfolgt, wenn auch ein Hauptwort direkt angeschlossen wird: He likes music. He likes **listening** to music. **Indirekt** wird angeschlossen: She is keen **on** computer games. She is keen **on playing** computer games.

He	**enjoys / loves likes**	watching TV.
We	**can't stand / hate don't like / dislike**	working overtime.

Die *ing*-Form wird nach Verben benutzt, die **Vorlieben** oder

Abneigungen ausdrücken.

2.1.2 Die *ing*-Form nach Verhältnis- oder Fügewörtern / The *ing*-form after prepositions → Unit 17, → Exercise 8

I must **apologise for being** late.
He **insisted on talking** French.
We **look forward to meeting** you in Dallas.
They didn't **object to going** to the seaside.

Diese Form steht immer nach **Verben**, die **fest** mit einer Präposition verbunden sind. Sie werden auch in dieser Form in Wörterbüchern aufgeführt.

I'm not **afraid of telling** the truth.
He's **interested in seeing** us soon.
They were **tired of saying** it again and again.

Auch nach Eigenschaftswörtern, die **fest** mit einer Präposition verbunden sind, **muss** die **ing-**Form verwendet werden,

How about going to Manchester? He **doesn't mind doing** homework.	sowie nach häufigen Wendungen („Wie steht's mit ...?", „Wie wär's, wenn ...?").

2.2 Die Befehlsform / Imperative → Unit 7

Go down King Street, then **turn** left into Park Lane. **Stop** talking.	Der Imperativ drückt einen **Befehl** oder eine **Aufforderung** aus. Er wird durch die Grundform englischer Verben ohne **to** gebildet.
Don't disturb the meeting. **Don't be** so noisy and **don't go into** the room.	Der verneinte Imperativ drückt ein **Verbot** aus. Er wird stets mit **don't** gebildet.
Let's go now.	Als Ersatz für die 1. Person des Plurals steht die Umschreibung mit **let**.

Will man seinen Willen höflicher ausdrücken, stehen noch andere Möglichkeiten zur Verfügung, wie z. B.: **Please**, **can / could** you tell me the way to the library? **Would** you give me a glass of water, please?

2.3 Modale Hilfsverben und Umschreibungsformen / Modal auxiliaries and replacements

2.3.1 *can/could – to be allowed to* → Unit 11, → Exercise 9

The seat is free. You **can** sit down. They **couldn't** leave Paris because of the strike.	**Can / could** bezeichnet oft die **Erlaubnis** (deutsch: kann/konnte, darf/durfte).
He **was allowed to** go home earlier. They **weren't allowed to** make photocopies.	Die Ersatzform wird verwendet, wenn die Erlaubnis **offiziellen Charakter** hat.

2.3.2 *can/could – to be able to* → Unit 11

I **can** lend you the money. Unfortunately your parents **can't / cannot** help you.	**Can** bezeichnet **Fähigkeiten** und **Möglichkeiten** und drückt aus, wozu jemand imstande oder nicht imstande ist.
We **could** run faster when we were younger. My grandfather **couldn't** read or write.	Diese **körperlichen** oder **geistigen** Fähigkeiten besaß man in der Vergangenheit oder hat sie in der Gegenwart.
The man **was able** to swim across the river. Next week my son **will be able to** swim.	Die Ersatzform wird nicht so häufig verwendet, muss aber für Aussagen in der Zukunft benutzt werden.

2.3.3 *must / have to / needn't / don't have to / mustn't* → Units 5 + 11, → Exercise 10

Aussage	You **must / have to** do the work now. We **must / have to** leave before midnight. Yesterday I **had to** post the letter. Tomorrow my colleague **will have to** do it.	Das Hilfsverb *must* und seine Ersatzform *to have to* drücken eine (starke) Verpflichtung aus. *Must* bleibt als modales Hilfsverb in der Gegenwart für alle Personen gleich. Das folgende Vollverb wird direkt, d. h. ohne *to* angeschlossen.

Die Ersatzform *to have to* wird, da **must** nur im Präsens verwendet wird, vor allem für die Bildung weiterer Zeiten benötigt.

Verneinung	You **mustn't / must not** forget it. We **mustn't / must not** work less.

Die verneinte Form **mustn't / must not** entspricht dem deutschen **„nicht dürfen"** und drückt ein Verbot aus.

Wollen Sie hingegen **„nicht müssen"** übersetzen, stehen in der englischen Sprache *needn't / need not* und die Verneinung von *to have to* zur Verfügung: You **needn't / don't have to** be good at sport to be popular.

Frage	**Must** you work overtime tonight? Why **must** they be so noisy.

Auch in der Frage wird zunehmend die Ersatzform **to have to** verwendet: **Do you have to** work overtime tonight?

2.3.4 *to have something done* → Unit 20

She has her hair cut. When did you have your motorbike repaired? We'd only just had our house painted.	Sie läßt sich ihr Haar schneiden. Wann hast du dein Motorrad reparieren lassen? Wir hatten gerade erst unser Haus streichen lassen.

Wenn man etwas machen läßt, drückt man dies durch *to have something done* aus.

2.4 Vollverben und *be* in der Gegenwart / Full verbs and *be* in the present simple → Units 1 + 19, → Exercises 11 and 12

2.4.1 Bildung / Formation

Aussage	I / You / We / They **live** in Great Britain. He / She stay**s** with us at Christmas. It give**s** him a lot of pleasure.

Bei **Vollverben** in der einfachen Form hat nur die dritte Person Einzahl eine Endung: **-s**, nach Zischlauten (= -s, -sh und -ch) **-es**.

Verneinung			
	I / You / We / They	**don't**	live in Paris.
	He / She	**doesn't**	like London.
	It	**doesn't**	worry me.

Bei der Verneinung wird vor dem Vollverb **don't** (= do not) eingefügt, in der 3. Person Einzahl **doesn't** (= does not).

Frage		
	Where **do**	you / they live?
	Where **does**	he / she live?
	Do	you / they see her very often?
	Does	he / she live in Brussels?
	Does	it hurt?

Bei Fragen wird vor dem Satzgegenstand (Subjekt) **do** eingefügt, in der 3. Person Einzahl **does**.
In der Kurzantwort mit **yes** oder **no** wird das eingefügte Hilfszeitwort wieder aufgenommen: Yes, I **do**. Yes, it **does**.
No, I **don't**. No, it **doesn't**.

Aussage				
	I	**'m**	(= **am**)	on my way home.
	You / We / They	**'re**	(= **are**)	in Rome.
	He / She / It	**'s**	(= **is**)	in my office.

Die Formen des Verbs **be** sind unregelmäßig.

Verneinung			
	I	**'m not**	in my office.
	You / We / They	**aren't**	at home.
	He / She / It	**isn't**	in the house.

An die Form von **be** wird **n't** (= **not**) gehängt. In der 1. Person Einzahl jedoch lautet die Kurzform **I'm not**.

Frage		
	Where **am**	I?
	Where **are**	you / they / we?
	How **is**	he / she / it?
	Is	he / she ill?
	Are	you / we / they fit?

Die Frage mit dem Zeitwort (Verb) **be** wird wie im Deutschen gebildet. In der Kurzantwort wird die gebildete Form wieder aufgenommen: Yes, I **am**. Yes, he **is**. Yes, they **are**.

2.4.2 Gebrauch / Use

(1)	For business people, time **is** money. Not many people **are** patient and **like** queueing.
(2)	She **works** for IBM and **is** head of the sales department. They **collect** stamps.
(3)	Paul **goes** to the theatre once a month. He **likes** Italian operas and German plays.

Mit dieser „einfachen" Zeitform des Verbs werden im Englischen (1) allgemeingültige Aussagen gemacht sowie Tatsachen und Erklärungen ohne Hinweise auf zeitliche Abläufe aufgeführt, (2) Berufe oder dauerhafte Beschäftigungen benannt und (3) gewohnheitsmäßige, sich wiederholende Handlungen erzählt.

2.5 Die vollendete Gegenwart / The present perfect simple → Units 2, 6 + 19, → Exercise 13

2.5.1 Bildung der einfachen Form / Formation

Zur Bildung des *present perfect* wird immer **have / has** benutzt, auch bei Verben, die im Deutschen mit **sein** verwendet werden.

Die Partizipform regelmäßiger Verben wird durch Anhängen von **-d** oder **-ed** an die Grundform des Verbs gebildet. Die Partizipform unregelmäßiger Verben müssen Sie gesondert lernen.

Aussage	I **have phoned** my sister. She **has posted** the letter He **has** never **been** to Rome. They **have** just **gone** home.

Have / has wird vor das Mittelwort der Vergangenheit eines Verbs, auch Partizip Perfekt genannt, gestellt.

Verneinung	I **haven't had** enough time. She **hasn't done** her homework.

Bei der Verneinung wird **-n't** (= **not**) an **have** oder **has** gehängt.

Frage	**Have** you ever **been** to Italy? **Has** she **written** the letter?

Bei der Frage rückt **have** oder **has** - wie im Deutschen - vor den Satzgegenstand.

Kurz-antwort	Yes, I **have** / she **has** / they **have**. No, I **haven't** / she **hasn't** / they **haven't**.

Bei den Kurzantworten wird das Hilfszeitwort **have** oder **has** wieder aufgenommen.

2.5.2 Gebrauch / Use

(1)	I **have been** to Naples twice, but I **have** never **been** to Rome. She **has** already **met** him once. We **have** never **read** such an interesting book.
(2)	I must say (that) he **has made** a terrible mistake. So we don't know what to do now. The President and his wife **have had** an accident. They're in hospital now. We **haven't done** our homework yet.
(3)	My wife **has known** him for 10 years. The firm **has made** a lot of money this year.

Die Zeit des *present perfect* nimmt im Englischen eine Sonderstellung ein, da sie nicht eindeutig den Zeitblöcken der **Gegenwart** oder der **Vergangenheit** zugeordnet werden kann. Sie drückt aus, (1) dass Dinge in der Vergangenheit geschahen, gleichgültig wann, und dass sie zur Biographie und Lebenserfahrung des Sprechers/der Sprecherin gehören ("*life experience*"). Sie beschreibt (2) Folgen und Resultate abgeschlossener Handlungen oder Ereignisse für die Gegenwart ("*past action, present result*") und (3) Handlungen und Vorgänge, die von der Vergangenheit bis zur Gegenwart andauern ("*up to now*").

2.5.3 *for* und *since* / *for* and *since* → Unit 2, → Exercise 14

He **has been** our neighbour *for* 12 years and **has worked** as a salesman *since* 1980.	Er ist seit 12 Jahren unser Nachbar und arbeitet seit 1985 als Handelsvertreter.

Die Beziehung der Zeitform *present perfect* zur Gegenwart wird besonders bei der Übersetzung deutscher Sätze mit „seit“ deutlich, deren Verben in der Gegenwart gebraucht werden.

– How long **has** he **been** out of work?
– He **has been** out of work *for* more than a year.
He **has been** out of work *since* last June.

Der Anfangspunkt dieser Zeitspanne, die sich bis in die Gegenwart erstreckt, wird durch *since* gekennzeichnet (*since* 1985, *since* January, *since* eleven o'clock, *since* I was a boy / girl ....), ihre bisherige Dauer durch *for* (*for* 12 years, *for* three weeks, *for* a quarter of an hour ...). Entsprechende Fragen werden mit *How long ...?* eingeleitet.

2.6 Die einfache Vergangenheit / The past simple → Units 3, 6 + 20, → Exercise 15

2.6.1 Bildung / Formation

Aussage	I **lived** in Rome when I was a child. He / she **started** work last week. We **went** to France two years ago. They **saw** her at the opera yesterday.
Verneinung	I **didn't** have enough time. She **didn't** work last August. They **didn't** come on time.
Frage	**Did** you watch TV last night? Where **did** she get that dress?
Kurz-antwort	Yes, I **did**. No, I **didn't**.

Um die einfache Vergangenheitsform zu bilden, wird bei regelmäßigen Verben die Endung **-ed** an die Grundform des Verbs gehängt. Die Vergangenheitsformen sind - bis auf den Sonderfall des Verbs *be* (Vergangenheit: *was / were*) – für alle Personen gleich. Verneinte Aussagen in der Vergangenheit macht man mit **didn't** und Verben in der Grundform.

Fragen in der Vergangenheit werden mit **did** gebildet.

Das Hilfszeitwort **did / didn't** wird in der Kurzantwort wieder aufgenommen.

2.6.2 Gebrauch / Use

When I **started** work 40 years ago, my job **was** very hard. We **did**n't have the machines which make factory work so much easier now. All we **had were** our own hands and some heavy tools. And we **had** to work 10 hours a day.

Sprechen wir über etwas Vergangenes, seien es Ereignisse oder Tätigkeiten, das keinen direkten Bezug zur Gegenwart hat, müssen wir die Vergangenheit (*past simple*) benutzen.

2.6.3 *used to* → Units 3 + 20, → Exercise 16

I **used to** smoke a lot.
We **used to** live downtown / in the country.
They **used to** be housewives.

used to drückt in Verbindung mit der **Grundform** eines Verbs aus, was **früher** dauernd und gewohnheitsmäßig geschah, **heute** aber nicht mehr der Fall ist.

2.7 Der Gebrauch von einfacher Vergangenheit und *present perfect* / The use of *past simple* and *present perfect* → Units 4 + 6, → Exercise 17

(1) In those days I **looked** young and handsome. (2) I **have** always **looked** young and handsome.	(1) Jugend und Schönheit sind vergänglich, d. h. der Sprecher / die Sprecherin empfindet sich jetzt nicht mehr als jung und schön. (2) Der Sprecher / die Sprecherin hält sich immer noch für jung und schön.
(3) The singer, Dana Shaw, **sang** in over 30 operas. (4) The singer, Dana Shaw **has sung** in over 30 operas.	(3) Dana Shaw hat in mehr als 30 Opern gesungen. Diese Zeit ist vorüber. (4) Dana übt ihren Beruf noch immer aus.
(5) **Did** you **see** Maria when you were in Denver? (6) **Have** you **seen** Maria? I want to tell her something.	(5) Hast Du Maria gesehen / getroffen, als Du in Denver warst? (6) Hast Du Maria gesehen = Weißt Du, wo sie jetzt ist? Ich möchte ihr etwas sagen. Die Übersetzung verdeutlicht, dass in Satz (5) von der Vergangenheit die Rede ist, während man in Satz (6) erfahren möchte, wo sich Maria jetzt aufhält.

2.8 Die vollendete Vergangenheit / The past perfect simple → Units 5, 6 + 20, → Exercise 18

2.8.1 Bildung der einfachen Form / Formation of the simple form

Aussage	He remembered (that) he **had / 'd played** the game before. By that time they **had / 'd finished** their work.	Diese Zeit wird für alle Personen mit **had** und dem Partizip Perfekt (past participle) gebildet. Die Kurzform von **had** lautet **'d**.
Verneinung	Barbara **hadn't worked** in an office before. I was sorry that I **hadn't seen** her.	Bei der Verneinung wird für alle Personen **hadn't** (= had not) verwendet.
Frage	**Had** you ever **been** to America before you emigrated there? **Had** they **turned** off all the lights before they left the house?	Die Frage mit dem Hilfszeitwort **had** wird wie im Deutschen gebildet und verwendet. Bei der Kurzantwort wird das Hilfsverb wieder aufgenommen: Yes, I / they **had**.

2.8.2 Gebrauch / Use

When Susan **had cleaned** the stairs, she decided to have a break. Bill's plum pudding tasted great. He **had** always **been** an excellent cook. Suddenly they realised (that) someone **had broken** into their flat.	Das **past perfect** bezeichnet Handlungen, die vor einem bestimmten Zeitpunkt der Vergangenheit einsetzten *(Vorzeitigkeit)*. Diese Zeit wird – wie im Deutschen – häufig in Erzählungen, Berichten und in der indirekten Rede benutzt.

2.9 Die einfache Form und die Verlaufsform der Gegenwart / The present simple and the present progressive → Units 9 + 19, → Exercise 19

Die Verlaufsform der Gegenwart wird mit der Gegenwart von **be** und der **ing-Form** von Verben gebildet. Beide Zeitformen werden zur Verdeutlichung unterschiedlicher Situationen und Sachverhalte verwendet.

Present simple	*Present progressive*
He **works** for an international magazine.	Today he**'s not working**, he **is writing** a letter to his aunt, while his children **are playing** in the garden.
The theatre **opens** at 6.30 p.m.	Look! They **are playing** badminton on the lawn.
He **likes** soccer, but his wife **doesn't**, she **prefers** tennis. I **don't know** what their hobbies are, I always **forget** to ask them.	Our team **is doing** extremely well this season. Leisure centres **are becoming** popular.

Die einfache Form bezeichnet gewohnheitsmäßige, sich wiederholende Handlungen, die Verlaufsform schildert den Verlauf einer „gegenwärtigen" Handlung oder Tätigkeit. Für Aussagen, die allgemein gültig sind, benutzt man die einfache Form. Die Verlaufsform drückt den Verlauf einer Handlung zu einem bestimmten Zeitpunkt oder in einem Zeitraum aus. Verben wie *forget, hate, know, like, understand* und *want*, die keine Tätigkeiten ausdrücken, werden in der einfachen Form verwendet. Die Verlaufsform drückt augenblickliches Interesse und Trends aus.

2.10 Die Verlaufsform der Vergangenheit / The past progressive → Units 11 + 20, → Exercise 20

2.10.1 Bildung / Formation

Aussage	They **were having** breakfast at 9 a.m.
Frage	**Was** he **waiting** for her at lunchtime?
Verneinung	We **weren't watching** TV when our mother came home.

Die Verlaufsform der Vergangenheit (erweiterte Form) wird mit **was / were** und der **-ing**-Form der Vollverben gebildet:

2.10.2 Gebrauch / Use

When he entered the room I **was reading** the newspaper.

Yesterday morning Greg and Norman **were playing** tennis.

Die Verlaufsform der Vergangenheit dient dazu, den **Verlauf eines Geschehens oder einer Tätigkeit** in der Vergangenheit anschaulich darzustellen.

Mr Miller **was reading**, his wife **was working** in the kitchen, and their children **were looking** at their stamps.
While Susan **was cleaning** the windows, Tom **was doing** the dishes.

Durch die erweiterte Form kann die Gleichzeitigkeit mehrerer Handlungen ausgedrückt werden.

When I **was looking** out of my window, a lorry suddenly **came** round the corner and **crashed** into my garage.

They **were working** in their garden when it **began** to rain.

Die im Verlauf befindliche Handlung wird in der Verlaufsform, die neu hinzutretende Handlung wird in der einfachen Form ausgedrückt. Beide Verbformen treten meist **zusammen** auf, wenn eine fortschreitende Handlung durch eine neue unterbrochen wird.

2.11 Die Zukunft mit *going to* / *going to* future → Units 13, 14 + 18, → Exercise 21

What **is going to** happen? It'**s going to** rain very soon. Look, the film'**s going to** start.
What **are** you **going to** do this afternoon? I'**m going to** write some letters and my wife'**s going to** meet some friends in town. We'**re going to** buy theatre tickets tomorrow. They'**re going to** finish the lesson.

Das **going to**-Futur bezieht sich häufig auf die **nahe** Zukunft und drückt aus, dass etwas wahrscheinlich oder gleich passieren wird.

Das **going to**-Futur wird besonders dann gebraucht, wenn der Sprecher eine **Absicht** oder ein **Vorhaben** ausdrücken möchte. Ob diese Absichten verwirklicht werden, steht nicht fest.

ACHTUNG!
Bei Verben der Bewegung wie **to go** und **to come** wird eine für die nahe Zukunft geplante oder beabsichtigte Handlung durch **to be** + **Partizip Präsens** (***ing*-Form**) ausgedrückt:
They **are going** to Brighton for the weekend. **Is** Susan **coming** tonight?

2.12 Die Zukunft mit dem *present progressive* / The *present progressive* for future → Units 13 + 18

What **are** you **doing** this evening? John **is playing** football, but I'**m staying** at home.
We'**re meeting** our friends after the concert tonight. She'**s taking** her exam in September.

Im Gegensatz zur **going to**-Form drückt diese Form **fest getroffene** Vereinbarungen aus.

Um Verwechslungen mit laufenden Handlungen auszuschließen, wird meist eine auf die Zukunft verweisende Zeitangabe benutzt.

2.13 Zukunft mit *will* / *Will*-future → Units 14 + 18, → Exercise 22

Das ***will*-future** wird mit ***will*** + Infinitiv (ohne ***to***) gebildet. In verneinten Aussagesätzen wird für alle Personen ***won't*** benutzt. ***Will*** zum Ausdruck der Zukunft wird benutzt,

When **will** we see you again? Pam **will** leave for Australia next month.	im Gegensatz zum Deutschen auch dann, wenn schon Zeitbestimmungen auf die Zukunft verweisen: „**Wann** sehen wir Dich / Sie wieder?",
The news **will** be on after the film. My daughter **will** be 16 next year.	um zukünftige Geschehnisse, die nicht vom Sprecher beeinflusst werden können, zu versprachlichen,
I hope she **will** soon be well again. Do you think (that) he **will** leave tomorrow? I suppose you **will** get the prize.	bei Verben, die auf die Zukunft weisen, wie z. B. **to expect**, **to hope**, **to imagine, to promise**, **to suppose** und **to think**,
Susan **will** be here in half an hour.	um **Vorhersagen** zu machen,
I'**ll** send you a postcard from India. We **will** look after your children and bring them home late.	um **Willenserklärungen** abzugeben oder etwas zu **versprechen** und
I'**ll** answer the phone.	um **spontane Entscheidungen** mitzuteilen.

2.14 Die einfache Gegenwart zum Ausdruck der Zukunft / The *present simple* for future → Unit 18, → Exercise 23

The film **starts** at 8.30. The train **leaves** at 5 o'clock.

Diese Zeitform wird verwendet, wenn zukünftige Ereignisse festgelegt sind, z. B. durch Fahrpläne (***timetable future***).

Ausnahmen und Sonderregeln: → Units 15 + 18

(a) in temporalen Nebensätzen / in time clauses

Hauptsatz (*will*)		Nebensatz (*present simple*)
She **will** leave	**as soon as** **before** **when**	he **telephones.**

In Nebensätzen mit **as soon as**, **before** und **when** wird die einfache Form der Gegenwart (***simple present***) benutzt, selbst wenn über zukünftige Geschehnisse oder Handlungen gesprochen wird: Sie wird aufbrechen, **sobald**, **bevor**, **wenn** er telefoniert = telefonieren **wird**.

(b) in Bedingungssätzen / in *if*-clauses

Hauptsatz (*will*)		Nebensatz (*present simple*)
I'**ll** certainly feel better	**if**	I take this medicine.
They **won't** lose weight	**if**	they don't eat less.

Das gleiche gilt für Bedingungssätze vom Typ 1.

3 Das Hauptwort / The noun

3.1 Der Genitiv / The genitive → Unit 18

3.1.1 Bildung / Formation

Fred**'s**	books	
the boy**'s**	toy	the colour **of** the car / cars
the boys**'**	toys	
the men**'s**	cars	the door **of** my house
the women**'s**	dresses	the buttons **of** his shirts

Im Englischen gibt es zwei Möglichkeiten, den Genitiv oder „Wes-Fall" auszudrücken:

1. Der **s-Genitiv** (**'s**) wird an den Namen oder die Bezeichnung von **Personen** angehängt (Fred's books).
   Ist ein Mehrzahl-**s** schon vorhanden, wird nur der Apostroph angehängt (the boys' toys).
2. **of** + Artikel / Pronomen + Sachbezeichnung in der Ein- oder Mehrzahl

3.1.2 Gebrauch / Use

the boy**'s** T-shirt the dog**'s** tail
an hour**'s** walk / yesterday**'s** newspaper
at the dentist**'s** / at the butcher**'s** at the Millers**'**

Der **s-Genitiv** wird bei **Personen** und manchmal auch bei **Tieren** verwendet.

Der **s-Genitiv** gibt auch ein **Zeitmaß** an und

bezeichnet **Örtlichkeiten** bei Praxen, Geschäften, Wohnungen etc.

ACHTUNG !
Mit ***one of*** wird jemand aus einer bestimmten Gruppe oder Anzahl herausgegriffen:
He's **one of** my friends. oder He's a friend **of mine**.

the side	**of**	the building
the Houses	**of**	Parliament
in the days the house	**of** **of**	Queen Elizabeth I our reporter living in London

Der ***of*-Genitiv** wird bei Sach**bezeichnungen**,

Sammelnamen und

bei Bezeichnungen für **Einzelpersonen**, denen eine Beifügung nachgestellt ist, verwendet.

4 Der Artikel / The article → Unit 4, → Exercise 24

4.1 Der unbestimmte Artikel / The indefinite article: *a / an*

4.1.1 Form und Aussprache / Form and pronunciation

	a [ə] vor Mitlauten	**an** = [ən] vor Selbstlauten
Einzahl	**a** boss **a** hamburger	**an** aunt **an** uncle
Mehrzahl	bosses hamburgers	aunts uncles
	a uniform [ə 'ju:nɪfɔ:m] **a** one-year old child [ə wʌn-jɪə əʊld tʃaɪld] **an** hour [ən aʊə] **an** 18-year-old boy [ən ˌei'ti:n-jɪə əʊld bɔɪ]	

Der unbestimmte Artikel lautet in der Einzahl immer **a** oder **an**. In der Mehrzahl fällt er, wie im Deutschen, weg: **ein** Auto – Autos; **a** car – cars.

Nicht die Schreibung, sondern die Aussprache ist entscheidend für den Gebrauch von *a/an*.

4.1.2 Der unbestimmte Artikel bei Zugehörigkeit zu Beruf, Nationalität usw. / The indefinite article and jobs, nationalities etc.

(1)	My aunt is **a** professor in Atlanta. She is **a** Mormon. Her son, **an** artist, has become **a** politician. He's **a** Democrat. Meine Tante ist Professorin in Atlanta. Sie ist Mormonin. Ihr Sohn, (ein) Künstler, ist Politiker (geworden). Er ist Demokrat.
(2)	They elected him mayor of the city. Er wurde zum Bürgermeister der Stadt gewählt.

(1) Der unbestimmte Artikel ordnet Einzelne(s) in eine Gruppe ein und wird – abweichend vom Deutschen – in Verbindung mit Berufen, Nationalitäten, Religionen, Parteien etc. verwendet.
(2) Bei Stellungen, die nur eine Person bekleidet, steht kein Artikel.

4.2 Der bestimmte Artikel / The definite article

4.2.1 Form und Aussprache / Form and pronunciation

Der bestimmte Artikel lautet in der Ein- und Mehrzahl **the**. Die Aussprache richtet sich nach dem folgenden Laut:

the book, **the** books	**the** union [ðə 'ju:njən]
the English book	**the** hour [ði aʊə]

[ðə] vor konsonantischem Anlaut
[ði; ði:] vor vokalischem Anlaut

4.2.2 Gebrauch / Use

(1) Der bestimmte Artikel hebt, wie im Deutschen, das Hauptwort aus einer größeren Zahl oder Gruppe gleichartiger Wesen oder Gegenstände heraus, oft in Verbindung mit einem Attribut (z. B. Adjektiv oder *of*-Fügung):

Give me **the blue** parcel / pencil, please. **The** doors **of the house** were wide open.

(2) Namen / Eigennamen bezeichnen in der Einzahl etwas Einzigartiges und sind schon ausreichend bestimmt. Deshalb tritt im Englischen auch **kein** bestimmter Artikel auf:

Susan often watches TV with **Pamela**. **Buckingham Palace** is a wonderful sight.

(3) Anders als im Deutschen entfällt der bestimmte Artikel bei bestimmten Wörtern wie **bed**, **church**, **class**, **college**, **hospital**, **market**, **school**, **town**, **university** und **work**, wenn auf ihre Zweckbestimmung und ihre Funktion Bezug genommen wird:

He went to university when he was 18.	Er ging zur (= zu **der**) Universität / auf **die** Universität als er 18 Jahre alt war.
The children are at school.	Die Kinder sind in **der** Schule.

Er wird **mit** den zuvor aufgeführten Wörtern benutzt, wenn von dem Gegenstand oder den Gebäuden die Rede ist:

Your bag is under **the** bed.	Ihre / Deine Tasche ist unter dem Bett.

5 Das Eigenschaftswort oder Adjektiv / The adjective → Units 6 + 10

5.1 Gebrauch / Use

– What's your sister like?	– Well, she's **tall** and **slim**. She has **black** hair.
– Is she **beautiful**?	– No, but she's very **smart**.
– How old is she?	– She's quite **young**.
– And is she **married**?	– No, she's **single**.
– Is she **rich**?	– Don't be **nosy** – mind your own business.

Nach Haupt- und Tätigkeitswörtern (Nomen und Verben) bilden die Adjektive die drittgrößte Wortklasse in der englischen Sprache. Eigenschaftswörter beschreiben – wie ihr Name treffend verdeutlicht – Eigenschaften oder Qualitäten von Personen, Plätzen, Dingen etc.

5.2 Steigerung von Adjektiven / Comparison of adjectives → Unit 6, → Exercise 25

fast – fast**er** – fast**est**	schnell – schnell**er** – schnell**ster**
hot – hott**er** – hott**est**	heiß – heiß**er** – heiß**ester**
early – earli**er** – earli**est**	früh – früh**er** – früh**ster**

1. Einsilbige Adjektive und zweisilbige Adjektive, die auf **-y** enden, werden durch die Endungen **-er** (1. Steigerungsstufe = Komparativ) und **-est** (2. Steigerungsstufe = Superlativ) gesteigert.

! Achten Sie bitte auf die Rechtschreibung bei den Steigerungsformen: Der **Endkonsonant** wird **verdoppelt**, wenn diesem ein betonter Vokal vorausgeht, wie auch bei big – bi**gg**er – bi**gg**est.
y wird zu **i**, wie auch bei happy – happ**i**er – happ**i**est.

attractive – **more** attractive – (**the**) **most** attractive
difficult – **more** difficult – (**the**) **most** difficult

2. Mehrsilbige Adjektive werden gesteigert, indem **more** und **(the) most** vorangestellt werden.

She is nicer **than** Susan.	Sie ist netter **als** Susan.
His car was more expensive **than** mine.	Sein Wagen war teurer **als** meiner.

3. In Vergleichen, die Unterschiede herausstellen, wird **than** vor das zweite Vergleichselement gestellt. **Than** entspricht dem deutschen **als**.

good – **better** – **best**	little – **less** – **least**
bad – **worse** – **worst**	much / many – **more** – **most**

4. Einige unregelmäßige Steigerungsformen von Adjektiven, die häufig benutzt werden, müssen auswendig gelernt werden.

6 Das Umstandswort oder Adverb / The adverb → Unit 10, → Exercise 26

6.1 Form und Bildung / Formation

Adjektiv	Adverb
a **beautiful** voice a **careful** driver a **quick** decision	to sing **beautifully** to drive **carefully** to decide **quickly**

Das Adjektiv bestimmt ein Substantiv , während das Adverb den Vorgang oder die Umstände einer Handlung bestimmt.

Mr Jones is a quick worker. He works **quickly**.
Her voice is beautiful. She sings **beautifully**.
They had a bad accident and were **badly** injured.

Von den meisten Eigenschaftswörtern oder Adjektiven lassen sich Adverbien ableiten, indem in der Regel -ly als Endung „angehängt" wird.

Beachten Sie:

-y wird zu **-ily**:	angry → angrily; happy → happily
Die Adjektivendung **-le** entfällt nach Konsonant:	simple → simply
Stummes End-**e** entfällt:	true → truly; whole → wholly

6.2 Häufigkeitsadverbien / Adverbs of frequency → Units 1 + 19

(1) I **usually** pay my bills at once, I **always** go to my bank after work.

(2) She has **never** had to wait in a queue and has **seldom** had problems getting tickets.

(3) Mark is **always** late, Peter is **usually** on time.

Häufigkeitsadverbien wie *always*, *ever*, *frequently*, *never*, *occasionally*, *often*, *rarely*, *seldom*, *sometimes* und *usually* stehen im Regelfall (1) vor dem einfachen Verb, (2) bei zusammengesetzten Zeiten hinter dem ersten Hilfsverb und (3) hinter einer einfachen Form von *be*.

6.3 Umstandwörter der Art und Weise / Adverbs of manner → Unit 10

happy – happi**ly**

simple – simp**ly**

full – fu**lly**

automatic - automatic**ally**

whole – whol**ly**

Bildung: Adjektiv + **-ly** = **abgeleitetes** Adverb.
Pamela is a quick runner. She runs **quickly**.
Auslautendes *y* wird nach Konsonant zu *i*.
Einsilbige Adjektive können das *y* behalten: *dryly* und *drily*.
Bei Konsonant + *le* erfolgt Vereinfachung zu *-ly*.
Keine Schreibung von dreifachem *l*.
-ally bei Adjektiven auf -ic: scientific / ally.
Stummes *e* entfällt, ebenso bei true – *truly*.

6.4 Unregelmäßige Umstandswörter / Irregular adverbs → Unit 10

He drove too **fast** and had an awful accident.
We had to work very **hard** indeed.
They speak French **well**.

fast = schnell
hard = viel, fest
well = gut

That's **nice**. It's becoming **expensive** to travel abroad. He feels **terrible**. It is getting **dark**. He has grown **old**. She looks **sad**. It seems **difficult** to me. The soup smells **awful**. It sounds **good**. The meal tastes **terrible**.

ACHTUNG! Mit bestimmten Verben steht das **Adjektiv** zur Bezeichnung einer Eigenschaft als Ergänzung zum Subjekt. Dies ist der Fall bei **to be**, **to become**, **to feel**, **to get**, **to grow**, **to look**, **to seem**, **to smell**, **to sound** und **to taste**.

! **to look** kann auch mit einem Umstandswort kombiniert werden:
She looks **well**. = Sie sieht gut (**gesund**) aus.
She looks **good**. = Sie sieht gut (**hübsch**) aus.

6.5 Steigerung von Umstandswörtern / Comparison of adverbs → Unit 10, → Exercise 27

Abgeleitete Umstandswörter mit der Endung **-ly** werden mit **more** und (the) **most** gesteigert, um Tätigkeiten und Geschehnisse zu vergleichen: Some workmen worked **more efficiently** than others, but the robot did the job the **most efficiently**.

Grundform	1. Steigerungsstufe	2. Steigerungsstufe
badly **little** **much** **well**	**worse** **less** **more** **better**	**worst** **least** **most** **best**
fast **hard** **soon**	**faster** **harder** **sooner**	**fastest** **hardest** **soonest**

AUSNAHMEN:

Einige Adverbien haben besondere Steigerungsformen

„Ursprüngliche", d. h. nicht abgeleitete Adverbien werden durch die Endungen **-er** und **-est** gesteigert.

7 Mengenangaben / Quantifiers

7.1 *much – many, a lot of, a little – a few* → Unit 12, → Exercises 28 and 29

much	*many*
I haven't got **much** time.	She hasn't got **many** friends.
Did you have **much** trouble getting here?	Has he got **many** colour photographs?
There's too **much** sugar in it. Learn as **much** as you can.	I've never seen so **many** luxury cars.

Much bezeichnet eine große **Menge**, **many** eine große **Zahl** oder **Anzahl**.
Much (= viel) und **many** (= viele) finden sich vorwiegend in verneinten Sätzen und in Fragesätzen. **Much** wird dabei mit „nicht zählbaren" Begriffen, **many** dagegen mit „zählbaren" Ausdrücken verbunden.
Nach **as**, **too**, **so** und **how** stehen **much** und **many** auch in bejahenden Sätzen.

a lot of
She has (got) **a lot of** time. – Has he got **a lot of** money? – No, he hasn't got **a lot of** money.

A lot of wird im gesprochenen Englisch in **allen** Satzarten verwendet, **muss** aber in Aussagesätzen benutzt und kann bei zählbaren und nicht zählbaren Begriffen verwendet werden, wenn **as**, **so** und **too** nicht vorhanden sind.

a little	*a few*
I still have **a little** time for you.	**A few** customers came early.

A little (= **ein wenig**) wird mit **nicht zählbaren** Begriffen verwendet,
a few (= **einige wenige**) mit zählbaren.

7.2 *some* und *any* → Unit 7

7.2.1 Verwendung mit anderen Hauptwörtern / Use in combination with nouns

Some und **any** werden in der Einzahl und in der Mehrzahl gebraucht.

(1)	I'd like **some** coffee, please. I need **some** money to pay for it.
(2)	**Some** people were watching TV I am going to buy **some** interesting books for him.

Some steht meist in Aussagesätzen und bezeichnet in der Einzahl eine **unbestimmte Menge** von etwas (1) und in der Mehrzahl eine **unbestimmte Anzahl** (2), entsprechend deutsch „etwas" (1) und „einige, ein paar" (2).

(3)	He hasn't got **any** friends. We haven't got **any** time to lose
(4)	Is there **any** cheese left? Have you got **any** apples?

Any wird überwiegend in verneinten (3) und in fragenden Sätzen verwendet (4) und entspricht deutsch „kein(e,er), bzw. „etwas" und „einige, ein paar".

! Wird **some** in englischen Fragesätzen benutzt, handelt es sich meist darum, dass man etwas anbietet, oder man erwartet als Antwort auf eine gestellte Frage ein JA: Would you like **some** tea?

7.2.2 Gebrauch als Einzelwörter / Use as pronouns

Some und **any** können auch wie Hauptwörter (Substantive) benutzt werden (1). Ihnen entsprechen **somebody – anybody**, **something – anything**, **someone – anyone** (2).

(1)	**Some** like it hot.	→	Einige mögen es heiß. (Filmtitel)
	Some of my friends will certainly help me.	→	**Einige** meiner Freunde werden mir bestimmt helfen.
(2)	– **Somebody** came to see you.	→	**Irgend jemand** kam, um Sie zu sprechen.
	– Was **anybody** in?	→	War **jemand** da?
	– Is there **anything** else, I can do for you?	→	Kann ich noch **etwas** für Sie tun?
	– Yes, there is **something** else.	→	Ja, da ist noch **etwas**. (Ich habe wirklich noch einen Wunsch.)
	– **Someone** must be responsible for the chaos.	→	**Irgend jemand** muss für das Chaos verantwortlich sein.
	– Do you think **anyone** would do that job?	→	Glauben Sie, dass **jemand** diese Arbeit tut/tun würde?

7.3 Die Quantität anzeigende Wörter / Quantifiers → Unit 8, Exercise 30

none of (them)	**some of (them)**
one of (them)	**a lot of (them)**
both of (them)	**most of (them)**
a few of (them)	**all of (them)**

He gave me **a few of** the papers.
I found **none of** them interesting.

Die links stehenden Ausdrücke geben in aufsteigender Reihenfolge (von 0 bis 100 % = alle) die Anzahl oder Menge von Personen oder Gegenständen an.

8.1 Besitzanzeigende Fürwörter / Possessive adjectives and pronouns → Unit 12, Exercise 31

I'm 50. **My** father is 75 years old.
You're quiet, but **your** sister is extremely noisy.
He's my friend. **His** name's Norman.
She's my friend. **Her** name's Susan.
It's a school. **Its** name's Aldington College.

We're a class of 10 people. **Our** teacher's Mike.
You're a class of 15 people. **Your** teacher is Alison.
They're brothers. **Their** family name is Wilson.

The possessive adjective

Sie erinnern sich sicher an den Gebrauch des „besitzanzeigenden Fürworts" **vor** einem Nomen. Wie ein Eigenschaftswort (Adjektiv) wird es – wie im Deutschen – vor ein Hauptwort gestellt, was seine englische Bezeichnung erklärt.

ACHTUNG! Das deutsche „Ihr/ihr" wird im Englischen verschieden wiedergegeben:

1. Where's **your** bag, Ms Johnson?	Wo ist **Ihre** Tasche, Frau Johnson?
2. Jane's 12, **her** brother's 15.	Jane ist zwölf, **ihr** Bruder ist 15.
3. This cat is nice. What's **its** name?	Diese Katze ist nett. Wie ist **ihr** Name?
4. They're brothers, **their** name is Wilson.	Sie sind Brüder, **ihr** Name ist Wilson.

This isn't my pencil. **Mine** is red.
I can't find my magazine. Can I have **yours**?
Where are his shirts? Those aren't **his**.
I've done my homework, but Sue hasn't done **hers**.

Your car is brand-new, **ours** isn't..
My birthday is in May. When are **yours**, Peter and Paul?
This isn't the Parkers' villa. **Theirs** is much bigger.

The possessive pronoun

Fürwörter können auch **allein** stehen und ein Hauptwort „vertreten": Auf diese Weise vermeiden wir die unschöne Wiederholung eines bereits genannten Nomens.

8.2 Rückbezügliche Fürwörter / Reflexive pronouns → Unit 9, Exercise 32

8.2.1 Form / Form

myself, yourself, himself, herself, itself, oneself	Einzahlformen enden auf **-self**,
ourselves, yourselves, themselves	die Mehrzahlformen auf **-selves**.

8.2.2 Gebrauch / Use

(1) Paul did the work **himself**.

(2) The house owners **themselves** have asked us to move in earlier.

Das Pronomen auf *-self, -selves* kann zur **Hervorhebung** benutzt werden. Wird ein Satzsubjekt verstärkend betont, tritt das Pronomen an das Satzende (1), sonst hinter das zu betonende Nomen oder Pronomen (2).

May I introduce **myself**? My name's …
Please, help **yourself**. The drinks are over there.
He has cut **himself** with the kitchen knife.

Das Pronomen wird rückbezüglich (reflexiv) verwendet, wenn Subjekt und Objekt eines Satzes dieselbe(n) Person(en) bezeichnen.

Viele reflexive deutsche Verben haben im Englischen eine **nicht reflexive** Entsprechung, wie z. B. **to change, to concentrate**, **to feel**, **to meet**, **to relax**, **to remember** und **to sit down**.

8.3 Beziehungsfürwörter oder Relativpronomen / Relative pronouns → Unit 16, Exercise 33

Marconi is the man	**who** **that**	invented the radio.
There's one shop	**which** **that**	stays open late.
I didn't like the actor	(**who**) (**that**)	I saw last time
That's a superstition	(**which**) (**that**)	we all know about.

Der Relativsatz bestimmt das vorhergehende Hauptwort: Marconi ist der **Mann**, **der / welcher** das Radio erfand. Es gibt ein **Geschäft, das / welches** spät geöffnet hat. Für Personen wird **who** oder **that**, für Sachen **which** oder **that** benutzt.

Bestimmende oder notwendige Relativsätze stehen im Gegensatz zum Deutschen **ohne** Komma. Hat der Relativsatz einen eigenen Satzgegenstand / ein eigenes Subjekt, **kann** das Relativpronomen entfallen.

9 Verhältniswörter / Prepositions → Unit 7, Exercise 34

Präpositionen sind Wörter, die in der Regel vor Haupt- und Fürwörtern stehen, Beziehungsverhältnisse ausdrücken und Satzglieder in den Satz einfügen. Deshalb werden sie auch **Fügewörter** genannt: **bei, über, unter, von …**

about	**along**	**before**	**by**	**in**	**of**	**over**	**through**	**up**
above	**around**	**below**	**down**	**into**	**off**	**past**	**to**	**with**
across	**as**	**beside**	**for**	**like**	**on**	**since**	**under**	**without**
after	**at**	**between**	**from**	**near**	**onto**	**till**	**until**	

Sie lassen sich in drei Hauptkategorien einteilen: (1) **Ort und Raum**, (2) **Zeit und Dauer,** (3) **Logik und Modalität**.
(1) Paul parked **in front of** the building. Pamela's car is **in** the car park **behind** the town hall.
(2) **On** Fridays he worked **until** midnight. His friends left the party **before** 11 p.m. They visited Toronto **in** 1994.
(3) We talked **about** that problem all day yesterday. **For** several reasons we should start **from** the very beginning.

Achtung:

by = bis (spätestens)	It must be ready **by** 5 p.m.
in = in (Ortsangabe)	He lives **in** Osnabrück. He has to stay **in** his office.
into = in (hinein) (Richtungsangabe)	She went **into** the school building.

10 Unregelmäßige Verben / Irregular verbs

be, was / were, have (has) been	sein	leave, left, have left	verlassen, abfahren
begin, began, have begun	beginnen	let, let, have let	lassen
break, broke, have broken	brechen	make, made, have made	machen
bring, brought, have brought	bringen	mean, meant, have meant	meinen, bedeuten
build, built, have built	bauen	meet, met, have met	treffen, begegnen
buy, bought, have bought	kaufen	put, put, have put	stellen, legen
come, came, have come	kommen	read, read, have read	lesen
do, did, have done	tun, machen	ring, rang, have rung	anrufen, klingeln
drink, drank, have drunk	trinken	say, said, have said	sagen
drive, drove, have driven	(Auto) fahren	see, saw, have seen	sehen
eat, ate, have eaten	essen	sell, sold, have sold	verkaufen
fall, fell, have fallen	fallen	show, showed, have shown	zeigen
feel, felt, have felt	(sich) fühlen	sing, sang, have sung	singen
find, found, have found	finden	sit, sat, have sat	sitzen
get, got, have got	bekommen	sleep, slept, have slept	schlafen
give, gave, have given	geben	speak, spoke, have spoken	sprechen
go, went, have gone	gehen, fahren	spend, spent, have spent	verbringen, ausgeben
have, had, have had	haben	stand, stood, have stood	stehen
hear, heard, have heard	hören	swim, swam, have swum	schwimmen
know, knew, have known	wissen, kennen	take, took, have taken	nehmen

Grammar exercises

Die Lösungen zu diesen Übungsseiten finden Sie auf Seite 149.

1 (Grammar 1.1): Ergänzen Sie die Sätze mit dem passenden Frageanhängsel.
Beispiel: *She speaks English and Swedish, doesn't she?*

1 You play golf, ……………………?
2 She's got a sister, ……………………?
3 We'll get there early, ……………………?
4 Terry doesn't drive, ……………………?
5 They had a wonderful time, ……………………?
6 They aren't married, ……………………?
7 It rained all day, ……………………?
8 The news sounded terrible, ……………………?

2 (Grammar 1.2): Eine Kollegin erwähnt eine bevorstehende Reise nach London. Sie stellen mit Erstaunen fest, dass Sie die gleichen Pläne haben. Reagieren Sie mit *So … I / Neither … I (Nor … I).*
Beispiel: *I think London's a wonderful city. So do I.*

1 I've been there twice. So …………………… .
2 I went there last summer. So …………………… .
3 But I didn't have time to see everything.
Neither …………………… .
4 I'd like to go there again this summer.
…………………… .
5 I won't stay at an expensive hotel.
…………………… .
6 I've got three weeks holiday this year.
…………………… .
7 I can't leave till the beginning of August.
…………………… .

3 (Grammar 1.3): Bilden Sie aus den angegebenen Satzteilen einen vollständigen Satz. Achten Sie dabei auf die richtige Wortstellung!

1 gets up / at about eight o'clock / always / My cousin Jane / every morning
My cousin Jane ……………………
……………………
2 doesn't / have / breakfast / any / often / She
She ……………………
……………………
3 can / a cup of coffee / later / at the office / always / She / have / in the morning
She ……………………
……………………
4 Jane / at the office / When / arrives / starts / at once / seldom / she / work
When ……………………
……………………
5 first / the newspaper / quite often / She / reads / makes / sometimes / she / a few / or / phone calls
She ……………………
……………………
……………………
6 starts / work / Jane / never / before / has / secretary / her / hot / a / brought / her / a / cup of coffee
Jane ……………………
……………………
……………………

4 (Grammar 1.4): Meine Schwester wohnt bei London. Stellen Sie Fragen über ihr Alltagsleben. Die Antworten auf die Fragen sind angegeben.

Ask about

1 her job
What does your sister do? / What job has she got?
"She works for a large American company."
2 her hobbies
……………………
"She doesn't have much time for hobbies, I'm afraid."
3 her favourite food
……………………
"She loves eating cheese salads."
4 where she goes on holiday
……………………
"She and her husband often fly to Italy."
5 what she reads
……………………
"Magazines, papers, books. Her favourite writer is Ruth Rendell."
6 what TV programmes she watches
……………………
"Mastermind – that's a quiz show."
7 her children
……………………
"She's got a boy and a girl, they're in their twenties."
8 where she lives.
……………………
"In Epsom, just near London."

5 (Grammar 1.5): Lesen Sie die Sätze. Sie beschreiben Situationen, die man verändern könnte, wenn …
Beispiel: Terry doesn't speak French, so he won't get the job.
If Terry spoke French, he'd (would) get the job.

1 Terry doesn't take much exercise. That's why he's too fat.
If .... more exercise,
he ....
2 Terry watches TV till midnight every evening. He always feels so tired.
If .... ,
he .... so tired.
3 He doesn't drive to work, because he can't park near his office.
If he .... his car to work, he
.... (have) a problem with parking.
4 Because he leaves home too late, he always misses the bus.
If .... earlier, he
.... the bus.
5 His boss doesn't want to give him more money. He thinks he must work harder.
Terry's boss .... more money if he
.... harder.
6 Terry isn't very happy. Perhaps he should change his job!
He .... a lot happier if he
.... his job.

6 (Grammar 1.5): Freunde kommen mit Problemen zu Ihnen. Erteilen Sie Ratschläge mit *If I were you, I would …*

1 I find it difficult to get to sleep.
If I were you, ... *(go)* later.
2 I've never got enough money.
If I .... , I .... *(spend)* so much.
3 I can't cook very well.
If .... , I .... *(buy)* a cookbook.
4 My neighbours are very noisy.
If .... , I .... *(speak)* to them about it.
5 I need a holiday.
If .... , I .... *(fly)* to Majorca for two weeks.
6 I think I'm getting fat.
If .... , I .... *(eat)* so much.

7 (Grammar 2.1): Was man gern und weniger gern hat. Ergänzen Sie das Interview mit den entsprechenden Verben: *(don't) mind / enjoy / like / love / can't stand / dislike / hate.*

– Excuse me. I'm from the local paper, the Daily Argus. We're doing some articles about what people like and dislike. Do you mind .... (1 *answer*) some questions?
– Not at all. Go on. But I haven't got so much time, I'm afraid.
– That's all right. What do you hate most?
– Well, to tell you the truth, I hate .... (2 *pay*) bills, but I'm sure that most people dislike .... (3 *do*) that. And I can't stand .... (4 *queue*), especially in banks, post offices and at the supermarket.
– What about at home? Do you like .... (5 *get*) phone calls late at night?
– No, that isn't such a problem. I enjoy .... (6 *use*) the phone, actually. What else? I don't like .... (7 *write*) letters, but I love .... (8 *get*) them from friends. I suppose a lot of people will say that. Oh, I forgot to tell you, I'm on the way to the dentist. I don't enjoy .... (9 *go*) there, I must say.

8 (Grammar 2.1.2): Bill ist jetzt 65 Jahre alt. Er hat im letzten Mai aufgehört, zu arbeiten. Da er nicht wusste, wie er seine Zeit verbringen sollte, besuchte er einen interessanten Kurs. Dort sollte er ein Formular ausfüllen. Ergänzen Sie die Antworten.

1 Which sports are you interested in?
I'm interested .... *(play)* tennis.
2 What do you enjoy most?
I enjoy .... *(work)* in the garden.
3 Do you make friends easily?
Yes, I'm fond .... *(meet)* people.
4 What are you bad at?
I'm bad .... *(cook)*.
5 Are you a good organizer?
Yes, in my last job I was responsible .... *(arrange)* all our parties.
6 Are you afraid of hard work?
No, I'm not afraid .... *(work)* hard!
7 Do you mind late nights?
No, I don't mind .... *(stay up)* late.

9 **(Grammar 2.3.1):** In diesen Sätzen geht es um eine offizielle Erlaubnis. Ersetzen Sie *can / could etc.* mit dem Ersatzverb *be allowed to*. Achten Sie auf die richtige Form des Verbs!

1 Because the teacher was ill, the children *(could)* .... go home early.
2 *(Can / your son)* .... stay out late every evening?
3 I'm sorry. You *(can't)* .... speak to the Minister tomorrow.
4 I *(couldn't)* .... drive a car until I was 18.
5 In some countries you *(can't)* .... take photos at airports or railway stations.
6 From next week visitors *(can)* .... visit every room in the palace.

10 **(Grammar 2.3.3):** Was ist richtig: ***mustn't*** oder ***needn't***? Setzen Sie die richtige Form ein.

1 You .... drive so fast. The sign over there says 30 miles an hour!
2 Tomorrow's a holiday, so my brother .... get up early.
3 Chan understands English very well, so you .... speak to him in Chinese.
4 This is the no-smoking area of the restaurant, so you .... light a cigarette here.
5 Our neighbours have told us that we .... play the piano after 10 o'clock at night.
6 It isn't raining, so you .... take your umbrella with you to the shops.
7 Sarah's got enough cash, so she .... go to the bank.

11 **(Grammar 2.4):** Lesen Sie die Antworten und bilden Sie die dazu passenden Fragen.

1 How many languages .... *(Margaret / speak)*? She speaks four languages.
2 .... *(she / need)* them in her job? Yes, she does.
3 Where .... *(she / work)*? In a bank.
4 What .... *(she / do)*? She gives advice about money problems.
5 What time .... *(she / finish)* her work? Usually at six, but she often works late.

12 **(Grammar 2.4):** Schreiben Sie die richtigen Formen der Gegenwart.

My husband and I (1 *like*) .... holidays very much, of course, but we (2 *not / go*) .... to other countries very often. Every summer we (3 *drive*) .... to the seaside and (4 *stay*) .... at one of the hotels there. We (5 *usually / be*) .... very lucky with the weather. Of course, people (6 *say*) .... that it (7 *rain / always*) .... a lot in England, but every year the sun (8 *always / shine*) .... Our friends in Germany (9 *not / believe*) .... this when we (10 *tell*) .... them. The hotel (11 *not / be*) .... very big – there (12 *be*) .... only about twenty rooms, but it (13 *be*) .... very comfortable. The other people in the hotel (14 *be*) .... very friendly and we (15 *play / sometimes*) .... cards together in the evening.

13 **(Grammar 2.5):** Bilden Sie Sätze mit *already* und *not yet. (…n't … yet)* wie im Beispiel. Verwenden Sie folgende Verben: *leave, knit, earn, sell, pay.*
Beispiel: *Bill's already had a bath, but he hasn't had his dinner yet.*

1 Sally's already .... all her bills, but Bert .... his bills yet.
2 Bert .... his house for £ 150,000, but Anita .... her house yet.
3 Anita .... a lot of money, but her sister .... much money yet.
4 Terry .... the house, but his wife .... the house yet.
5 Sue .... two pullovers, but I .... any pullovers yet.

14 **(Grammar 2.5.3):** Ein befreundetes Ehepaar erzählt Ihnen über Robert und seine Frau. Stellen Sie Fragen mit *how long* und der vollendeten Gegenwart. Streichen Sie in der Antwort die falsche Form (*since* oder *for*) durch.

1 We **know** Robert very well.
Oh, yes. How long .... him?
For / Since three years.
2 He **lives** with his wife in King St.
How long .... there?
For / Since 1989.
3 Robert **works** for a computer company.

How long .... there?
For / Since ages.

4 He **has** a sports car.
Really? How long .... it?
For / Since May.

5 He and his wife **are** members of the local tennis club.
Oh, how long .... members?
For / Since a year.

15 (Grammar 2.6): Bilden Sie Sätze in der Vergangenheit mit den angegebenen Verben. Achten Sie darauf, dass immer eine Satzhälfte verneint werden muss. Lesen Sie den Beispielsatz.

1 **go / spend:** Vera ***went*** to Rome for two weeks, but she ***didn't spend*** any time in museums.
2 **take / have:** She .... a raincoat with her, but she .... an umbrella.
3 **eat / drink:** Vera .... a lot of Italian food, but she .... any red wine.
4 **meet / see:** Vera .... some friends in Rome, but she .... any film stars.
5 **find / walk:** She .... the way to the Vatican, but she .... to the Forum.
6 **buy / wear:** She .... a new dress in Rome, but she .... it every day.
7 **send / write:** Vera .... postcards to her friends, but she .... any letters.

16 (Grammar 2.6.3): Was hat Percy früher getan und was macht er jetzt? Bilden Sie Sätze wie im Beispiel.
Beispiel: *Percy – playboy; now: not spend much money. Percy used to be a playboy, but now he doesn't spend much money.*

1 Percy – got up at – 11 a.m; now: get up – very early
2 drink whisky; now: only – drink water
3 smoke – 40 cigarettes a day; now: not smoke
4 not take any exercise; now: run five miles every day
5 not eat – fruit; now: always – eat – two apples for lunch
6 drive – big car; now: ride a bike to work
7 not go to bed before midnight; now: go to bed – ten o'clock

17 (Grammar 2.7): Lesen Sie den folgenden Text. Wählen Sie die richtige Verbform und streichen Sie die falsche durch. Nur **eine** ist richtig!

When I was about 18, I *(1) travelled / have travelled* to Spain for the first time. Of course, since then I *(2) was in / have been to* Spain a few times. But this first visit *(3) was / has been* very special for me. At that time I *(4) didn't know / haven't known* any Spanish. After that visit I *(5) decided / have decided* to take lessons. I *(6) learnt / have learnt* the language very well since that first visit. I *(7) wanted / have wanted* to go back to Spain for a long time now and next summer I can again spend two weeks in Madrid! I *(8) heard / have heard* that the city *changed / has changed* a lot since my first visit.

18 (Grammar 2.8): Tragen Sie die richtige Form des Verbs (einfache oder vollendete Vergangenheit) ein.

1 When Melanie *(finish)* .... her work, she *(feel)* .... very tired.
2 The robbers *(run away)* .... with the money by the time the police *(arrive)* ....
3 After Boris *(take)* .... a cookery course, he *(cook)* .... wonderful meals for his friends.
4 I *(not/eat)* .... paella before I *(go)* .... to Spain.
5 When Philip *(answer)* .... all the questions, he *(put)* .... his books away.
6 She *(buy)* .... a dress for £ 250 before the shop *(begin)* .... to reduce their prices.
7 They *(see)* .... the film at the cinema after a friend *(tell)* .... them about it.
8 I *(try)* .... to phone her yesterday, but then I suddenly *(remember)* .... that she *(go)* .... away.

19 (Grammar 2.9): Wie lautet die richtige Form des Verbs – einfache Form oder Verlaufsform?
Beispiel: *Mary (drink)* .... *coffee nearly every day but today she (drink)* .... *tea.* ➔ *Mary drinks coffee nearly every day but today she's drinking tea.*

– Hello, Tony. There's a letter for you this morning.
– Oh, thanks. What a nice stamp! Ah – the letter's from Pat – she (1 *spend*) .... her holiday in Barbados at the moment. She (2 *go*) .... there every summer. She (3 *like*) .... the place and she (4 *know*) .... a lot of people there. Well, she says in this letter that she (5 *have*) .... a good time. She (6 *play*) .... tennis most afternoons.
– I (7 *not/understand*) .... Isn't it too hot for tennis?
– Well, perhaps it's table tennis. She (8 *play*) .... quite well.

– What's the food like?
– She (9 *not often/eat*) .... at the hotel. She says that they (10 *not / cook*) .... the food she (11 *like*) ....
– (12 *she / stay*) .... at an expensive hotel?
– I (13 *think*) .... it must be quite expensive. It's got a fitness centre and a swimming pool. Listen to this. She says: "I (14 *write*) .... this letter by the pool, I (15 *drink*) .... a rum with a lot of ice, the sun (16 *shine*) .... and I (17 *want*) .... to stay here for ever."
– That's typical of your sister! She (18 *always / write*) .... the same!

20 (Grammar 2.10): Welche Form des Verbs ist richtig?

1 At 8 o'clock last night my parents *watched / were watching* TV and I *did / was doing* my homework.
2 My father *washed / was washing* the car when it *started / was starting* to rain.
3 Andrew had a date with Fiona. But when he *arrived / was arriving* at the station, she *did not wait / was not waiting* for him.
4 While we *listened / were listening* to the news yesterday, we *heard / were hearing* about the accident.
5 – I *sat / was sitting* in the bus last night in Oxford Road and I saw you outside the Odeon Cinema. What *did you do / were you doing*?
– Oh, we *tried / were trying* to get tickets for that new Chinese film, but it was hopeless. About a hundred people *stood / were standing* in the queue.
6 Old Mrs Peters *cross / was crossing* the road when she *fell / was falling* and *hurt / was hurting* her leg.

21 (Grammar 2.11): Morgen ist Johnny sehr beschäftigt. Lesen Sie seine Notizen und schreiben Sie auf, was er vorhat (Zukunft mit *going to*).

Beispiel: write some letters
Johnny's going to write some letters tomorrow.

1 meet some friends in town
....
2 have a drink with Annie
....
3 phone the dentist
....
4 have a swim
....
5 buy a video cassette
....

22 (Grammar 2.13): Wie wird die Welt im Jahre 2020 aussehen? Machen Sie Vorhersagen mit *will be* und *won't be*. Achten Sie darauf, dass Sie *there will be / there won't be* mit Substantiven *(there'll be an accident)* verwenden und *it will be / it won't be* mit Adjektiven *(it'll be hot)*.

What will the world look like in the year 2020? Many people say that (1) .... more cars on the roads and the air (2) .... a lot dirtier. Very pessimistic people say that (3) .... enough jobs for everybody. (4) .... easy to find one. But let's be optimistic. Experts say (5) .... easier to do your shopping. You (6) .... able to stay at home and shop by computer. (7) .... necessary to leave your house. But (8) .... boring to live like that? (9) .... less chance of meeting new people. Experts may be wrong, of course. In my opinion, (10) .... fascinating to live in the year 2020!

23 (Grammar 2.14): Ergänzen Sie die richtige Form des Verbs (einfache Gegenwart oder Zukunft mit *will*)

1 I'd like to speak to Mr Blakeney when he .... *(arrive)*
2 We .... *(leave)* the house as soon as the rain .... *(stop)*.
3 Before you .... *(use)* this machine, please read the handbook very carefully.
4 As soon as I .... *(know)* the answer to your questions, I .... *(send)* you a fax.
5 They .... *(phone)* us from the shop when they .... *(want)* to bring our new TV.
6 If you want to leave early tomorrow morning, I suppose you .... *(have)* breakfast before everybody .... *(get up)*.

24 (Grammar 4): Ergänzen Sie den Text mit *a, an,* und *the*. In einigen Fällen muss man den Artikel weglassen.

Carol worked as (1) .... nurse at (2) .... Lancaster Hospital. One day (3) .... young man had (4) .... car accident and they took him to (5) .... hospital. It was (6) .... hospital where Carol worked. (7) .... young man was very ill and he needed (8) .... lot of help. Carol looked after him. She used to bring him (9) .... different newpapers and

(10) .... interesting magazines. He talked about his job as (11) .... university teacher. She talked about her work as (12) .... nurse. After (13) .... month he was better. He didn't want to leave (14) .... hospital, because he liked Carol so much. (15) .... end of (16) .... story is that they are now happily married and have (17) .... eight-year-old boy.

25 **(Grammar 5.2):** In der Werbung ist immer alles bestens *(best, biggest, fastest, most attractive etc.)*. Vervollständigen Sie die Werbeaussagen mit folgenden Eigenschaftswörtern im Superlativ: *cheap, fast (X2), interesting, little, attractive, good, expensive.*

1 The Tiger Supremo is the .... car in the world, 0 to 100 in 3 seconds!
2 This week's special offers at low prices – they're the .... in town!
3 Do you want the most for the .... money?
4 The .... museums in the world are just a few minutes from your hotel.
5 This week only – our .... watches at half-price!
6 Liverpool in under three hours! Intercity trains are the .... way to travel.
7 The dresses from our store in Oxford Street are the .... you can buy.
8 Is it time for a holiday? We can offer you the .... for your money!

26 **(Grammar 6):** Streichen Sie das falsche Wort durch.

My brother lives quite (1) *happy / happily* in a small house near London. He catches the morning train to the City every day. He prefers the train. He says that it gets him to work (2) *quick / quickly* and (3) *easy / easily*. The train service is still quite (4) *good / well*, although the monthly ticket is now rather (5) *expensive / expensively*. He says he can work (6) *good / well* on the train if it isn't too (7) *full / fully*. When there are too many people on the train, he sometimes feels (8) *terrible / terribly* and that makes him (9) *angry / angrily*. He works very (10) *hard / hardly* in his London office all day. Sometimes he doesn't even have time for lunch. In the summer he may go to a local open-air café where the food tastes (11) *wonderful / wonderfully*. He often arrives home after it gets (12) *dark / darkly*.

27 **(Grammar 6.5):** Lesen Sie jeweils den ersten Satz und vervollständigen Sie dann den zweiten Satz mit einer Steigerungsform des Adverbs *(more quickly, faster etc.)*

1 You weren't very careful with this work.
You must work .... *(careful)* next time!
2 I'm sorry, I can't understand you.
Can you speak .... *(clear)*, please?
3 I have to be at the airport in 10 minutes.
Please drive .... *(fast)*.
4 Your sister can't see very well, can she?
Well, she can see .... *(good)* with her new glasses.
5 That old chair isn't very comfortable.
You can sit .... *(comfortable)* in this one.
6 What's that terrible noise?
It's my brother. He sings .... *(bad)* than anyone else in the family.

28 **(Grammar 7.1):** Schreiben Sie *much* oder *many* in diesen Fragen und verneinten Sätzen.

1 How .... time have you got?
2 There weren't .... people at the concert.
3 We didn't have .... trouble with our baggage.
4 They couldn't give us very .... information.
5 She didn't buy .... clothes on holiday.
6 There isn't .... sugar in this coffee.
7 Have you got .... friends?
8 There isn't .... news in this paper.
9 We didn't see .... police at the match.
10 Do you have .... homework?

29 **(Grammar 7.1):** Jetzt schreiben Sie Aussagesätze für Sätze 2, 3, 5, 6, 8 und 9 in der letzten Übung. Verwenden Sie *a lot of*.

30 **(Grammar 7.3):** Lesen Sie die Sätze. Setzen Sie die passenden *quantifiers (both of, all of, none of, some of, a lot of, most of, a few of, one of)* ein.

1 His two brothers are older than he is.
.... his brothers are older than he is.
2 About six of seven of my friends like dancing.
.... my friends like dancing.
3 About 10,000 people were at the concert.
.... people were at the concert.
4 90% of the questions were difficult.
.... the questions were difficult.

5 Every student came to the lesson.

.... the students came to the lesson.

6 Three or four of these books look interesting.

.... these books look interesting.

7 My friends can't speak Italian.

.... my friends can speak Italian.

8 'Psycho' is the Hitchcock film that made millions.

.... Hitchcock's films made millions.

31 (Grammar 8.1): Ergänzen Sie die Sätze mit einem Possessivpronomen *(mine, yours etc.)*

1 I'm sorry. I haven't got a pen. Can I borrow .... for a minute, Ted?

2 I didn't have an umbrella when I went out to lunch, so Tessa lent me ....

3 I think we'll have to buy a new microwave oven. .... has got something wrong with it.

4 – Who do those glasses belong to, you or Billy?
– Well, I've got my glasses here, so they must be ....

5 Now they've got a baby, the Barclays are moving into a new flat. .... is too small for them.

6 Oh, here's the coffee! I'm very thirsty. Now, which cup is ....?

32 (Grammar 8.2): Ergänzen Sie das folgende Party-Gespräch mit den passenden Reflexivpronomen *(myself etc.)*

Hello, Margaret, hello, Peter. I hope that you're enjoying (1) .... Try some of this fruitcake. My wife made it (2) .... And you're drinking my special beer. I make it (3) .... in the kitchen, it's very easy, you know. Are you hungry? There are some cheese sandwiches on the table. Help (4) ...., Margaret, I know you like cheese. My son isn't here, I'm sorry. When we have a party, he shuts (5) .... in his bedroom! He hates parties. By the way, do you know our neighbours? They're both architects – they designed their house (6) ...., it looks great! They also designed this room for us. We're hopeless – we couldn't do it (7) ....! Now, can the two of you look after (8) .... for a few minutes. I've got to open another bottle of wine …

33 (Grammar 8.3): In diesem Text fehlen die Relativpronomen. Finden Sie das passende Pronomen. Wo kann man das Pronomen weglassen?

Some years ago, a friend invited me to an old country house (1) .... he had just bought. The train (2) .... I caught was slow and I arrived at the country station very late. There weren't many people (3) .... wanted to get out. I picked up the bag (4) .... was on the seat next to me and got out of the train. I stood there and looked around. There was no one to meet me. I looked for a taxi (5) .... could take me to my friend's house, but I couldn't find any taxis outside the station. There wasn't anybody (6) .... I could ask for a lift. It was now dark. The map (7) .... I had in my pocket was useless. But I remembered that my friend lived near the end of the road (8) .... passed the station. I decided to walk. I walked to the top of the hill and found the road (9) .... went to my friend's house. The house (10) .... I saw in front of me was dark. It was all very strange …

34 (Grammar 9): Lesen Sie die Sätze und wählen Sie die richtige Präposition.

I was born (1) *at / in / on* midnight (2) *at / in / on* December 24th. It was a cold night (3) *at / un / on* winter and it was difficult to find a doctor (4) *at / in / on* Christmas. My father drove my mother (5) *at / in / into* the nearest town and stopped (6) *before / in / in* front of the hospital. He ran (7) *in / into / on* the building and looked for a doctor who was working (8) *at / in / on* night. The doctor looked (9) *at / on / to* my mother and asked my father to wait. That was (10) *at / in / on* eleven o'clock. An hour later I was born. My parents often talk (11) *about / at / on* that winter night (12) *at / in / on* 1958.

Key Grammar exercises

1 1 don't you, 2 hasn't she, 3 won't we, 4 does he, 5 didn't they, 6 are they, 7 didn't it, 8 didn't it

2 1 So have I. 2 So did I. 3 Neither/ Nor did I. 4 So would I. 5 Neither/ Nor will I. 6 So have I. 7 Neither/ Nor can I.

3 1 My cousin Jane always gets up at about eight o'clock every morning. 2 She doesn't often have any breakfast. 3 She can always have a cup of coffee at the office later in the morning. 4 When Jane arrives at the office, she seldom starts work at once. 5 She quite often reads the newspaper first or she sometimes makes a few phone calls. 6 Jane never starts work before her secretary has brought her a hot cup of coffee.

4 2 What are her hobbies?/Does she have any hobbies?/Has she got any hobbies? 3 What is her favourite food? 4 Where does your sister go on holiday?/Where does she spend her holiday? 5 What does she read?/Does she read ...? 6 What TV programmes does she watch? 7 How many children has she got? / How old are her children? 8 Where does she live?

5 1 If he took, wouldn't be; 2 If he didn't watch so much TV, he wouldn't feel; 3 If he drove, he would have; 4 If he left home, he wouldn't always miss; 5 would give him, if he worked; 6 He would be, if he changed

6 If I were you, 1 I'd (= would) go to bed later. 2 I wouldn't spend so much. 3 I'd buy a cookbook. 4 I'd speak to them about it. 5 I'd fly to Majorca for 2 weeks. 6 I wouldn't eat so much.

7 1 answering, 2 paying, 3 doing, 4 queuing, 5 getting, 6 using, 7 writing, 8 getting, 9 going

8 1 in playing, 2 working, 3 of meeting, 4 at cooking, 5 for arranging, 6 of working, 7 staying up late

9 1 were allowed to, 2 is your son allowed to, 3 won't be allowed to, 4 wasn't allowed to, 5 aren't allowed to, 6 will be allowed to

10 1 mustn't drive, 2 needn't get up, 3 needn't speak, 4 mustn't light, 5 mustn't play, 6 needn't take, 7 needn't go

11 1 does Margaret speak? 2 Does she need, 3 does she work? 4 does she do? 5 does she finish

12 1 like, 2 don't go (do not go), 3 drive, 4 stay, 5 are usually, 6 say, 7 always rains, 8 always shines, 9 don't believe (do not believe), 10 tell 11 isn't (is not), 12 are, 13 is, 14 are, 15 sometimes play

13 1 Sally's already paid ..., but Bert hasn't paid his bills yet. 2 Bert's already sold ..., but Anita hasn't sold her house yet. 3 Anita's already earned ..., but her sister hasn't earned much money yet. 4 Terry's already left ..., but his wife hasn't left ... yet. 5 Sue's already knitted ..., but I haven't knitted ... yet.

14 1 have you known/For, 2 has he / have they lived/Since, 3 has he worked/For, 4 has he had/Since, 5 have they been/For

15 2 took /didn't have, 3 ate / didn't drink, 4 met / didn't see, 5 found /didn't walk, 6 bought /didn't wear, 7 sent / didn't write

16 1 Percy used to get up at 11 a.m., but now he gets up very early. 2 He used to drink whisky, but now he only drinks water. 3 He used to smoke 40 cigarettes a day, but now he doesn't smoke. 4 He didn't use to take any exercise, but now he runs five miles every day. 5 He didn't use two eat any fruit, but now he always eats two apples for lunch. 6 He used to drive a big car, but now he rides a bike to work. 7 He didn't use to go to bed before midnight, but now he goes to bed at ten o'clock.

17 1 travelled, 2 have been to, 3 was, 4 didn't know, 5 decided, 6 have learnt, 7 have wanted, 8 have heard/ has changed

18 1 had finished/felt, 2 had run away/arrived, 3 had taken/ cooked, 4 had not eaten/went, 5 had answered/put, 6 had bought/began, 7 saw/had told, 8 tried/remembered/ had gone

19 1 she's spending, 2 goes, 3 likes, 4 knows, 5 she's having, 6 plays, 7 don't understand, 8 plays, 9 doesn't often eat, 10 don't cook, 11 likes, 12 Is she staying, 13 think, 14 'm writing, 15 'm drinking, 16 is shining, 17 want, 18 always writes

20 1 were watching/was doing, 2 was washing/started, 3 arrived/was not waiting, 4 were listening/heard, 5 was sitting/were you doing/were trying/were standing, 6 was crossing/fell/hurt

21 1 He's going to meet some friends. 2 He's going to have a drink with Annie. 3 He's going to phone the dentist. 4 He's going to have a swim. 5 He's going to buy a video cassette.

22 1 there'll be (there will be), 2 will be, 3 there won't be, 4 It won't be, 5 it'll be (it will be), 6 will be, 7 It won't be, 8 won't it be, 9 There'll be (will be), 10 it'll be (it will be)

23 1 arrives, 2 we'll leave/stops, 3 use, 4 know,/'ll send, 5 'll phone/want, 6 'll have/gets up

24 1 a, 2 –, 3 a, 4 a, 5 –, 6 the, 7 The, 8 a, 9 –, 10 –, 11 a, 12 a, 13 a, 14 – / (the), 15 The, 16 the, 17 an

25 1 fastest, 2 cheapest/best, 3 least, 4 most interesting/ best, 5 most expensive/best, 6 fastest/best, 7 cheapest/ most/attractive/best, 8 best

26 Richtig ist: 1 happily, 2 quickly, 3 easily, 4 good, 5 expensive, 6 well, 7 full, 8 terrible, 9 angry, 10 hard, 11 wonderful, 12 dark

27 1 more carefully, 2 more clearly, 3 faster, 4 better, 5 more comfortably, 6 worse

28 1 much, 2 many, 3 much, 4 much, 5 many, 6 much, 7 many, 8 much, 9 many, 10 much

29 2 were a lot of people, 3 we had a lot of trouble, 5 bought a lot of clothes, 6 there's a lot of sugar, 8 there's a lot of news, 9 we saw a lot of police

30 1 Both of his brothers, 2 Some of my friends/A few of my friends, 3 A lot of people, 4 Most of the questions, 5 All of the students, 6 A few of these books / Some of these books, 7 None of my friends, 8 One of Hitchcock's films

31 1 yours, 2 hers, 3 ours, 4 his, 5 theirs, 6 mine

32 1 yourselves, 2 herself, 3 myself, 4 yourself, 5 himself, 6 themselves, 7 ourselves, 8 yourselves

33 1 which/that, 2 (which)/(that), 3 who/that, 4 which/ that, 6 (that), 5 which/that, 8 which/that, 7 (that)/ (which), 10 (which)/(that), 9 which/that
Entfallen kann das Relativpronomen in den Sätzen: 2, 6, 7 und 10.

34 1 at midnight, 2 on December 24th, 3 in winter, 4 at Christmas, 5 into the nearest town, 6 in front of the hospital, 7 ran into the building, 8 at night, 9 looked at my mother, 10 at eleven o'clock, 11 talk about, 12 in 1958.

How to say it

Eine Zusammenfassung wichtiger Redemittel

Die *kursiv* gesetzten Redewendungen sind etwas formeller oder sehr höflicher Sprachstil.

Abneigung ausdrücken → Unit 15
I *dislike* / don't like (eating) fruit.

Angebote aussprechen → Unit 6
Shall I carry that for you?
Let me do that for you.
Can I help you?
Would you like some sugar with your tea?
Yes, please.
That's very kind of you. / You're very kind.
Thank you. (usw., s. *danken*)

Begründungen abgeben → Unit 10
I went on holiday in August so that I could enjoy the good weather.
I went on holiday in August (in order) to enjoy the good weather.
I went on holiday in August because I wanted to enjoy the good weather.

Begrüßungen aussprechen und darauf reagieren → Units 2 + 9
Hello. / Hi. / How do you do?
Nice to meet you. / How do you do?
Hi, there! I've heard a lot about you.
Hi, I haven't seen you for ages.

Bitten äußern → Unit 6
Can you do that for me, please?
Do you think you could possibly help me, please?
Would you carry that for me, please?

Briefanreden und -schluß → Unit 13
Dear Mum,
Dear Peter,
Dear Mr Richards,
With love,
Best wishes,
Yours sincerely,

Danken und darauf reagieren → Unit 12
Thanks (a lot / very much).
Thank you (*very much indeed*).
That's okay / *quite all right*. / You're welcome.

Einkaufen → Unit 12
What size do I take?
Does it / Do they fit me?
Does the colour suit me?
How much is this shirt?
How much are these trousers?
Can I try it / them on, please?

Einladungen aussprechen, annehmen und abschlagen → Unit 18
Would you like (to have) a cup of coffee?
How about having a cup of coffee together?
Shall we have a cup of coffee together after work?
That's very kind of you.
I'm afraid I can't.
I'd love to.

(Sich) Entschuldigen und auf Entschuldigungen reagieren → Unit 11
I'm (very) sorry that I'm late.
That's all right. / It doesn't matter.

Komplimente machen → Unit 19
What a pretty dress!
You're a very good cook!
You did a good job of work!

Meinung ausdrücken → Unit 16
Personally speaking, I think ... / don't like it.
What's your opinion? / What do you think?
I think ...

Möglichkeit ausdrücken → Unit 14
I hope / think / expect he will read it.
Perhaps he will read it.
He probably will read it.
He may / might read it.
I'm sure he will read it.

Ratschläge geben → Unit 17
If I were you, I would go there.
What about going there?
I (really don't) think you should go there.
Why don't you go there?
I suggest ...ing ...
You could go there.

(Im) Restaurant → Unit 15
What would you like to eat/drink?
Would you like white wine?
Would you prefer beer?
Could we order (a starter / a main course / a dessert), please?

How to say it

I'd like a tomato salad, please.
I think I'll have a beer, please.
Could you bring me some bread, please?
Cheers!
Can / Could I have the bill, please?
Do you take credit cards?

Soziale Konventionen → Unit 20

Cheers.
Bless you.
Good luck.
Congratulations!

Telefonieren → Unit 4

Hello, this is …
Good morning, … speaking.
Can I speak to …?
Could you put me through to …, please?
Wait a minute, I'll tell … you're on the phone.
Could you hold on a moment, please?
I'm sorry … has just gone out.
I'm afraid … is not in at the moment.
Can I take a message?
Would you like to leave a message?
You can ring back later if you like.
Would you like to call back later?

(Sich) Verabschieden → Units 9 + 13

Good-bye. / Bye. / Bye-bye.
See you tomorrow.
Take care.
Have a good trip.
With love,
Best wishes,
Yours sincerely,

Vorlieben ausdrücken → Unit 15

I enjoy / like / love (eating) fruit.

Vorschläge machen und darauf reagieren → Unit 1

Let's take a taxi.
Why don't you phone your brother?
We could borrow mother's car.
Whar about going to the bank during your lunch-hour?
Shall we ask mother if we can borrow her car?
Yes, that's a good idea.
Yes, let's.
We can't do that.
I don't really want to.

(Sich und andere) Vorstellen → Unit 2

My name's …
I'm …
Let me introduce myself: I'm …
I would like to introduce you to …
I'd like you to meet …
This is …

Warnungen und Verbote aussprechen → Unit 5

You can't leave the door open.
You shouldn't leave the door open.
Please don't leave the door open.
You mustn't leave the door open.
Don't forget to lock the door.

(Nach dem) Weg fragen und Wegbeschreibungen geben → Unit 7

Excuse me, can/could you tell me the way to the post office, please?
Take the first road on the left / right.
Go along James Street.
Turn left / right at the bank.
It's opposite / past / next to the station.

Widersprechen → Unit 3

I'm sorry but that's wrong.
I'm afraid I must disagree with you.
I'm sorry I can't agree with you.
Look, you can't say that.

Zustimmen → Units 9 + 16

I'm sure you're right.
Yes, that's very true.
You're quite right.
So / Neither / Nor do I.
I do, too. / I don't either.

Zweck/Beschaffenheit erfragen und angeben → Unit 8

What's it for?
It's for …ing.
What's it made of?
It's made of …

Pronunciation

In dem nachfolgenden Wortschatzanhang wird die Aussprache in eckigen Klammern nach jedem Eintrag angegeben. Dazu wird eine spezielle Lautschrift verwendet, deren wichtigste Symbole hier erläutert werden.

Symbol	Beispielwort	Aussprache
ə	numb**er**	wie e in Deutsch *singe*
ɪ	**i**n	wie *i* in Deutsch *in*
ɪə	h**ere**	wie *ie* in Deutsch *hier*
iː	m**ee**t	wie *ie* in Deutsch *Knie*
e	y**e**s	etwa wie *e* in Deutsch *fett*
eɪ	d**ay**	nicht wie Deutsch *ei*, sondern [e] + [ɪ]
eə	wh**ere**	wie *air* in Deutsch *fair*
æ	th**a**nks	zwischen deutschem *a* und *ä*
aɪ	n**i**ce	wie *ei* in Deutsch *Eile*
aʊ	h**ow**	wie *au* in Deutsch *flau*
ɑː	f**a**ther	wie *ah* in Deutsch *Kahn*
ɒ	c**o**ffee	wie *o* in Deutsch *Motte*
ɔɪ	b**oy**	wie *eu* in *deutsch*
ɔː	f**our**	wie *o* in Deutsch *Borke*
ʌ	c**o**me	wie *a* in Deutsch *Klatsch*
ʊ	l**oo**k	wie *u* in Deutsch *Butter*
ʊə	t**our**ist	[ʊ] + [ə]
əʊ	n**o**	[ə] + [ʊ]
uː	t**oo**	etwa wie *u* in Deutsch *Tuch*
ɜː	**ear**ly	etwa wie ö in Deutsch *Segeltörn*
v	ha**v**e	wie *v* in Deutsch *Virus*
θ	**th**anks	wie ein gelispeltes *ss* in Deutsch *Biss*
ð	**th**is	wie ein gelispeltes *s* in Deutsch *Sand*
s	**s**eat	wie *ß* in Deutsch *Muße*
z	plea**s**e	wie *s* in Deutsch *Museum*
ʃ	**sh**e	wie *sch* in Deutsch *fesch*
ʒ	televi**s**ion	wie *g* in Deutsch *Regie*
tʃ	**ch**eers	wie *tsch* in Deutsch *Klatsch*
dʒ	**G**erman	[d] + [ʒ]
ŋ	so**ng**	wie *ng* in Deutsch *singen*
r	**r**epeat	nicht wie ein deutsches r, sondern vorn im Munde gesprochen
w	**w**e	nicht wie ein deutsches w, sondern durch die Lippen wie [uː]

Der hochgestellte Strich ˈ steht in Wörtern mit mehr als einer Silbe vor dem Teil des Wortes, der am stärksten betont wird. Der tiefgestellte Strich ˌ bedeutet, daß die folgende Silbe auch etwas betont wird.

Dictionary

Hier finden Sie alle Wörter und Wendungen des Buches, die über die ca. 1000 Wörter der *Grundbaustein*-Liste *(ICC Certificate in English, Stage 1)* hinausgehen, in alphabetischer Reihenfolge. Neben dem englischen Stichwort finden Sie die Aussprache und die deutsche Übersetzung.

A

a.m. = ante meridiem [eɪ‿'em] vormittags
abbreviation [əˌbriːvɪ'eɪʃn] Abkürzung
aboriginee [ˌæbə'rɪdʒəniː] Ureinwohner/in
above [ə'bʌv] oberhalb, drüber, *hier:* oben
accept [ək'sept] annehmen, akzeptieren
account [ə'kaʊnt] Konto
act out [ækt 'aʊt] spielen, agieren
action ['ækʃn] Handlung
activity [æk'tɪvətɪ] Beschäftigung: **leisure activity** Freizeitbeschäftigung
actor ['æktə] Schauspieler
add [æd] hinzufügen
adopt [ə'dɒpt] adoptieren
adult ['ædʌlt] Erwachsener
adult ['ædʌlt] erwachsen
advantage [əd'vɑːntɪdʒ] Vorteil
adventure [əd'ventʃə] Abenteuer
advert(isement) [əd'vɜːt(ɪsmənt)] Anzeige, Annonce
advertise ['ædvətaɪz] Werbung machen für
advice [əd'vaɪs] Ratschlag
affection [ə'fekʃn] Zuneigung, *hier:* angenehme Erinnerung
afford [ə'fɔːd] sich leisten
age [eɪdʒ] Lebensalter, Zeitalter: **old age** hohes Alter
agency ['eɪdʒənsɪ] Agentur, Dienststelle
agree [ə'griː] zustimmen: **agree on** sich einigen auf
aim [eɪm] Ziel, Absicht
alcohol ['ælkəhɒl] Alkohol
alike [ə'laɪk]: **look alike** einander ähnlich sehen
American [ə'merɪkən] amerikanisch(-e, -er, -es); Amerikaner/in
amuse [ə'mjuːz] belustigen, erfreuen, amüsieren
anniversary [ˌænɪ'vɜːsərɪ] Geburtstag
announce [ə'naʊns] ankündigen
announcer [ə'naʊnsə]: **(radio) announcer** (Rundfunk-)Sprecher/in
annual ['ænjʊəl] jährlich
anonymous [ə'nɒnɪməs] anonym
antique [æn'tiːk] Antiquität
apartment [ə'pɑːtmənt] Wohnung *(in Wohnblock)*
apologise [ə'pɒlədʒaɪz] sich entschuldigen
appear [ə'pɪə] erscheinen
appointment [ə'pɔɪntmənt] Verabredung, Termin: **make an appointment** einen Termin ausmachen
apron ['eɪprən] Schürze
area ['eərɪə] Gegend
arena [ə'riːnə] Arena, Kampfplatz
arrange [ə'reɪndʒ] planen, verabreden
arrangement [ə'reɪndʒmənt] *hier:* Plan, Vereinbarung
arrest [ə'rest] einsperren
article ['ɑːtɪkl] Artikel
artist ['ɑːtɪst] Künstler/in: **talked-about artist** Künstler/in, über den/die man spricht
ask [ɑːsk] *hier:* (Geld) verlangen: **how much do I ask for ...?** wie viel verlange ich für ...?
associate [ə'səʊʃɪeɪt] in Zusammenhang bringen, assoziieren
at first [ət 'fɜːst] zuerst
athlete ['æθliːt] Leichtathlet/in, Sportler/in
atmosphere ['ætməsfɪə] Stimmung, Atmosphäre
attention [ə'tenʃn] Aufmerksamkeit
attract [ə'trækt] anziehen, auf sich ziehen
attraction [ə'trækʃn] Anziehungspunkt
attractive [ə'træktɪv] anziehend, verlockend
au pair (girl) [əʊ 'peə (ˌgɜːl)] Aupair-Mädchen
audience ['ɔːdjəns] Zuhörer, Publikum
Australian [ɒ'streɪljən] australisch(-e, -er, -es); Australier/in
Austria ['ɒstrɪə] Österreich
Austrian ['ɒstrɪən] österreichisch(-e, -er, -es); Österreicher/in
automatical [ɔːtə'mætɪkəl] automatisch, selbsttätig
automobile ['ɔːtəməbiːl] Auto *(amerik.)*
average ['ævərɪdʒ] durchschnittlich
avoid [ə'vɔɪd] vermeiden

B

babysit ['beɪbɪsɪt] auf Kinder aufpassen
backache ['bækeɪk] Rückenschmerzen
bake [beɪk] backen: **baked potato** gebackene Kartoffel
balcony ['bælkənɪ] Balkon
bald [bɔːld] kahl, kahl geschoren
balloon [bə'luːn] Ballon; *hier:* Ballon fliegen: **hot-air ballooning** Fahren mit dem Fesselballon
ban [bæn] verbieten
bark [bɑːk] bellen
basic ['beɪsɪk] grundsätzlich, einfach
Bavaria [bə'veərɪə] Bayern
bazaar [bə'zɑː] Bazar, Markt
beach [biːtʃ] Strand
beauty ['bjuːtɪ] Schönheit
bedsit ['bedˌsɪt] Ein-Zimmer-Apartment
behalf [bɪ'hɑːf]: **on behalf of** im Namen von
behave [bɪ'heɪv] sich benehmen
Belgian ['beldʒən] belgisch(-e, -er, -es); Belgier/in
Belgium ['beldʒəm] Belgien
below [bɪ'ləʊ] unterhalb, *hier:* unten
bi-lingual [baɪ'lɪŋgwəl] zweisprachig
bill [bɪl] Geldschein, Banknote *(amerik.)*
bird [bɜːd] Vogel
biscuit ['bɪskɪt] Keks
bit [bɪt] Stückchen, bisschen
bite (bit, bitten) [baɪt (bɪt, 'bɪtn)] beißen (biss, gebissen)
bitter ['bɪtə] bitter; *hier:* dunkles Bier
bleed (bled, bled) [bliːd (bled, bled)] bluten (blutete, geblutet)
bleeding ['bliːdɪŋ] Blutung
blond [blɒnd] blond
blow (blew, blown) up [bləʊ (bluː, bləʊn)] in die Luft sprengen
board [bɔːd] (Holz-)Diele, Brett: **board game** Brettspiel
board (a ship, plane) [bɔːd] (ein Schiff, Flugzeug) betreten
bonfire ['bɒnfaɪə] Freudenfeuer
border ['bɔːdə] Kante, Rand, Grenze
bored [bɔːd]: **feel bored** gelangweilt sein
boring ['bɔːrɪŋ] langweilig
bow [baʊ] sich verneigen
bowl [bəʊl] Schüssel, Napf, Schale
bracket ['brækɪt] Klammer
brave [breɪv] tapfer, mutig
break [breɪk] Pause, *hier:* Kurzurlaub: **lunch break** Mittagspause
break-in ['breɪk‿ɪn] Einbruch
bride [braɪd] Braut
bright [braɪt] leuchtend: **bright red** knallrot
Briton ['brɪtn] Brite, Engländer
broadcast ['brɔːdkɑːst] senden, Sendung
brochure ['brəʊʃə] Broschüre, Prospekt
building ['bɪldɪŋ] Gebäude
Bulgaria [bʌl'geərɪə] Bulgarien

bull [bʊl] Stier, Bulle: **bull-fight(ing)** Stierkampf
bungalow ['bʌŋgələʊ] Bungalow
burglar ['bɜːglə] Einbrecher/in
bus-ride ['bʌs ˌraɪd] Busfahrt

C

calculate ['kælkjʊleɪt] berechnen, ausrechnen
call to see [ˌkɔːl‿tə 'siː] vorbeischauen bei, kurz besuchen
canteen [kæn'tiːn] Kantine
capital ['kæpɪtl] Hauptstadt
car park ['kɑː ˌpɑːk] Parkplatz
care [keə]: **health care** Gesundheitsvorsorge
career [kə'rɪə] Karriere
carefree ['keəfriː] sorglos, ohne Sorgen
carpet ['kɑːpɪt] Teppich
cart [kɑːt] Karren, Einkaufswagen *(amerik.)*
cash [kæʃ] Bargeld: **be short of cash** zu wenig Geld haben
cash [kæʃ]: **cash a cheque** einen Scheck einlösen
cathedral [kə'θiːdrəl] Dom, Kathedrale
cause [kɔːz] verursachen
caviar ['kævɪɑː] Kaviar
celebrate ['selɪbreɪt] feiern
celebration [ˌselɪ'breɪʃn] Feier
celebrity [ˌse'lebrətɪ] berühmte Persönlichkeit
cellar ['selə] Keller
central ['sentrəl] zentral, in der Mitte, im Zentrum
century ['sentʃʊrɪ] Jahrhundert
certain ['sɜːtn] sicher
chain [tʃeɪn] Kette
champagne [ˌʃæm'peɪn] Sekt, Champagner
championship ['tʃæmpɪənˌʃɪp] Meisterschaft
change [tʃeɪndʒ] Veränderung
change [tʃeɪndʒ] tauschen, wechseln: **change ends** *(Sport)* die Seiten wechseln
channel ['tʃænl] Kanal, Sender
character ['kærəktə] Kennzeichen, Charakter
charge (money) [tʃɑːdʒ] (Geld) verlangen
cheer [tʃɪə] Beifall klatschen, jubeln, anfeuern
chef [ʃef] Küchenchef, Koch
cheque [tʃek] Scheck: **cash a cheque** einen Scheck einlösen
chestnut ['tʃesnʌt] Rosskastanie
chief [tʃiːf] Häuptling
childhood ['tʃaɪldhʊd] Kindheit
chimney sweep ['tʃɪmnɪ ˌswiːp] Schornsteinfeger
China ['tʃaɪnə] China
Chinese [ˌtʃaɪ'niːz] chinesisch(-e, -er, -es); Chinese, Chinesin
chips [tʃɪps] Pommes frittes
chocoholic [ˌtʃɒkə'hɒlɪk] schokoladesüchtig
choice [tʃɔɪs] Auswahl
chronological [ˌkrɒnə'lɒdʒɪkl] chronologisch
circle ['sɜːkl] Kreis, Ring
citizen ['sɪtɪzn] Bürger: **senior citizen** ältere/r Mitbürger/in, Senior/in
classical ['klæsɪkl] klassisch
clause [klɔːz] Nebensatz
cleaner ['kliːnə] *hier:* Besitzer einer Reinigung
clear [klɪə] *hier:* freimachen
climate ['klaɪmɪt] Klima
clock [klɒk] *hier:* Wanduhr
close [kləʊs] nahe, eng
cloud [klaʊd] Wolke
club [klʌb] Verein, Club
co-star [kəʊ'stɑː] Mitspieler/in
coach [kəʊtʃ] Trainer/in
colleague ['kɒliːg] Kollege, Kollegin
collect [kə'lekt] sammeln
collection [kə'lekʃn] Sammlung
colony ['kɒlənɪ] Kolonie
colonist ['kɒlənɪst] Siedler
column ['kɒləm] Säule, Rubrik, Spalte
comedy ['kɒmədɪ] Lustspiel, Komödie
communicate [kə'mjuːnɪkeɪt] mitteilen, sich verständigen
community [kə'mjuːnətɪ] Gemeinschaft, Gemeinde
company ['kʌmpənɪ] Firma, Gesellschaft, Konzern
compare [kəm'peə] vergleichen
compartment [kəm'pɑːtmənt] (Zug-)Abteil
competition [ˌkɒmpɪ'tɪʃn] Wettbewerb, *hier:* Preisausschreiben
competitor [kəm'petɪtə] Teilnehmer/in an Wettbewerb
complain [kəm'pleɪn] jammern, sich beschweren
complete [kəm'pliːt] völlig, vollständig
compliment ['kɒmplɪmənt] Lob, Anerkennung, Kompliment
compliment ['kɒmplɪmənt] Kompliment aussprechen
comprehension [ˌkɒmprɪ'henʃn] *hier:* Textverständnis
computer [kəm'pjuːtə] digitaler Rechner, Computer: **computer-literate** der Computer-Sprache kundig sein; **computer-phobia** Angst vor dem PC; **computerised car** Auto, das einen Computer hat
concentrate ['kɒnsəntreɪt] sich konzentrieren
condense [kɒn'dens] sich niederschlagen, kondensieren
connect [kə'nekt] verbinden
connection [kə'nekʃn] Verbindung
conservation [ˌkɒnsə'veɪʃn] Bewahrung, Wiederherstellung
contact ['kɒntækt] Verbindung, Kontakt
contact ['kɒntækt] sich wenden an
contain [kən'teɪn] beinhalten, enthalten
contest ['kɒntest] Wettbewerb
continue [kən'tɪnjuː] fortfahren, weitermachen
conversation [ˌkɒnvə'seɪʃn] Gespräch, Unterhaltung
cool [kuːl] kühlen
cool [kuːl] kühl, lässig, toll
copy ['kɒpɪ] Kopie, *hier:* Exemplar, Stück
corn [kɔːn] Mais *(amerik.)*
corporation [ˌkɔːpə'reɪʃn] Körperschaft
correct [kə'rekt] richtig
cottage ['kɒtɪdʒ] Bauernhaus, Ferienhaus
cotton ['kɒtn] Baumwolle
council ['kaʊnsl] Rat; Stadtverwaltung: **council housing** Wohnungsbeschaffung durch die Gemeinde; **council-owned** im Besitz der Stadt
count [kaʊnt] zählen
counter ['kaʊntə] Ladentisch
countryside ['kʌntrɪsaɪd] Landschaft
couple ['kʌpl] Paar
court [kɔːt] *hier:* Spielfeld
cousin ['kʌzn] Cousin, Cousine
crash [kræʃ] Zusammenstoß, Unfall
crazy ['kreɪzɪ] verrückt
credit ['kredɪt] Kredit, Darlehen
crisis ['kraɪsɪs] Krise
critic ['krɪtɪk] Kritiker/in
cross out [ˌkrɒs 'aʊt] durchstreichen
crowd [kraʊd] Menge
culture ['kʌltʃə] Kultur
currency ['kʌrənsɪ] Währung
custom ['kʌstəm] Sitte, Brauch: **customs** Zoll
cycle ['saɪkl] Rad fahren: **cycle path** Radweg; **cycling holiday** Fahrradurlaub

D

dairy ['deərɪ] Milchgeschäft
day out ['deɪ 'aʊt] Ausgehtag
daydream ['deɪdriːm] Tagtraum
deal [diːl] Handel
decadent ['dekədənt] verderbt, dekadent
decide [dɪ'saɪd] entscheiden
decision [dɪ'sɪʒn] Entscheidung
decorate ['dekəreɪt] schmücken
define [dɪ'faɪn] bestimmen, definieren
definite ['defɪnɪt] bestimmt, fest, fix
degree [dɪ'griː] Grad
delicatessen [ˌdelɪkə'tesn] Feinkostgeschäft
deliver [dɪ'lɪvə] *hier:* liefern
Denmark ['denmɑːk] Dänemark
depart [dɪ'pɑːt] abfahren
department [dɪ'pɑːtmənt] Abteilung: **fashion department** Modeabteilung
departure [dɪ'pɑːtʃə] Abfahrt

describe [dɪ'skraɪb] beschreiben
design [dɪ'zaɪn] Entwurf, Design
designer [dɪ'zainə] Modeschöpfer/in
detail ['diːteɪl] Einzelheit
develop [dɪ'veləp] entwickeln
dialect ['daɪəlɪkt] Mundart, Dialekt
diary ['daɪərɪ] Tagebuch
difference ['dɪfrəns] Unterschied
diploma [dɪ'pləʊmə] Diplom, Studienabschluss
direct [dɪ'rekt, daɪ'rekt] unmittelbar, direkt
direction [dɪ'rekʃn] *hier:* Anweisung, Wegbeschreibung
disadvantage [ˌdɪsəd'vɑːntɪdʒ] Nachteil
disagree [ˌdɪsə'griː] nicht übereinstimmen, widersprechen
disappear [dɪsə'pɪə] verschwinden
discover [dɪ'skʌvə] entdecken
discuss [dɪ'skʌs] bereden, diskutieren
discussion [dɪ'skʌʃn] Diskussion, Aussprache
disease [dɪ'ziːz] (schwere) Krankheit
dish [dɪʃ] *hier:* Gericht
dishwasher ['dɪʃˌwɒʃə] Geschirrspüler
dislike [dɪs'laɪk] nicht mögen, missfallen
dissatisfied [dɪs'sætɪsfaɪd] unzufrieden
divorce [dɪ'vɔːs] sich scheiden lassen
divorced [dɪ'vɔːst] geschieden
document ['dɒkjʊmənt] Dokument, Formular: **sign a document** ein Formular unterschreiben
documentary [ˌdɒkju'mentərɪ] *hier:* Dokumentarfilm
downtown ['daʊntaʊn] im Stadtzentrum *(amerik.)*
dozen ['dʌzn] Dutzend
dramatic(al) [drə'mætɪk(l)] dramatisch, aufregend
draw (drew, drawn) [drɔː (druː, drɔːn)] zeichnen (zeichnete, gezeichnet)
dream [driːm] Traum
dress [dres] sich anziehen, kleiden
drill ['drɪl] bohren
drive [draɪv] Auffahrt, Einfahrt *(amerik.)*
driver's license [ˌdraɪvəz 'laɪsəns] Führerschein *(amerik.)*
driving licence [ˌdraɪvɪŋ 'laɪsəns] Führerschein
dungarees [dʌŋgə'riːz] Latzhosen
dust [dʌst] abstauben

E

earn (money) [ɜːn] (Geld) verdienen
earring ['ɪəˌrɪŋ] Ohrring
earth [ɜːθ] Erde
eater ['iːtə] Esser
education [ˌedʒʊ'keɪʃn] Erziehung, Schulbildung
elderly ['eldəlɪ] älter
elevator ['elɪveɪtə] Aufzug *(amerik.)*
embassy ['embəsɪ] Botschaft
emigrate ['emɪgreɪt] auswandern
emperor ['empərə] Kaiser
employee [emplɔɪ'iː] Angestellte/r
encourage [ɪn'kʌrɪdʒ] ermutigen, bestärken
end [end] Ende, *hier:* Rand des Spielfelds: **change ends** *(Sport)* die Seiten wechseln
energetic [ˌenə'dʒetɪk] energisch, energiegeladen
entertainment [ˌentə'teɪnmənt] Unterhaltung, Zerstreuung
enthusiastic [ɪnˌθjuːzɪ'æstɪk] begeistert, begeisterungsfähig
environment [ɪn'vaɪərənment] Umwelt
escalator ['eskəleɪtə] Rolltreppe
estate [ɪ'steɪt] *hier:* Immobilie: **housing estate** Wohnsiedlung; **estate agent** Immobilienmakler/in
ethnic ['eθnɪk] ethnisch: **ethnic mix** Völkergemisch
Europe ['jʊərəp] Europa
European [ˌjʊərə'piːən] europäisch(-e, -er, -es); Europäer/in
eve [iːv] Vorabend: **New Year's Eve** Sylvester
event [ɪ'vent] Ereignis
exam [ɪg'zæm] Abschlussprüfung, Examen: **pass an exam** ein Examen bestehen
exchange student [ɪk'stʃeɪndʒ 'stjuːdənt] Austauschstudent/in
excited [ɪk'saɪtɪd] aufgeregt, erregt
exciting [ɪk'saɪtɪŋ] aufregend
exclusive [ɪk'skluːsɪv] ausschließend, besonders, exklusiv
execute ['eksɪkjuːt] hinrichten
execution [ˌeksɪ'kjuːʃn] Hinrichtung
exercise ['eksəsaɪz] Übung: **do exercise(s)** Gymnastik machen
exhibition [ˌeksɪ'bɪʃn] Ausstellung
exotic [ɪg'zɒtɪk] fremdartig, exotisch
expect [ɪk'spekt] erwarten
experience [ɪk'spɪərɪəns] Erfahrung, Erlebnis
expert ['ekspɜːt] Fachmann, -frau, Experte, Expertin
explanation [ˌeksplə'neɪʃn] Erklärung
express [ɪk'spres] ausdrücken
expression [ɪk'spreʃn] Ausdruck
extract ['ekstrækt] *hier:* Textauszug

F

fabric ['fæbrɪk] Gewebe, Stoff
facility [fə'sɪlətɪ] Möglichkeit, Angebot, Einrichtung
fact [fækt] Tatsache: **in fact** in Wirklichkeit, tatsächlich
fail [feɪl] scheitern, verfehlen: **fail an exam** eine Prüfung nicht bestehen
fair (hair) [feə] hell (Haar)
fanatic [fə'nætɪk] besessen, fanatisch
fancy-dress ['fænsɪ ˌdres] Maskenkostüm
fantastic [fæn'tæstɪk] fabelhaft
fashion ['fæʃn] Mode: **fashion department** Modeabteilung
fatty ['fætɪ] fetthaltig, fettreich
favourite ['feɪvərɪt] Lieblings-
fax [fæks] ein Fax senden
federal ['fedərəl] bundesstaatlich, föderativ: **Federal Reserve** amerik. Bundesnotenbank
feel (felt, felt) sorry for [ˌfiːl (felt, felt) 'sɒrɪ fɔː] Mitleid haben (hatte, gehabt) mit
female ['fiːmeɪl] weiblich
ferry ['ferɪ] Fähre
figure ['fɪgə] *hier:* Figur, Puppe
filling-station ['fɪlɪŋ ˌsteɪʃn] Tankstelle
final ['faɪnl] abschließend: **final exam** Abschlussprüfung
finals ['faɪnlz] Endspiel, Finale
finance [faɪ'næns] Gelddinge, Finanzen
finish ['fɪnɪʃ] beenden
Finland ['fɪnlənd] Finnland
fireman ['faɪəmən] Feuerwehrmann
fireworks ['faɪəˌwɜːks] Feuerwerk
firm [fɜːm] Firma, Unternehmen
fish [fɪʃ] fischen, angeln
fit [fɪt] passen
flat [flæt] flach
flexi-time ['fleksɪtaɪm] Gleitzeit
fluent ['fluːənt] flüssig
focus ['fəʊkəs] Brennpunkt
fool [fuːl] Dummkopf, Narr
foot [fʊt]: **square foot** *(Fläche)* Quadratfuß
footballer ['fʊtˌbɔːlə] Fußballspieler/in
force ['fɔːs] Kraft: **police force** Polizeikräfte
form [fɔːm] Formular
formal ['fɔːml] förmlich, formell
fox [fɒks] Fuchs: **fox-hunting** Fuchsjagd
France [frɑːns] Frankreich
freeze (froze, frozen) [friːz (frəʊz, 'frəʊzn)] gefrieren (gefror, gefroren)
freezer ['friːzə] Tiefkühltruhe, Gefrierfach
French [frentʃ] französisch(-e, -er, -es); Franzose/ Französin
frequency ['friːkwənsɪ] Häufigkeit
fridge [frɪdʒ] Kühlschrank
friendly ['frendlɪ] freundlich
frozen food ['frəʊzn 'fuːd] Tiefkühlware
frying-pan ['fraɪɪŋpæn] Bratpfanne
function ['fʌŋkʃn] Aufgabe, Funktion
furniture ['fɜːnɪtʃə] Möbel

G

gallery ['gælərɪ] *hier:* Kunstgalerie
gamble ['gæmbl] um Geld spielen, zocken

game [geɪm]: **board game** Brettspiel
gardening ['gɑːdnɪŋ] Gartenarbeit
gas [gæs] Benzin *(amerik.)*
gate [geɪt] Tor
German ['dʒɜːmən] deutsch(-e, -er, -es); Deutsche/r
Germany ['dʒɜːmənɪ] Deutschland
globe [gləʊb] Weltkugel, Globus
gloves [glʌvz] Handschuhe
go (went, gone) [gəʊ (went, gɒn)] gehen (ging, gegangen): **go with my hair** zu meinem Haar passen; **go wrong** schief laufen
gold [gəʊld] Gold
goods [gʊdz] Güter, Waren
government ['gʌvnmənt] Regierung
granddaughter ['græn,dɔːtə] Enkelin
grandson ['grænsʌn] Enkel
graph [grɑːf] Schaubild, Grafik
grass [grɑːs] Gras
Greece [griːs] Griechenland
Greek [griːk] griechisch(-e, -er, -es); Grieche, Griechin
greet [griːt] grüßen
greeting ['griːtɪŋ] Begrüßung, Gruß
groceries ['grəʊsərɪz] Lebensmittel
ground [graʊnd] Erdboden, *hier:* im Freien
grow (grew, grown) [grəʊ (gruː, grəʊn)] wachsen (wuchs, gewachsen), anbauen
guard [gɑːd] Wache, Wachmann
guess [ges] raten
guitar [gɪ'tɑː] Gitarre
gymnastic team [dʒɪm'næstɪk 'tiːm] Gymnasikmannschaft, -team: **gymnastics** Gymnastik

H

habit ['hæbɪt] Gewohnheit
ham [hæm] Schinken
hamper ['hæmpə] Geschenkkorb
hand [,sekənd'hænd]: **second-hand** gebraucht
handle ['hændl] umgehen mit
handler ['hændlə] Person, die umgeht mit
handsome ['hænsəm] stattlich, gutaussehend
handy ['hændɪ] geschickt, praktisch
hardly ['hɑːdlɪ] kaum
hate [heɪt] hassen
heading ['hedɪŋ] Überschrift, Überbegriff
headline ['hedlaɪn] Schlagzeile, Überschrift
headscarf (headscarves) [,hed'skɑːf (,hed'skɑːvz)] Kopftuch
health [helθ] Gesundheit: **health care** Gesundheitsvorsorge
healthy ['helθɪ] gesund
helmet ['helmɪt] Helm
helpful ['helpfʊl] hilfsbereit
high-life ['haɪ'laɪf] Vergnügen, Spaß
history ['hɪstərɪ] Geschichte
hit (hit, hit) [hɪt (hɪt, hɪt)] treffen (traf, getroffen)
hole [həʊl] Loch
home [həʊm] Heim, *hier:* Heimat
homeless ['həʊmlɪs] obdachlos
homework ['həʊmwɜːk] Hausaufgabe: **do homework** Hausaufgaben machen
honey ['hʌnɪ] Honig
honeymoon ['hʌnɪmuːn] Flitterwochen
hoover ['huːvə] Staub saugen
horseshoe ['hɔːsʃuː] Hufeisen
hot [hɒt] *hier:* scharf
housewarming party ['haʊs,wɔːmiŋ 'pɑːtɪ] Einzugsfest
housing ['haʊsɪŋ] Wohnung, Unterkunft: **council housing** Wohnungsbeschaffung durch die Gemeinde; **housing estate** Wohnsiedlung
huge [hjuːdʒ] riesig
humane [hjuː'meɪn] menschlich, human
hunt [hʌnt] jagen: **fox-hunting** Fuchsjagd

I

ice [aɪs] Eis: **ice-fishing** Angeln im Eis
iceberg ['aɪsbɜːg] Eisberg
Iceland ['aɪslənd] Island
icy ['aɪsɪ] eisig, Eis-
ideal [aɪ'dɪəl] ideal, vorbildlich
identity [aɪ'dentətɪ] Identität: **identity card** Personalausweis
idiom ['ɪdɪəm] feststehender Ausdruck, Redewendung
idol ['aɪdl] Vorbild, Idol
if so [ɪf 'səʊ] wenn dem so ist, wenn ja
igloo ['ɪgluː] Iglu
imagine [ɪ'mædʒɪn] sich vorstellen, annehmen
immediately [ɪ'miːdɪətlɪ] sofort
immigration [ɪmɪ'greɪʃn] Einwanderung: **immigration form** Einwanderungsformular
import ['ɪmpɔːt] Einfuhr, Import
improve [ɪm'pruːv] verbessern
include [ɪn'kluːd] enthalten, umfassen, einschließen
including ... [ɪn'kluːdiŋ] einschließlich ...
incorrect [ɪnkə'rekt] nicht richtig, falsch
independence [,ɪndɪ'pendəns] Unabhängigkeit
independent [,ɪndɪ'pendənt] unabhängig
India ['ɪndjə] Indien
Indian ['ɪndjən] indisch(-e, -er, -es); Inder/in; *hier:* Indianer
influence ['ɪnflʊəns] Einfluss
institute ['ɪnstɪtjuːt] Einrichtung, Institut
intend [ɪn'tend] beabsichtigen, vorhaben
intension [ɪn'tenʃn] Vorhaben, Absicht
inter- ['ɪntə] *(Vorsilbe)* zwischen: **inter-school** zwischen zwei Schulen
interest ['ɪntrəst] Interesse: **pay interest** Zinsen bezahlen
interest ['ɪntrəst] interessieren
interrupt [ɪntə'rʌpt] unterbrechen
interview ['ɪntəvjuː] befragen
introduce to [,ɪntrə'djuːs_tə] (Person) vorstellen
invent [ɪn'vent] erfinden
inverted commas [ɪn'vɜːtəd 'kɒməz] Anführungszeichen
invitation [,ɪnvɪ'teɪʃn] Einladung
invite [ɪn'vaɪt] einladen
involve [ɪn'vɒlv] einbeziehen, beteiligen
Ireland ['aɪələnd] Irland
Irish ['aɪrɪʃ] irisch(-e, -er, -es); Ire, Irin
(ir)regular [(ɪ)'regjʊlə] (un)regelmäßig
island ['aɪlənd] Insel
issue ['ɪʃuː] Thema, Anliegen, (Zeitungs-)Ausgabe
issue ['ɪʃuː] verfassen, herausgeben
Italian [ɪ'tæljən] italienisch(-e, -er, -es); Italiener/in
Italy ['ɪtəlɪ] Italien
item ['aɪtəm] Gegenstand, Stück, *hier:* Punkt

J

jacket ['dʒækɪt] Jacke, Blouson, Jackett
Japanese [,dʒæpə'niːz] japanisch(-e, -er, -es); Japaner/in
jar [dʒɑː] Glas: **jar of marmalade** Glas Orangenmarmelade
job-sharing [,dʒɒb'ʃeərɪŋ] Teilzeitarbeit
join [dʒɔɪn] mitmachen, beitreten
journal ['dʒɜːnl] Zeitschrift
journalist ['dʒɜːnəlɪst] Journalist/in
journey ['dʒɜːnɪ] Reise
jump [dʒʌmp] Sprung
jump [dʒʌmp] springen
jungle ['dʒʌŋgl] Dschungel, tropischer Wald

K

keep (kept, kept) [kiːp (kept, kept)]: **keep an eye on** im Auge behalten (behielt, behalten)
kid [kɪd] *hier:* Kind
kiss [kɪs] küssen
kit [kɪt] Ausrüstung, Handwerkszeug
kiwi ['kiːwiː] Kiwivogel, -frucht
knit [nit] stricken

L

ladder ['lædə] Leiter
lager ['lɑːgə] helles Bier
landlord ['lænlɔːd] Vermieter, Gastwirt
large [lɑːdʒ] groß
law [lɔː] Gesetz: **son-in-law** Schwiegersohn
lawn [lɔːn] Rasen: **lawn-mower** Rasenmäher
layout (of a letter) ['leɪaʊt] äußere Form (eines Briefes)
leader ['liːdə] Führer/in
leadership ['liːdəʃɪp] Führung, Leitung
leaf (leaves) [liːf (liːvz)] Blatt, Laub
leaving party ['liːvɪŋ 'pɑːtɪ] Abschiedsfeier
legend ['liːdʒənd] Legende
leisure ['leʒə] Muße, Freizeit: **leisure activity** Freizeitbeschäftigung
lend (lent, lent) [lend (lent, lent)] verleihen (verlieh, verliehen)
lettuce ['letɪs] Kopfsalat
liberation [ˌlɪbə'reɪʃn] Befreiung: **liberation front** Befreiungsfront
library ['laɪbrərɪ] Bücherei
licence ['laɪsəns] Erlaubnis, Lizenz
life-size ['laɪf'saɪz] lebensgroß, in Originalgröße
lifestyle ['laɪfstaɪl] Lebensweise, Lebensstil
lighthouse ['laɪthaʊs] Leuchtturm
like this [laɪk 'ðɪs] auf diese Weise, so
limit ['lɪmɪt] Grenze, Beschränkung, Endpunkt
literate ['lɪtərət]: **computer-literate** der Computer-Sprache kundig sein
literature ['lɪtərətʃə] Literatur
local ['ləʊkl] örtlich, aus der Gegend
lock [lɒk] zusperren, verschließen
look alike [lʊk ə'laɪk] einander ähnlich sehen
lost-and-found office ['lɒst ənd 'faʊnd ˌɒfɪs] Fundbüro
luck [lʌk] Zufall, Glücksfall: **good luck** Glück
lunch break [ˌlʌntʃ 'breɪk] Mittagspause
luxurious [lʌg'ʒʊərɪəs] luxuriös
luxury ['lʌkʃərɪ] Luxus

M

magazine [ˌmægə'ziːn] Zeitschrift, Blatt
mail order ['meɪl ˌɔːdə] Bestellung per Post: **mail-order service** Versandhaus
main [meɪn] hauptsächlich, Haupt-
make (made, made) [meɪk (meɪd, meɪd)] machen (machte, gemacht): **make a reservation** reservieren lassen; **make an appointment** einen Termin ausmachen; **make up a story** sich eine Geschichte ausdenken
male [meɪl] männlich
mall [mɔːl] Einkaufszentrum *(amerik.)*
manufacturer [ˌmænjʊ'fæktʃərə] Hersteller, Fabrikant
Maori ['maʊrɪ] Ureinwohner Neuseelands
marathon ['mærəθn] Marathon
marital status ['mærɪtl ˌsteɪtəs] Familienstand
mark [mɑːk] (Schul-)Note
market (an idea) ['mɑːkət] (eine Idee) vermarkten
married ['mærɪd] verheiratet: **get married** sich verheiraten
marry ['mærɪ] heiraten
mascot ['mæskət] Talismann, Maskottchen
mask [mɑːsk] Maske
master ['mɑːstə] meistern, beherrschen
match [mætʃ] passen, zuordnen
maths (= mathematics) [mæθs] Mathematik
may (might) [meɪ (maɪt)] dürfen (dürfte)
meaning ['miːnɪŋ] Bedeutung
medal ['medl] Medaille, Orden
meditate ['medɪteɪt] meditieren
medium ['miːdɪəm] *hier:* Massenmedium
member ['membə] Mitglied
membership ['membəʃɪp] Mitgliedschaft
mend [mend] reparieren, flicken
message ['mesɪdʒ] Nachricht
method ['meθəd] Verfahren, Methode
microwave ['maɪkrəˌweɪv] Mikrowellenherd
mid- [mɪd] Mitte: **mid-twenties** Mitte zwanzig
midnight ['mɪdnaɪt] Mitternacht
milky ['mɪlkɪ] milchig
million ['mɪljən] Million
millionaire/ss [ˌmɪljə'neər/es] Millionär/in
mineral water [ˌmɪnərəl 'wɔːtə] Mineralwasser
mini ['mɪnɪ] Mini-, klein
miniature ['mɪnɪtʃə] Miniatur-, klein
mint [mɪnt] Minze
minus ['maɪnəs] minus
mirror ['mɪrə] Spiegel
missing ['mɪsɪŋ] fehlend, vermisst, gesucht wird
mix (= mixture) [mɪks] Mischung
mix up [mɪks 'ʌp] verwechseln
mobile ['məʊbaɪl] beweglich, tragbar
model ['mɒdl] Fotomodell: **modelling agency** Agentur für Fotomodelle
mom [mɒm] Mammi, Mutter
monopoly [mə'nɒpəlɪ] Monopol
moon [muːn] Mond
movie theater ['muːvɪ 'θɪətə] Kino *(amerik.)*
multi-function(al) [ˌmʌltɪ 'fʌŋʃən(l)] vielseitig verwendbar
murder ['mɜːdə] Mord
murderer ['mɜːdərə] Mörder/in
museum [mjuː'zɪəm] Museum
mysterious [mɪ'stɪərɪəs] geheimnisvoll
mystery ['mɪstərɪ] Geheimnis

N

name [neɪm] nennen
national ['næʃənl] national, staatlich: **national day** Nationalfeiertag
nationality [næʃə'nælətɪ] Staatsangehörigkeit, Nationalität
nature ['neɪtʃə] Natur
neat [niːt] ordentlich, sauber, gepflegt
neighbourhood ['neɪbəhʊd] Nachbarschaft
nephew ['nevjuː] Neffe
Netherlands ['neðələndz] Niederlande
New Zealand [njuː 'ziːlənd] Neuseeland
niece [niːs] Nichte
not ... either ['nɒt ... 'aɪðə] auch nicht
notice ['nəʊtɪs] Mitteilung, Anschlag
noun [naʊn] Hauptwort, Substantiv
nowadays ['naʊədeɪz] heute, heutzutage
number ['nʌmbə] Nummer
number ['nʌmbə] abzählen, nummerieren
nurse [nɜːs] Krankenschwester, Kindermädchen

O

obligation [ˌɒblɪ'geɪʃən] Verpflichtung
occasion [ə'keɪʒn] Gelegenheit, Anlass
occasional [ə'keɪʒənl] gelegentlich
occupation [ɒkjʊ'peɪʃn] Beschäftigung, *hier:* Beruf
ocean ['əʊʃn] Weltmeer, Ozean: **Atlantic Ocean** Atlantik; **Indian Ocean** Indischer Ozean; **Pacific Ocean** Pazifik
odd [ɒd] merkwürdig, überschüssig: **do odd jobs** Gelegenheitsarbeiten erledigen
official [ə'fɪʃl] amtlich, offiziell
Olympic [ə'lɪmpɪk] olympisch
on-screen [ˌɒn'skriːn] mit stehendem Bildschirm
open top (bus) [ˌəʊpən 'tɒp] (Bus) mit offenem Dach
opening ['əʊpənɪŋ] Eröffnung
opera ['ɒprə] Oper: **soap opera** Fernsehserie, Seifenoper

opinion [ə'pɪnjən] Meinung
opponent [ə'pəʊnənt] Gegner/in
opposite ['ɒpəzɪt] Gegenteil
order ['ɔ:də] Ordnung, Reihenfolge
organise ['ɔ:gənaɪz] organisieren, in Gang bringen
origin ['ɒrɪdʒɪn] Ursprung, Herkunft
out of work [aʊt əv 'wɜ:k] arbeitslos
over ['əʊvə] über
overtime ['əʊvətaim] Überstunden
overview ['əʊvəvju:] Überblick
overweight [ˌəʊvə'weit] Übergewicht
own [əʊn] besitzen
owner ['əʊnə] Besitzer/in

P

p.m. = post meridiem [ˌpi: 'em] nachmittags
pack(et) ['pækɪt] Päckchen, Packen
paint [peɪnt] Farbe
paintbrush ['peɪntbrʌʃ] Pinsel
painting ['peɪntiŋ] Gemälde
palace ['pælɪs] Palast
pale [peɪl] blass
pancake ['pænkeɪk] Pfannkuchen
parliament ['pa:ləmənt] Parlament
part [pɑ:t] Rolle: **take part in** teilnehmen, eine Rolle spielen
particular [pə'tɪkjʊlə] bestimmt, besonders
pass [pɑ:s]: **pass an exam** ein Examen bestehen; **pass time** Zeit verbringen, *hier:* vergeht
passage ['pæsɪdʒ] (Text-)Abschnitt
path [pɑ:θ] Pfad, Weg: **cycle path** Radweg
pay [peɪ] Bezahlung
pay interest ['peɪ 'ɪntrəst] Zinsen bezahlen
payment ['peɪmənt] Zahlung
percentage [pə'sentɪdʒ] Prozentsatz
permission [pə'mɪʃn] Erlaubnis
personal ['pɜ:snl] persönlich
pet [pet] Haustier
phobia ['fəʊbɪə]: **computer-phobia** Angst vor dem PC
phone-in programme [fəʊn 'ɪn prəʊgræm] Programm zum Anrufen
photographer [fə'tɒgrəfə] Fotograf/in
phrase [freɪz] Redewendung
pick [pɪk] pflücken, *hier:* auswählen
pie [paɪ] Pastete
pig [pɪg] Schwein
pilot ['paɪlət] Pilot
place [pleɪs] *hier:* Haus, Wohnung
planet ['plænɪt] Planet
plant [plɑ:nt] Pflanze
plaster ['plɑ:stə] Pflaster
player ['pleɪə] Spieler
please [pli:z] *hier:* erfreuen
pleasure ['pleʒə] Freude, Vergnügen
plenty ['plentɪ] reichlich, sehr viel
plus [plʌs] plus, mehr als: **the 60-plus group** die Altersgruppe über sechzig
pocket ['pɒkɪt] (Hosen-)Tasche: **pocket-money** Taschengeld
point [pɔɪnt] Punkt, Stichpunkt: **point of view** Standpunkt, Meinung
poisonous ['pɔɪzənəs] giftig
polish ['pɒlɪʃ] putzen, polieren
polite [pə'laɪt] höflich
politeness [pə'laɪtnɪs] Höflichkeit
Polynesian [ˌpɒlɪ'ni:zjən] polynesisch(-e, -er, -es); Polynesier/in
pop [pɒp] Pappi, Vater
pop [pɒp]: **pop song** leichte Musik, Schlager; **pop star** Schlagersänger
popular ['pɒpjʊlə] beliebt
population [ˌpɒpjʊ'leɪʃn] Bevölkerung
porter ['pɔ:tə] *hier:* Gepäckträger
Portugal ['pɔ:tʃʊgl] Portugal
Portuguese [ˌpɔ:tʃʊ'gi:z] portugiesisch(-e, -er, -es); Portugiese, Portugiesin
position [pə'zɪʃn] Stelle, Position
positive ['pɒzətɪv] positiv
possibility [ˌpɒsə'bɪlətɪ] Möglichkeit
postage ['pəʊstɪdʒ] Porto
poster ['pəʊstə] Plakat
postman ['pəʊstmən] Briefträger
practical ['præktɪkl] praktisch, brauchbar
practise ['præktɪs] üben
predict [prɪ'dɪkt] vorhersagen
prediction [prɪ'dɪkʃn] Vorhersage
prefer [prɪ'fɜ:] bevorzugen
preparation [ˌprepə'reɪʃn] Vorbereitung
present ['preznt] *hier:* Gegenwart
president ['prezɪdənt] Präsident
previous ['pri:vɪəs] vorhergehend, früher
priest [pri:st] Priester, Geistlicher
Prime Minister [praɪm 'mɪnɪstə] Premierminister, Regierungschef
primitive ['prɪmɪtɪv] einfach, primitiv
prison ['prɪzn] Gefängnis
private ['praɪvɪt] privat: **private school** Privatschule
prize [praɪz] Prämie, Preis, Gewinn
probable ['prɒbəbl] wahrscheinlich, möglicherweise
produce [prə'dju:s] herstellen, hervorbringen
product ['prɒdʌkt] Erzeugnis, Produkt
professional [prə'feʃnl] Berufstätige/r
progress ['prəʊgres] *hier:* Verlauf: **in progress** im Verlauf
project ['prɒdʒekt] Plan, Vorhaben, Projekt: **job-training project** Projekt zur beruflichen Bildung
promise ['prɒmɪs] versprechen
prostitute [prɒstɪ'tju:t] Hure, Prostituierte
protest [prə'test] Einspruch erheben, protestieren
proud of ['praʊd‿əv] stolz auf
provide [prə'vaɪd] versorgen, *hier:* zur Verfügung stellen
psychologist [saɪ'kɒlədʒɪst] Psychologe, Psychologin
psychotherapist [ˌsaɪkəʊ'θerəpɪst] Psychotherapeut/in
public ['pʌblɪk] Öffentlichkeit
public ['pʌblɪk] öffentlich: **public school** exklusives (Privatschul-)Internat; **public transport** öffentlicher Nahverkehr
publicity [pʌ'blɪsətɪ] Öffentlichkeit, Werbung
pumpkin ['pʌmkɪn] Kürbis
punch [pʌntʃ] Punsch
put (put, put) [pʊt (pʊt, pʊt)]: **put out a fire** ein Feuer löschen (löschte, gelöscht)
puzzle ['pʌzl] Rätsel

Q

question ['kwestʃən] ausfragen, verhören
queue [kju:] Schlange stehen

R

race [reɪs] Rennen
race [reɪs] laufen, jagen, rennen: **snail-racing** Schneckenrennen
racket ['rækɪt] Tennisschläger
rare [reə] selten
re- [ri:] *(Vorsilbe)* wieder
re-phrase [ˌri:'freɪz]: **re-phrase a sentence** einen Satz erneut formulieren
re-train [ˌri:'treɪn] sich weiterbilden
re-write [ˌri:'raɪt] nochmal schreiben
reach [ri:tʃ] erreichen
react [rɪ'ækt] reagieren
real ['ri:əl] wirklich, echt
realise ['rɪəlaɪz] wahrnehmen, bemerken
reality [rɪ'ælətɪ] Wirklichkeit: **virtual reality** virtuelle, künstliche Wirklichkeit
receive [rɪ'si:v] empfangen, erhalten
recently ['ri:sntlɪ] vor kurzem
receptionist [rɪ'sepʃənɪst] Empfangsdame, -sekretär/in, Portier
recipe ['resɪpɪ] (Koch-)Rezept
recognise ['rekəgnaɪz] (wieder-) erkennen
record ['rekɔ:d] (Band-)Aufnahme; *hier:* Höchstleistung, Rekord: **on record** *hier:* aufgezeichnet
record [rɪ'kɔ:d] Platte aufnehmen
refuse [rɪ'fju:z] verweigern
related to [rɪ'leɪtɪd] *hier:* verwandt mit
relationship [rɪ'leɪʃnʃɪp] Verbindung, Beziehung
relax [rɪ'læks] sich entspannen
relaxation [ˌri:læk'seɪʃn] Entspannung

religion [rɪ'lɪdʒən] Religion
remind s.o. to [rɪ'maɪnd] jdn. daran erinnern zu
renovate ['renəveɪt] herrichten, renovieren
renovation [ˌrenə'veɪʃn] Reparatur, Renovierung
repair [rɪ'peə] richten, reparieren
repeat [rɪ'piːt] wiederholen
replace [rɪ'pleɪs] ersetzen
reply [rɪ'plaɪ] Antwort
reply [rɪ'plaɪ] entgegnen, antworten
report [rɪ'pɔːt] Bericht: **weather report** Wetterbericht
report [rɪ'pɔːt] berichten
reservation [rezə'veɪʃn] Reservierung: **make a reservation** reservieren lassen
respect [rɪ'spekt] Achtung, Respekt
respect [rɪ'spekt] achten, respektieren
restroom ['restˌruːm] Toilette *(amerik.)*
result [rɪ'zʌlt] Ergebnis
retire [rɪ'taɪə] pensioniert werden
retired [rɪ'taɪəd] im Ruhestand, pensioniert
retirement [rɪ'taɪəmənt] Rückzug, Pensionierung
return [rɪ'tɜːn] zurückkommen
reward [rɪ'wɔːd] Entgelt, Belohnung
rice [raɪs] Reis
ride [raɪd] Fahrt
right [raɪt] Recht
rise (rose, risen) [raɪz (rəʊz, 'rɪzn)] ansteigen (stieg an, angestiegen)
robot ['rɒbɒt] Roboter
role [rəʊl] Rolle
roll [rəʊl] Brötchen, Semmel
roller-skates ['rəʊlə'skeɪts] Rollschuhe
romance [rəʊ'mæns] Romanze, romantische Geschichte
romantic [rəʊ'mæntɪk] romantisch
Rome [rəʊm] Rom
route [ruːt] Strecke
routine [ruː'tiːn] Gewohnheit, Pflicht
rub [rʌb] reiben
rule [ruːl] Spielregel, Regel
run (ran, run) [rʌn (ræn, rʌn)] laufen (lief, gelaufen): **run a centre** ein Zentrum leiten; **run-down** heruntergekommen
runner ['rʌnə] Läufer/in
Russia ['rʌʃə] Russland
Russian ['rʌʃən] russisch(-e, -er, -es); Russe, Russin

S

safe [seɪf] sicher
sail [seɪl] segeln
saint [seɪnt] heilig
salary ['sælərɪ] Gehalt
salesperson (salespeople) ['seɪlzpɜːsn] Verkäufer/in
sample [saːmpl] Beispiel, Muster, Kostprobe
saying ['seɪɪŋ] Redensart
scare [skeə] Angst, Beunruhigung
scene [siːn] Szene, Auftritt
schedule ['ʃedjuːl] Fahrplan, Stundenplan
scheme [skiːm] Plan, Projekt
school [skuːl] Schule: **private school** Privatschule; **public school** exklusives (Privatschul-)Internat; **secondary school** höhere Schule, Gymnasium
scientific [ˌsaɪən'tɪfɪk] wissenschaftlich
score [skɔː] Punktestand, Spielstand
Scotsman ['skɒtsmən] Schotte
screen [skriːn] Bildschirm
season ['siːzn] Jahreszeit: **season ticket** jahreszeitlich befristete Karte
second-hand [ˌsekənd'hænd] gebraucht: **second-hand book store** Antiquariat
secondary school ['sekəndərɪ skuːl] höhere Schule, Gymnasium
Secretary General [ˌsekrətrɪ 'dʒenrəl] Generalsekretär
secrete ['siːkrɪt] geheim, heimlich, versteckt
secure [sɪ'kjʊə] sicher
see [siː]: **call to see** vorbeischauen bei, kurz besuchen
seldom ['seldəm] selten
self-employed [ˌself ɪm'plɔɪd] selbstständig
self-service [ˌself 'sɜːvɪs] Selbstbedienung
senior ['siːnjə] älter, ranghöher, leitend: **senior citizen** ältere/r Mitbürger/in, Senior/in
sensation [sen'seɪʃn] Sensation
separate ['seprət] sich trennen; **(live) separated** getrennt (lebend)
separate ['seprət] (ab)getrennt, einzeln
series ['sɪəriːz] Serie
service ['sɜːvɪs] einen Dienst erweisen: **service a car** ein Auto warten
several ['sevrəl] einige, ein paar
sex [seks] Geschlecht
shade [ʃeɪd] Schatten
shaded ['ʃeɪdɪd] schattiert, dunkel unterlegt
shake (shook, shaken) [ʃeɪk (ʃʊk, 'ʃeɪkn)] schütteln (schüttelte, geschüttelt), wackeln: **shake hands** sich die Hand geben
shamrock ['ʃæmrɒk] Kleeblatt
share [ʃeə] teilen: **job-sharing** Teilzeitarbeit
shelf (shelves) [ʃelf (ʃelvz)] (Wand-) Brett, Regal
shilling ['ʃɪlɪŋ] Schilling
shock [ʃɒk] erschüttern, bestürzen
shocking ['ʃɒkɪŋ] erschreckend, schockierend
short of ['ʃɔːt əv] knapp an
shorthand ['ʃɔːthænd] Kurzschrift, Stenografie
show [ʃəʊ] Unterhaltungsprogramm, Show
shy [ʃaɪ] scheu, schüchtern
similar ['sɪmɪlə] ähnlich
sincerely [sɪn'sɪəlɪ]: **yours sincerely** mit freundlichen Grüßen, hochachtungsvoll
site [saɪt] Gelände: **camping site** Campingplatz
size [saɪz] (Kleider-)Größe
skate [skeɪt] Schlittschuh laufen
sketch [sketʃ] Stegreifspiel, Sketch
sketch [sketʃ] skizzieren, umreißen
skill [skɪl] Eignung, Geschick
skyscraper ['skaɪskreɪpə] Wolkenkratzer
slip [slɪp] schlüpfen, schleichen, gleiten
snail [sneɪl] Schnecke: **snail-racing** Schneckenrennen
snake [sneɪk] Schlange
soap opera ['səʊp ˌɒprə] Fernsehserie, Seifenoper
soldier ['səʊldʒə] Soldat
solve [sɒlv]: **solve a problem** ein Problem lösen
son-in-law ['sʌnɪnlɔː] Schwiegersohn
sorry ['sɒrɪ]: **feel sorry for** Mitleid haben mit
sound [saʊnd] klingen
space [speɪs] Raum, Weltraum
spaceship ['speɪsʃɪp] Raumschiff
Spain [speɪn] Spanien
Spanish ['spænɪʃ] spanisch(-e, -er, -es); Spanier/in
speaker ['spiːkə] Sprecher/in
speciality [ˌspeʃɪ'ælətɪ] Besonderheit, Spezialität
speech [spiːtʃ] Rede, Sprache
spice [spaɪs] Gewürz
spicy ['spaɪsɪ] würzig
spill [spɪl] verschütten, verstreuen
spirit ['spɪrɪt] Geist, Gesinnung
split (split, split) up [ˌsplɪt 'ʌp] auseinanderbrechen (brach, gebrochen)
spoil [spɔɪl] verderben
spoilsport ['spɔɪlspɔːt] Spielverderber
spontaneous [spɒn'teɪnɪəs] spontan, ungezwungen
sport(s) [spɔːt(s)] Sport: **non sports** *hier:* unsportlich
square [skweə] Quadrat: **square foot** *(Fläche)* Quadratfuß
stab [stæb] einstechen auf
star [stɑː] Stern, (Bühnen-)Star
state [steɪt] Staat
statement ['steɪtmənt] Feststellung, Stellungnahme
station ['steɪʃn] Bahnhof: **radio station** Rundfunksender
statistics [stə'tɪstɪks] Statistik
stay [steɪ] Aufenthalt
stay [steɪ] bleiben, untergebracht sein
step [step] Schritt, Treppenstufe
stereo ['sterɪəʊ] Stereoanlage
store [stɔː] Laden, Geschäft *(amerik.)*
store [stɔː] einlagern, speichern

strange [streɪndʒ] fremd, komisch
stranger ['streɪndʒə] Fremde/r
stress [stres] Anspannung, Stress
string [strɪŋ] Schnur, Kordel
stripper ['strɪpə] Striptease-Tänzer/in
studies ['stʌdɪz] Studium
study ['stʌdɪ] studieren, lernen
subject ['sʌbdʒɪkt] *hier:* Schulfach
success [sək'ses] Erfolg
successful [sək'sesfʊl] erfolgreich
suggest [sə'dʒest] vorschlagen, anregen
suitable ['su:təbl] passend, brauchbar
superstition [ˌsu:pə'stɪʃn] Aberglaube
support [sə'pɔ:t] Unterstützung
surprise [sə'praɪz] überraschen
suspicious [sə'spɪʃəs] verdächtig, misstrauisch
swap [swɒp] tauschen
Sweden ['swi:dn] Schweden
Swedish ['swi:dɪʃ] schwedisch(-e, -er, -es); Schwede, Schwedin
sweep [swi:p]: **chimney sweep** Schornsteinfeger
sweetener ['swi:tənə] Süßstoff
Swiss [swɪs] schweizerisch(-e, -er, -es); Schweizer/in
Switzerland ['swɪtsələnd] Schweiz
symbol ['sɪmbl] Sinnbild, Symbol

T

tablet ['tæblɪt] Tablette
talent ['tælənt] Begabung, Talent
talented ['tæləntɪd] talentiert
talked-about [ˌtɔ:kt ə'baʊt]: **talked-about artist** Künstler/in, über den/die man spricht
taste [teɪst] probieren, schmecken
tatoo [tə'tu:] Tätowierung
tatoo [tə'tu:] tätowieren
tax [tæks] besteuern
tea-bag [ti:'bæg] Teebeutel
tea-room [ti:'ru:m] Kaffeehaus auf englische Art
teach (taught, taught) [ti:tʃ (tɔ:t, tɔ:t)] lehren (lehrte, gelehrt), unterrichten
technical ['teknɪkl] technisch
technology [tek'nɒlədʒɪ] Technologie
teen (= teenager) [ti:n] Jugendliche/r unter zwanzig
teleshopping ['telɪʃɒpɪŋ] Einkaufen über das Fernsehen
tent [tent] Zelt
term [tɜ:m] Fachausdruck
thanksgiving [ˌθæŋks'gɪvɪŋ] Erntedankfest
theme [θi:m] Thema, Motto
theory ['θɪərɪ] Theorie
therapy ['θerəpɪ] Therapie
thinking ['θɪŋkɪŋ] *hier:* Geistesgegenwart
thousand ['θaʊznd] tausend
throw (threw, thrown) [θrəʊ (θru:, θrəʊn)] werfen (warf, geworfen)
tin [tɪn] *hier:* Blechdose
tip [tɪp] Hinweis, Tipp, Spitze
tired ['taɪəd]: **be tired of** satt haben
title ['taɪtl] Überschrift, *hier:* Bezeichnung
tobacco [tə'bækəʊ] Tabak
tongue [tʌŋ] Zunge
total ['təʊtl] ganz, völlig
touch [tʌtʃ] berühren
tournament ['tɔ:nəmənt] Turnier
tower ['taʊə] Turm
traditional [trə'dɪʃənl] herkömmlich, konservativ: **traditional Maori music** Volksmusik der Maori
tragedy ['trædʒɪdɪ] Trauerspiel, Tragödie
train [treɪn] abrichten, trainieren
training ['treɪnɪŋ] Ausbildung, Training
transport [træn'spɔ:t]: **public transport** öffentlicher Nahverkehr
treasure ['treʒə] Schatz
treat [tri:t] behandeln, umgehen mit
treatment ['tri:tmənt] Behandlung
trick [trɪk] Kunstgriff, Streich: **play a trick on** einen Streich spielen
trolley ['trɒlɪ] Einkaufswagen *(amerik.)*
trophy ['trəʊfɪ] Trophäe
trouble ['trʌbl] Ärger, Problem
trouble ['trʌbl] beunruhigen, belästigen: **don't trouble yourself** bemühen Sie sich nicht
try [traɪ] Versuch
tunnel ['tʌnl] Tunnel
turkey ['tɜ:kɪ] Truthahn
turn [tɜ:n]: **turn down** leiser drehen; **turn up** lauter drehen
twins [twɪnz] Zwillinge

U

U.K. (= United Kingdom) [ˌju:'keɪ, ju:ˌnaɪtɪd 'kɪŋdəm] Vereinigtes Königreich
U.S.A. (= United States of America) [ˌju: es 'eɪ] USA
ugly ['ʌglɪ] hässlich
un- [ʌn] *(Vorsilbe)* un-, -los, nicht
uncover [ʌn'kʌvə] aufdecken
unemployed [ˌʌnɪm'plɔɪd] arbeitslos, ohne Anstellung
unhealthy [ʌn'helθɪ] ungesund
uniform ['ju:nɪfɔ:m] Uniform
United Nations [ju:ˌnaɪtɪd 'neɪʃnz] Vereinte Nationen
unlock [ʌn'lɒk] aufsperren
untidy [ʌn'taɪdɪ] unordentlich
up-to-date ['ʌptədeɪt] modern, aktuell
upstate New York [ʌp'steɪt] im Norden des Staates N.Y.

V

vacation [və'keɪʃn] Urlaub, Ferien *(amerik.)*
van [væn] Lieferwagen
vegan ['vi:gən] Veganer/in
vegetables ['vedʒtəblz] Gemüse
vegetarian [vedʒɪ'teərɪən] Vegetarier/in
Venetian [və'ni:ʃn] venezianisch
verse [vɜ:s] Vers
video ['vɪdɪəʊ] mit Video aufzeichnen
Vietnam [ˌvjet'næm] Vietnam
Vietnamese [ˌvjetnə'mi:z] vietnamesisch(-e, -er, -es); Vietnamese, Vietnamesin
view [vju:] Aussicht, Ansicht: **point of view** Standpunkt, Meinung
viewer ['vju:ə] Zuschauer, *hier:* Guckloch
violet ['vaɪələt] Veilchen
virtual reality ['vɜ:tʃʊəl ˌrɪ'ælətɪ] virtuelle, künstliche Wirklichkeit
visitor ['vɪzɪtə] Besucher/in, Gast
vitamin ['vɪtəmɪn] Vitamin
vote [vəʊt] Stimm-, Wahlrecht: **give the vote to** das Wahlrecht geben
vote (for) [vəʊt] wählen, stimmen (für)
voucher ['vaʊtʃə] Gutschein

W

Wales [weɪlz] Wales
wander ['wɒndə] wandern
warning ['wɔ:nɪŋ] Warnung
waterfall ['wɔ:təfɔ:l] Wasserfall
wave [weɪv] zuwinken: **a friendly wave** freundliches Zuwinken
weak [wi:k] schwach
wedding ['wedɪŋ] Hochzeit
weight [weɪt] Gewicht
well-dressed [ˌwel'drest] gut gekleidet
Welsh [welʃ] aus Wales, walisisch(-e, -er, -es); Waliser/in
wheel [wi:l] Rad
while [waɪl] Zeitspanne, Weile
widowed ['wɪdəʊd] verwitwet
wireless ['waɪəlɪs] Radio
wooden ['wʊdən] hölzern, aus Holz
work [wɜ:k]: **out of work** arbeitslos; **work-shy** arbeitsscheu; **workaholic** arbeitssüchtig, arbeitskrank
worm [wɜ:m] Wurm
worth [wɜ:θ] wert
wrestler ['reslə] Ringer

Y

youngster ['jʌŋstə] Jugendliche/r
yours sincerely [ˌjɔ:z sɪn'sɪəlɪ] mit freundlichen Grüßen, hochachtungsvoll
youth [ju:θ] Jugend: **youth club** Jugendclub

Z

zoo [zu:] Zoo

Index

Hier finden Sie eine Liste grammatischer Begriffe mit Fundstellen in der Grammatik. Wir haben bewusst unterschiedliche Begriffe aufgenommen (deutsch, englisch und lateinisch), damit Sie möglichst schnell und ohne Umweg zum Ziel kommen.

Acknowledgements

We are grateful to the following for permission to reproduce copyright material:

Photographs:

action press, Hamburg: page 69 (middle left)
Archiv für Kunst und Geschichte, Berlin: page 11 (No 2)
Beate Andler-Teufel, München: pages 3, 79 (background), 86 (baby), 98 (background), 99 (right)
Barnaby's Picture Library, London: pages 23 (No 4, 6), 38 (Big Ben, bottom right), 38 (top right by D. Murdoch), 54 (bottom right), 70 (background)
Bavaria Bildagentur, Gauting: pages 6 (top right), 18 (top), 59 (No 1 by Dieter Gebhardt), 67
Gareth Boden, Hertford: pages 22, 23 (top right), 27 (right), 63, 82 (top right)
Reinhard Brendli, München: page 23 (No 1)
British Tourist Authority, London: page 42 (bottom left)
Dr. Sonia Brough, Oxford: pages 23 (No 3), 27 (left), 39 (bottom), 70 (coke, juice, beer), 71 (garlic, butter, suncream, coffee), 82 (middle right)
J. Allen Cash, London: page 79 (top right)
Central Order, Köln: page 79 (bottom left)
Deutsches Museum, München: pages 59 (No 2, 3, 4, 5, 6), 98 (bottom)
Deutsche Presseagentur, Frankfurt: pages 18 (bottom left by Georgsen), 50
Eastern Daily Press, Norwich: page 102 (bottom right)
Sally+Richard Greenhill, London: pages 38 (bottom left), 46 (background), 47 (top left)
W. Hackenberg, München: page 78 (middle left)
IFA Bilderteam GmbH, München: pages 1, 5, 9, 13, 21, 25, 29, 33, 41, 45, 49, 53, 61, 65, 69 (background), 73, 81, 85, 89, 93 (all by Brandt), 11 (No 3 by Comnet), 11 (No 1 by TPL), 42 (bottom right), 42 (top right by Heinz Koch), 42 (middle centre by LDW), 58 (middle by Barnes), 86 (disco by Bumann)
The Image Bank, München: pages 34 (background by Carlos Navajas), 34 (No C by Tom Knipps), 42 (middle right by Ian Royd), 42 (middle left by John P. Kelly), 46 (middle by Weinberg-Clark), 55 (top left by Charles Weckler), 58 (bottom right by Pamela J. Zilly)
Indisches Fremdenverkehrsamt, Frankfurt: pages 78 (bottom left), 78 (Gandhi)
Christopher Jones, Bristol: page 101
Kensington International Hotel, London: page 55 (middle left)
König+Neurath, Karben: page 14
Bettina Lindenberg, München: pages 2, 26 (women), 39 (top), 62 (bottom left), 70 (bottle)
Langenscheidt-Longman, München: page 34 (No B)
Kirsten Mannich, München: page 42 (bottom middle)
Mirror Syndication International, London: page 62 (middle)
Dr. Annegret Pago, Markt Schwaben: page 23 (No 7)
PhotoPress, Stockdorf: pages 78 (Indian shop by Galvin), 79 (bottom right by Brigitte Bott)
Radio Arabella, München: page 26 (radio studio)
Rogers, Coleridge & White, London: page 90 (middle by Dan Farson)
Royal Mail National, London: page 90 (top by Beryl Cook)
Ulrike Scheidler, Haimhausen: pages 18 (right), 19
Marion Schweitzer Photo-Agentur, München: page 98 (middle)
Stockfood, München: pages 71 (bottom left by Harry Bischof), 79 (top left)
Tony Stone Bilderwelten, München: page 34 (No A by Michael Busselle), 38 (top left by John Lamb), 39 (middle by Ed Pritchard), 43, 54 (top right by John Lawrence)
Superbild Bildarchiv Erich Bach, Grünwald: page 99 (earth)
Ugly Models, London: page 94 (top)
Ullstein Bilderdienst, Berlin: page 38 (Cartier by Waltraud Frentz), 58, (top right by Frank G. Quade)
John Walmsley, Guildford: page 6 (middle, top left)
Williams Press, London: page 94 (middle, bottom)
Zefa Zentrale Farbbild Agentur GmbH, Düsseldorf: page 86 (middle right by Oskar), page 98 (top by Kelly/Mooney)
Cover photographs: Bavaria Bildagentur, Gauting

Illustrations:

Jürgen Bartz, München: pages 18, 34 (right), 35, 46, 49, 58
Silvie Christoph, Berlin: page 74
Conny Jude, London: pages 2, 10
Brian Marshall, Glasgow: pages 101 (top), 102 (top), 103 (top), 104 (top)
Elke Naumann, München: page 78
Chris Ryley, Chigwell: pages 4, 8, 11, 12, 16, 20, 24, 28, 30, 31 (left), 34 (left), 36, 37, 42, 44, 48, 51, 52, 56, 64, 68, 72, 76, 92, 96
Herbert Schulmeyer, Köln: pages 1, 5, 9, 13, 15, 41, 45, 53, 61, 73, 81, 85

Texts:

Addison Wesley Longman Group, Harlow: The big match (p. 105); The quiet young man (p. 106); The house on the hill (p. 107); Japanese Red (p. 108)

We should be grateful for any information which might assist us in tracing the copyright owners of sources which we have been unable to acknowledge.

Mit unseren Begleitmaterialien zu English Network zu optimalen Lernerfolgen

Unsere **Homestudy-Cassette** bzw. **-CD** enthält alle Übungen aus dem Homestudy-Teil.
Unsere **Textcassette** bzw. **-CD** enthält Hörtexte, die für den Gruppenunterricht mit Kursleiter/in gedacht sind. Wenn Sie diese Texte zu Hause nacharbeiten möchten, dann empfiehlt sich die Anschaffung.
Unsere **Nachschlagegrammatik** unterstützt Ihren Lernweg sinnvoll durch alle Network-Bände. Vergessene Grammatik kann so jederzeit nachgeschlagen werden. Das Workbook stellt zusätzlich Übungsmaterial bereit.

Ich bestelle hiermit:

English Network Refresher

O **Homestudy-Cassette**
(Best.-Nr. 3-526-**57 502**-9 / DM 16,90* / öS 125,–* / sFr. 16,00*)
O **Homestudy-CD**
(Best.-Nr. 3-526-**57 516**-9 / DM 16,90* / öS 125,–* / sFr. 16,00*)

O **Textcassette**
(Best.-Nr. 3-526-**57 501**-0 / DM 19,80* / öS 147,–* / sFr. 19,00*)
O **Text-CD**
(Best.-Nr. 3-526-**57 515**-0 / DM 19,80* / öS 147,–* / sFr. 19,00*)

O **Nachschlagegrammatik**
(begleitet alle Network-Bände)
(Best.-Nr. 3-526-**50 412**-1 / DM 19,80* / öS 145,–* / sFr. 19,00*)
O **Workbook 1 zur Nachschlagegrammatik**
(einsetzbar zu Network Refresher)
(Best.-Nr. 3-526-**50 413**-X / DM 10,80* / öS 79,–* / sFr. 10,50*)

Unterschrift/Datum (Absender auf Vorderseite ---->)

* Preisänderung vorbehalten
- Zutreffendes ist angekreuzt -

Ich bestelle hiermit:

English Network Refresher

O **Homestudy-Cassette**
(Best.-Nr. 3-526-**57 502**-9 / DM 16,90* / öS 125,–* / sFr. 16,00*)
O **Homestudy-CD**
(Best.-Nr. 3-526-**57 516**-9 / DM 16,90* / öS 125,–* / sFr. 16,00*)

O **Textcassette**
(Best.-Nr. 3-526-**57 501**-0 / DM 19,80* / öS 147,–* / sFr. 19,00*)
O **Text-CD**
(Best.-Nr. 3-526-**57 515**-0 / DM 19,80* / öS 147,–* / sFr. 19,00*)

O **Nachschlagegrammatik**
(begleitet alle Network-Bände)
(Best.-Nr. 3-526-**50 412**-1 / DM 19,80* / öS 145,–* / sFr. 19,00*)
O **Workbook 1 zur Nachschlagegrammatik**
(einsetzbar zu Network Refresher)
(Best.-Nr. 3-526-**50 413**-X / DM 10,80* / öS 79,–* / sFr. 10,50*)

Unterschrift/Datum (Absender auf Vorderseite ---->)

* Preisänderung vorbehalten
- Zutreffendes ist angekreuzt -

Absender:

____
Name/Vorname

____
Straße/Nr.

____
PLZ/Ort

Bitte liefern Sie die angekreuzten Titel über die Buchhandlung

____
Name/Straße

____
PLZ/Ort

(Sollte keine Buchhandlung genannt sein, erfolgt die Lieferung über eine Buchhandlung unserer Wahl.)

Antwort

An den Verlag
Langenscheidt-Longman
Postfach 40 11 20

80711 München

Absender:

____
Name/Vorname

____
Straße/Nr.

____
PLZ/Ort

Bitte liefern Sie die angekreuzten Titel über die Buchhandlung

____
Name/Straße

____
PLZ/Ort

(Sollte keine Buchhandlung genannt sein, erfolgt die Lieferung über eine Buchhandlung unserer Wahl.)

Antwort

An den Verlag
Langenscheidt-Longman
Postfach 40 11 20

80711 München